Jerusalem
Betrayed

Jerusalem Betrayed

*Ancient Prophecy and Modern Conspiracy
Collide in the Holy City*

By Mike Evans

WORD PUBLISHING
Dallas·London·Vancouver·Melbourne

PUBLISHED BY WORD PUBLISHING
Dallas, Texas

All Scripture references are from the New International Version (NIV) of the Bible.

Library of Congress Cataloging-in-Publication Data
Evans, Mike, 1947–
    Jerusalem betrayed : ancient prophecy and modern conspiracy collide in the holy city / by Mike Evans.
        p.   cm.

    ISBN 0-8499-4002-8
    1. Jerusalem–History.   2. Jerusalem–History–Religious aspects.   3. Jewish-Arab relations–1973–   I. Title.
DS109.9.E93   1997   96-37036
956.94'42–dc21   CIP

7 8 9 QKP 9 8 7 6 5 4 3 2 1

Printed in the United States of America

Dedication

To the unsung heroes who have followed their convictions and stood courageously in support of Jerusalem and the Holy Land, and to all the unacknowledged friends who have worked diligently through the years to build a bridge of love that spans time and distance with their good deeds and compassion for the People of the Book.

For Zion's sake I will not keep silent,
for Jerusalem's sake I will not remain quiet,
till her righteousness shines out like the dawn,
her salvation like a blazing torch.
Isaiah 62:1

Contents

Part II   Dispersion and Discord

Part III   Prophecy Unfolding

This is the word of the LORD concerning Israel. The LORD, who stretches out the heavens, who lays the foundation of the earth, and who forms the spirit of man within him, declares: "I am going to make Jerusalem a cup that sends all the surrounding peoples reeling. Judah will be besieged as well as Jerusalem. On that day, when all the nations of the earth are gathered against her, I will make Jerusalem an immovable rock for all the nations. All who try to move it will injure themselves. . . . Then the leaders of Judah will say in their hearts, 'The people of Jerusalem are strong, because the LORD Almighty is their God.'

"On that day I will make the leaders of Judah like a firepot in a woodpile, like a flaming torch among sheaves. They will consume right and left all the surrounding peoples, but Jerusalem will remain intact in her place."

—Zechariah 12:1–3, 5–6

Introduction

A Torch Among Sheaves

December 9, 1996, 7:00 P.M. Children were coming from all over Jerusalem—the innocent victims of terrorism. A lovely Israeli woman in her late thirties wore a heart-shaped locket around her neck with a picture of her brother on it. The young man had been killed by terrorists a few months earlier.

A small girl clutched her ragged doll. Her mother and father both had been killed by terrorists. I was there on the last night of Hanukkah to bring a little joy to these children in the form of gifts for each of them. They came to the front, their eyes sparkling with happiness.

I looked into the eyes of these beautiful, innocent little lambs and thought about the politicians sitting in their plush offices around the world, making bureaucratic decisions that would ultimately cause the loss of hundreds more innocent lives, leaving thousands more children orphaned and alone.

I could not speak of it then, but just hours earlier, in the biblical town of Bethel, I had stood in the midst of several thousand Jewish mourners, including my longtime friend Benjamin Netanyahu, the prime minister of Israel, to mourn the brutal murder of a beloved Jewish mother ambushed by Palestinians on her way home to celebrate Hanukkah with her family. Her twelve-year-old son was also killed. Her husband and four other children were horribly wounded in the attack.

A mother of nine, gunned down. Her children will never again know the joy of sharing the special moments of their lives with her. As I stood on the frigid, rocky hillside and watched the mourners pass by, I noticed a soldier weeping. He wore the long side curls of an orthodox Jew. Something about his tears and his torn jacket broke my heart, and I couldn't bear to see him standing there all alone. I put my arm around his shoulder to comfort him.

He told me his father had come from Russia to build a life for his family. His father and brother had been killed by terrorists only a week earlier. I had no idea that the crew for our television special, "Jerusalem: City of Tears," had filmed that funeral just days before I encountered him weeping on this desolate hillside.

For what crimes were this young soldier's father and brother killed? Only this: they were Jewish.

As I was finishing up the final pages of this work, an Israeli friend asked me, "Mike, why did you title your book *Jerusalem Betrayed?*"

Immediately a flood of images filled my mind as I paused to reflect on his question. So many years, so many tears, so many painful memories; but my answer had to be direct. "Because Jerusalem *has* been betrayed." America and the economic power-brokers of the world have cut deals with the Arab sheiks who live in opulence beyond comprehension, and nations who run their governments by the power of the bullet—not the ballot box—have set out to humiliate and destroy the people of God.

"Somebody has to tell the true story," I said, "and that is the mission of this book."

Sooner or later the world will have to acknowledge what is being done to the City of God in the name of "foreign relations" and "peace in the Middle East." The warfare the nations are waging against Israel takes many forms. And these patterns of duplicity among so many powers raise a multitude of questions about recent disasters, bombings and terrorist attacks, including the unsolved, mysterious circumstances surrounding the crash of TWA Flight 800 in which 230 people lost their lives. I deal with numerous questions and situations like these throughout the book.

As you read this book, you may feel anger and resentment at times. In places, I hope you will feel tenderness and compassion, or perhaps hurt and disappointment. I do not apologize for these things or for the incidents detailed here that will provoke your emotions; I only hope that what you discover about the land of Israel, and the plot to undermine this ancient culture, will compel you to some kind of action.

Being both a Christian journalist and a friend of Israel gives me a certain perspective on events transpiring in the Middle East, and that perspective shapes my analysis of those events. As you will discover in this book, I believe that Jerusalem has been betrayed. And, ultimately, it will all come down to Jerusalem—because the City of God is at the heart of the Middle East conflict. Though they may not share my opinions, and certainly not my theology, I hope many of my Jewish friends in America and Israel will read this book. Please keep in mind that this book is written from a Christian perspective to a Christian audience.

A COSTLY GIFT

On January 15, 1997, a historic agreement was signed. Forty-eight hours later, Israeli troops redeployed from the biblical city of Hebron, leaving eighty percent of the city in the control of the Palestinian Authority, including the Jewish holy sites. I have known Israel's prime minister, Benjamin Netanyahu, for seventeen years. He is a man of principle and courage who has faced one of the most gut-wrenching issues the leader of a nation will ever face. I know that he could never have given up eighty percent of the City of the Patriarchs unless such tremendous pressure were brought to bear that he sincerely felt it was his only option. Indeed, press reports say that the long stalemate over the Hebron agreement was finally broken as a result of "American hardball diplomacy." Dennis Ross, the president's special envoy, told the Israeli and Palestinian negotiators that the United States had "finally lost its patience."

A few days later, Washington, D.C. threw a big party for the Clinton inauguration—lavish balls where celebrities and politicians rubbed shoulders with dedicated campaign workers and corporate donors. Well-wishers across the world showered President Clinton with congratulations and expensive gifts. But I can't help thinking that Israel has given the president the most expensive gift of all. I also can't help thinking that the timing was not coincidental. Was it just a quirk that the administration "lost patience" and pushed through a bitterly-disputed Israeli-Palestinian agreement only five days before the beginning of President Clinton's second term? Or was it intentionally coerced as a costly inaugural gift for a controversial president who needed a foreign policy victory?

This book has been written as a critical warning, a declaration with all the passion I can summon, to warn that the United States has taken a wrong turn. My purpose is to warn those who will listen that events unfolding in the Middle East could push Israel into a catastrophe of immense proportions and bring the judgment of God on America for our role in manipulating this explosive international situation. Can we wait and watch the destruction of Israel without lifting a hand or crying out? Can we just sit idly by?

It is my prayer that as a result of reading this book you will be challenged to "pray for the peace of Jerusalem" and to get involved in compassionate humanitarian causes for the reconciliation of both Arab and Jew. I trust that the story of Jerusalem, the revelation of ancient mysteries, and the personal narrative that will unfold for you in these pages may help to point you in that direction.

Adonai Oz Leamo Yitein, Adonai Yevarech et Amo Bashalom

The Almighty will give His people strength, the Almighty will bless His people with peace.

Psalm 29:11

Mike Evans
Jerusalem, Israel

Part I:
The Politics
of Peace

One

A Whispered Conversation

I was in Geneva to attend a specially-convened session of the Forty-third General Assembly of the United Nations. At 7:30 Tuesday evening, after a long and tiresome day, I had gone downstairs to the Hilton Hotel restaurant to have dinner and collect my thoughts. As I relaxed, sipping my coffee, I gradually became aware of two men speaking in English in the booth behind me.

I couldn't help overhearing parts of their conversation, but suddenly I became alarmed as I recognized the subject of their discussion. The speaker was obviously American and a diplomat. His companion was a well-dressed Middle Easterner, most likely an influential Arab prince.

"Everything is under control back in Washington," the American was saying, "and Harry's working on the agreement with the Japanese. There's a meeting set up at the Tokyo Club. I've just come from a Club of Rome meeting, and we have the support of our partners throughout Europe. . . ."

I was shocked as I realized what these men were whispering about. I grabbed the pen from my shirt pocket and began jotting down notes as fast as I could. Then the American made a statement that not only seized my attention but pierced my heart.

"We should have Jerusalem in your hands by '96—at the very latest by 2000," the American said. "We're certain we can get you a good piece of Israel by '95."

What on earth had I stumbled onto—the set of a third-rate spy movie? Or were these men actually brokering a behind-the-scenes deal to transfer Jerusalem and other parts of Israel into Arab hands?

To my surprise and his, I ran into the American just a few days later at the airport as I was preparing to leave Geneva. He was checking in at the airline counter beside me. I hesitated briefly but, finally, I could restrain myself no longer. I turned toward him and said, "You don't know who I am, but I know who *you* are and what you're planning to do to Jerusalem." Then I repeated everything I had overheard him say in the restaurant.

The color drained from his face. "You're scaring me," he said. "Who are you?"

I looked the man straight in the eye and said, "Don't fear me. Fear God. He that keepeth Israel neither slumbers nor sleeps."

I'm certain now that this chance meeting was no coincidence. And it was not simply an accident that I overheard that conversation I have to believe that God had put me in the right place at the right time. And that whispered conversation, on the evening of December 13, 1988, was the hard evidence proving that my fear of a conspiracy to rob Israel of the lands and birthright that are rightfully hers—to deprive Jerusalem of her status as Israel's capital—was right on target

Perhaps I should not have been shocked, for the conspiracy has been going on for many years now. But for me, overhearing that startling dialogue in a Geneva restaurant was the confirmation of what I and many others have long suspected

A CHRONICLE OF CRUELTY

For centuries the Jews have struggled and given their lives to regain their ancient homeland. Through a succession of wars and bitter conflicts, and with bloody skirmishes in virtually every decade since the 1920s, Israeli Jews have managed to hold on to their land. But never have the nations of the Middle East, and the many others who long so desperately to evict the Jews from the Holy Land, had so much cooperation from America and Europe as they have today. The carving up of Israel has already started, and the choicest part—Jerusalem, the City of David—appears to be on the verge of being devoured.

Throughout the bloodiest pages of history, the people of Jerusalem have been betrayed time and time again. The three-thousand-year chronicle of this ancient capital is an ageless story of victory and defeat, conquest and carnage, bloodshed and betrayal. The City of David has changed hands twenty-six times and has been leveled to the ground on five separate occasions. And still, it remains today one of the most coveted pieces of real estate on earth and the one city most ardently sought after by the enemies of God.

For decades Jerusalem has been a bone in the throat of the architects of the new world order. Too often their plans are covert and sinister. These people generally work under cover. Organizers like the two I overheard at the Geneva Hilton don't want their schemes to be known. World opinion would soon be against them, if the truth were known. But they are patient.

They are committed to a gradual wearing-down of our resolve. Yet events in the Middle East are proceeding with feverish intensity, and a steady stream of pernicious disinformation is being fed to the people of the world. Almost daily, news reports are circulated by the media that gloss over the outrages committed by Palestinians while portraying Jewish families as fanatics and zealots.

The entire world has been mobilized under the banner of "Peace in the Middle East." But the future of Jerusalem and the survival of this ancient city hang in the balance. By the time you read these words, the Holy City could once again be cut through the heart with barbed wire. World leaders are using financial leverage and economic blackmail to pressure the government of Israel into giving away more territory in the false hope of an arbitrated peace.

But please understand that the pushers of world peace have no intention of stopping with the West Bank or Gaza. They will not stop with Hebron or Tel Aviv or Haifa or the Golan Heights. Even as I listened to the two diplomats plotting their "end run around national sovereignty" in Geneva, I knew then that the city of Jerusalem and the entire nation of Israel had already been promised to the Arab nations, discreetly, behind the scenes. And the architects of the new world order plan to make good on that promise.

Will the reality of all these mounting tensions lead to some type of earth-shaking explosion in the near future? Will the truth of the ancient prophecies collide before our eyes with the modern conspiracy to divide and conquer the City of God? And what is the real truth behind the headlines coming out of the Middle East? Has Jerusalem been betrayed, not by war, but by the "peace process" itself?

The land-for-peace swap meet being conducted under international auspices will not bring an end to armed aggression in Zion. No lasting peace will ever come to these ancient lands without first securing the safety of the people of Israel by dealing with the ongoing threat of Palestinian violence. So far all their peace initiatives have only escalated the amount of terrorism in the region.

Since the peace accords were signed with such fanfare in Washington by Yitzhak Rabin and Yasser Arafat, more than 230 people have been killed by Arab terrorists. They call this the "peace process." It may be a *process,* but it's definitely not *peace.* In reality it is simply a well-planned attempt to change the balance of power in the Middle East and to undermine Jewish autonomy.

Even the most cursory consideration of what has happened over just the last decade should demonstrate that these events are more than coincidence. Franklin Roosevelt once said, "In politics, nothing happens by accident. If it happens, you can bet it was planned that way." The overwhelming magnitude of what's happening today in the Middle East is more than chance or circumstance alone could possibly explain.

THE GREAT GIVEAWAY

Just ten years ago Yasser Arafat and the Palestine Liberation Organization were still hijacking airplanes and terrorizing innocent people, in one case throwing Leon Klinghoffer, a wheelchair-bound passenger on the Italian cruise ship *Achille Lauro,* overboard to his death. Most Israelis found the notion of negotiating with Palestinian terrorists repugnant, and there was certainly no rush to give away land in the name of peace. Yet just ten years later, Israel ceded control of major land areas to the same terrorist organization. Armed and funded by the United States and its new world order partners, the PLO operates on the world stage under the thinnest veneer of legitimacy.

Clearly a dramatic shift has taken place in the focus of world attention. Previously, the attention focused on the Israeli-Arab conflict, with Israel portrayed as David, the little shepherd boy, standing courageously against the wicked giant. But today the world's attention has been refocused. Now the more common portrait is that of Israel as Goliath and the beleaguered Palestinian Arabs as hapless victims. You may ask: Did this dramatic change of focus come about on its own, or was it carefully orchestrated by those who have a larger agenda? Is it purely by coincidence that for over a decade now we have witnessed a systematic weakening of the Jewish position in the Holy Land? Or, as FDR's maxim would suggest, was the whole thing planned from the start?

One detail should be clear, however. Israel did not come up with the idea of the great giveaway on her own. After all, Arabs occupied the West Bank and Gaza prior to 1967, and there was no peace then. So why should Israel think that giving the land to the Arabs—land they never rightfully possessed in the first place—would suddenly bring peace? Israelis, who understood just how preposterous such a proposition had to be, did not decide to give away their land. This was forced on them by others.

Israel did not come up with the idea of negotiating with terrorists, either. Foreign policy under the Bush administration, led by Secretary of State James A. Baker, played a key role in maneuvering Israel to negotiate directly with the PLO. It was a new tactic for the U.S. Under the Reagan administration, the secretary of state pursued a strict policy of *never* negotiating with terrorists. Oliver North was nailed to a congressional cross for violating that policy in Nicaragua. But just a few years later the same State Department was pushing Israel to bargain with the most notorious of all terrorists, the PLO.

While Israel was willing to grant autonomy to Palestinians living in Israeli territory, they were adamant about negotiating only with resident Palestinians, and *not* with Yasser Arafat or the PLO, which was headquartered at that time in Tunis, on the north coast of Africa. The PLO was regarded, rightfully, as a terrorist organization. But now that, too, has changed.

The last decade started out with frustrated Palestinian youths throwing stones at Israeli soldiers. But it ended with a full-fledged

Palestinian army firing automatic weapons on Israeli troops. It started with Israel's territory intact and her borders secure, but it ended with Israel reduced almost to pre-1967 borders, and with her security seriously threatened.

To get a better idea of just how dramatic the changes in Israel have been over the past ten years, consider this brief synopsis of events since 1987:

- 1987—Palestinians launch the *intifada,* or "Arab Uprising," against Israel

- 1988—In Geneva the Forty-third General Assembly of the United Nations focuses on problems in the Middle East; the United States recognizes the PLO; Israeli elections put conservative Likud Party in power

- 1989—Four-point peace initiative proposed by Israel, including a call for Palestinian elections for municipal government; initiative rejected by Arab nations and undermined by Bush-Baker administration in the U.S.

- 1990—Bush administration continues to bypass the Likud government in Israel and conducts foreign policy with members of the Labor Party, perceived by the Arab nations as more likely to make territorial concessions

- 1991—Israel, attacked by Iraqi Scud missiles during the Gulf War, is kept from intervening by the U.S.; Madrid Peace Conference convened to promote peace in the Middle East; Israel, branded as the chief obstacle to peace, is pressured to negotiate with PLO representatives

- 1992—U.S. freezes ten billion dollars in loan guarantees to Israel designated for resettling massive influx of Soviet immigrants; Likud Party defeated by more liberal Labor Party in Israeli elections; Norway helps initiate secret negotiations between members of Israeli government and PLO

- 1993—Declaration of Principles signed between Israel and the PLO

- 1994—Gaza Strip and Jericho turned over to PLO control; Yasser Arafat, Yitzhak Rabin, and Shimon Peres receive Nobel Peace Prize

- 1995—Interim Agreement turns most of the West Bank over to PLO control; Prime Minister Yitzhak Rabin assassinated

- 1996—Increased Arab terrorism against Israel escalates; scheduled deployment from Hebron postponed by Israel; Likud Party returned to power in elections; in September, Palestinian police, armed with weapons provided by Israel under the peace process, fire on Israeli soldiers trying to disperse Arab rioters; widespread violence follows and civil war narrowly averted

THE HIGH PRICE OF COMPROMISE

This chronicle of aggression raises two important questions. First, what caused such dramatic upheaval in the short span of ten years? Second, who is behind it all? The short answer to the first question is economic blackmail. If Israel did not decide independently to give away her lands and negotiate with terrorists, then what happened to convince the Israeli government to do that? Could it be that the leadership in Israel had been pressured economically until they were forced to capitulate?

It is important to remember that Israel is a tiny nation less than one-third the size of the nation of England, and with a population of just six-and-a-half million people. But the gross domestic product of Israel, at approximately sixty billion, is just six and one-half percent the size of Great Britain's. Due to its small domestic market, the Israeli economy depends heavily on exports to Europe and North America. Israel maintains trade agreements with both the United States and the European Union, which accounts for some eighteen billion in annual export revenues. If her financial resources were cut off, the economy of Israel would be crippled. Almost half of all Israeli exports are sold in Europe. Another thirty-two percent goes to North and South America. But if those markets were suddenly closed, the economy and the welfare of that tiny nation would implode.

Israel receives financial assistance from the United States under the congressionally-mandated USAID program, initiated to assist in implementation of the historic Camp David Accords negotiated by Jimmy Carter between Israel and Egypt. This program comes in the form of cash transfers and loan guarantees rather than traditional monetary assistance. Israel uses its annual grant of $1.2 billion, in turn, to purchase goods and services from the U.S. and to repay its debts to this country. While the United States is Israel's largest benefactor, Germany, France, Switzerland, and the Netherlands are also participants.

These relationships create undeniable bonds between Israel and her trading partners. When the United States and other nations ask Israel to make territorial concessions, there is tremendous economic incentive to give in to the requests. When President Bush froze the ten billion in U.S. loan guarantees in 1992, for example, it created havoc in Israel. The resulting stalemate played a major factor in defeating the Likud Party in the national elections that year.

If the United States and Europe were to present a united front and tell Israel, "We're going to take you down, just like we did the Soviet Union," it would not be taken as an idle threat. Israel would have to acquiesce in whatever demands were made upon her, or face the prospect of total economic collapse.

Aware of the tremendous influence that can be brought to bear on a small government by American and European interests, Yasser Arafat routinely works to enlist the support of these powerful nations in pressuring the Israeli government, including the prime minister and the Knesset, for ever greater territorial concessions. A shrewd manipulator of public opinion, the PLO leader will apply pressure to Israel from any outside force, friend or foe, when negotiations are not going his way. In mid-1996 Arafat told the Associated Press that "international arbitration is needed to push forward the peace process." Translation: "Put more pressure on Israel." And the nations complied.

NEGOTIATING UNDER PRESSURE

These days Arafat's call for international arbitration of the Israeli-Palestinian conflict is finding increased support from many nations who want a slice of the Middle East pie. A recent policy paper from the James A. Baker III Institute for Public Policy at Rice University, in oil-rich Houston, calls for a "division of labor between the United States and Europe . . . to enhance the prospects for peace" in the Middle East. The Baker Institute not only says that "the United States government has a critical political role to play as the 'honest broker'" in the peace process, but suggests that "a parallel and equally important role for the Europeans and the World Bank to help stabilize the situation is also called for."

But the United States and Europe are not the only countries that should play a major role in the Middle East, according to the Baker Institute. The study calls for the G7+1 nations to "serve an important declaratory role." (The G7 nations are the United States, Canada, France, Germany, Italy, the United Kingdom, and Japan; the G7+1 designation adds Russia to the slate of world powerbrokers.) "Japan depends heavily on oil from the Middle East, and has a major interest in the stability of the region. They can and should play a major economic role," the Baker Institute proposes.

The United States, the European Union, the World Bank, Japan. Is it just coincidence that the nations of the world are vying for political and economic clout in Israel and the Middle East? Is it merely humanitarian? Is it statesmanship and diplomacy aimed at peace in our world? Or could it be that we are about to witness the monumental collision of ancient prophecies and modern conspiracy in the Holy City of Jerusalem?

As I have watched the acceleration of global involvement in the affairs of Israel, there is no doubt in my mind that we are on just such a prophetic countdown. The world is moving ever closer, pressing in on Jerusalem. The nations are coming together against Israel, raising their fortifications against the City of David, just as it was prophesied in the pages of God's Word more than two thousand years ago.

Not since 1947, when the United Nations voted to partition Palestine and make Jerusalem an international enclave, have all the nations of the world convened to debate the future of the Holy City. But since the Madrid Peace Conference in 1991, it has been a regular occurrence. The entire world has been unified in an attempt to divide up the Bible lands and to strip Jerusalem from the hands of the Jews.

From Madrid the nations went to Moscow, where another conference to determine the future of the Middle East was attended, not only by the regional participants, but by representatives of the United States, Russia, Japan, Italy, France, Germany, Ireland, Great Britain, Canada, Netherlands, Belgium, Luxembourg, Finland, Sweden, Norway, Denmark, India, China, Greece, Turkey, Spain, Portugal, Switzerland, and Australia.

I believe that many of the significant events that have transpired in the nation of Israel over the last decade occurred because somebody—or a group of somebodies—planned them that way. From terrorist attacks to international pressure to economic blackmail, there is no question that there is a purpose and a plan behind the heartbreaking events unfolding in the Holy City.

This is not a popular viewpoint, of course. Many important people in places of great influence believe that Israel is a cancer which threatens their plans for peace in the Middle East. For anyone to buck the politically correct tide running against Israel would mean social and professional ostracism, so these critics scoff at the facts. Rather than deal with the reality of the situation, they wage a war of words, labeling anyone who supports the God-given right of Israel over her historic homeland as a "Zionist lap dog," a "fanatic right-winger," or a conspiracy theorist who rustles every bush and kicks every rock looking for imaginary bogeymen.

Such people scoffed at Columbus when he announced that the world was a ball and not a pancake. Columbus upset the intellectuals of his day by challenging their complacent view of the universe. Many were afraid they would lose social prestige if they listened to him. Others simply wouldn't believe the world was round. Their attitude was, "Don't confuse us with the facts. Our minds are already made up."

In many ways, that same attitude prevails today. Intellectuals, liberals, and the mainstream media don't want to think about the reality of an international conspiracy to divide and dismember the city of Jerusalem. And they certainly don't want to hear that all these events which often seem so sporadic and random are, in fact, described with pinpoint accuracy in Bible prophecy. The images portrayed by the prophets many centuries ago offer a sobering portrait of the world today. Perhaps it's time for the intellectual ostriches to pull their collective heads out of the sand and ponder this reality.

The honest seeker of truth will discover that there is an international plot to steal Jerusalem from the Jews and to put it into Arab hands. It is a collusion that involves, knowingly or not, some of the biggest names and most powerful interests in the world today. Jerusalem is at center stage of an unfolding drama. And behind the international cast of collaborators is a master conspirator who is directing the play. Operating invisibly, but always present behind the curtain, is a player whose stakes are highest of all, manipulating the collaborators like actors on a colossal stage. Most of them do not even suspect that they are acting out the final scenes of the last desperate drama of planet earth—and, tragically, right on cue.

Jerusalem is the one obstacle to the world system whose financial control will ultimately fall into the hands of one man. That man, the chief conspirator against the City of Peace, is already active behind the scenes. Soon he will come forward to take his bow. Initially he will be applauded as the one who brings order and resolution to the problems of the Middle East. Mark your calendars, because this man will claim to have the perfect peace plan. His plan will be praised not only by Israel, but by the U.S., the European nations, and the entire world. Many who are reading this book will watch this "man of peace" on CNN and news outlets across the globe as he begins to take control over all business, banking, and other vital issues.

But this chief conspirator only wears the mask of a peacemaker. In reality he is a totalitarian who will have no qualms about fomenting civil wars, economic depressions, and racial hatred when it suits his purpose. His goal will be a monopoly of absolute control over the affairs of men and, ultimately, to destroy the world as we know it.

Does such a scenario sound insane, bizarre, unrealistic? Surely it must in today's world, and at a time in history when society has been assured that "man is the measure of all things."

But consider how the peace and tranquility of our lives has vanished over the past forty years. Consider how tragedies, bombings, missile attacks, murders, and scandals at the highest levels of power have reshaped our thinking about the innate goodness of mankind. And consider how at least two generations of Americans have been reprogrammed and utterly convinced that there is no such thing as absolute truth. One man's meat is another man's poison. All realities are equal. In such a world, it is easy to be deceived.

The first job of the chief conspirator is to convince the nations that no such conspiracy exists. Every conspirator must be an accomplished liar as well as a farsighted planner. No one could be fooled if the conspirator came to the forefront and acknowledged that his intent was absolute dictatorial control of Israel through duplicity and deception, and then, ultimately, to gain absolute power over the governments of the world.

In the early days of Adolf Hitler's rise to power in Germany, no one would ever have believed that he was conspiring to commit genocide against the Jewish people. His means were radical, but Hitler was an idealist with plans for changing the world. Germany and most of Europe bought his ideas and scoffed at those who offered more somber warnings. After the fact, however, everyone acknowledges that Hitler was a madman, a demon, a man possessed by dark and diabolical forces. His central purpose was the extermination of the Jews, and that's exactly what he did. Six million of them paid with their lives because the world refused to believe that a shrewd German politician could be an evil conspirator. And those who did believe it did nothing about it.

Today Israel is caught in a conspiratorial bear trap. The ultimate conspirator may not reveal himself for the judgment of the world, but he continues nevertheless to work his plans, patiently, systematically, to destroy the security and ultimately the freedom of that nation.

Already there are false prophets in the land, as there were in the days of Jeremiah, who are crying "peace, peace." But there is no real peace. The signing of peace accords between Israelis and Palestinians, scripted and choreographed so brilliantly by Washington, is not the dawning of new hope for the Middle East, as so many passionately believe. It is a delusion, a false hope, and a dangerous lie. The peace brokers are themselves key players in the undermining of the nation of Israel and the betrayal of Jerusalem.

It is no coincidence that the United Nations repeatedly passes resolutions against Israel. It is not a coincidence that international peace conferences are convened almost weekly to give the nations a forum for their wrath against Israel and its Holy City. Brilliantly planned and conceived, it is actually the fulfillment of the ancient prophecies, a tragedy that will consume the nations in their conspiracy against Jerusalem.

TWO

Next Year in Jerusalem

The 1973 oil embargo literally raped America and the western world, costing us hundreds of billions of dollars and making life unbearable for months. Then the Arab oil producers used the billions they wrested from us as they mouthed the clever words, "The status of Jerusalem must be determined by negotiations!"

Remember the names of this fabled city? The City of David, the City of God, the City of Truth, Jerusalem the Joyful, the Faithful City, the Lion of God, the Dwelling of Righteousness. It is a city of seventy names, the oldest capital in the world, mentioned 657 times in the Hebrew Bible and 157 times in the New Testament. Jerusalem, "the navel of the earth." The city beloved by Jews around the world as the center of their hope and faith. The bridge between Asia, Europe, and Africa. Now being trodden under foot by the Gentiles.

But God said, "If I forget you, O Jerusalem, may my right hand forget its skill" (Psalm 137:5).

Jerusalem has experienced more sorrow in the last three thousand years than any city in the world, as twenty-six empires conquered and occupied her, leveling the Jewish capital to the ground five separate times. Yet, in the midst of it, Jews cry out, "Next year in Jerusalem!" They utter the words at the Seder, on the eve of Passover. Again, they cry out at the end of Yom Kippur, the Day of Atonement, three times each day. Traditional believers face to the East, fast, and pray for the return of the Jews to the Holy City. In the Amidah, the silent part of the prayer, they say, "May our eyes behold thy return to Zion in mercy."

Similarly, in the grace after meals, traditional Jews pray that "The Almighty might rebuild Jerusalem speedily in our days." In 1991 when "Operation Solomon" took place, many Ethiopian Jews were brought back to the land of the Bible. They only knew two words in Hebrew, *Yerushalayim* and *shalom*—the name "Jerusalem" and the word of greeting which means "peace." Everything in the life of a Jew, the very scarlet thread of Judaism and the Jewish people, runs through the heart of Jerusalem, the holiest of cities for both Christians and Jews for two thousand years.

Two of the Seven *Bra Chot* (seven blessings) recited at Jewish ceremonies, pray for the return of Zion's children to Jerusalem. They pray that the sound of joy may once again be heard in her streets. The custom of breaking the wine glass at the conclusion of a ceremony is a symbolic commemoration of the destruction of the Temple at Jerusalem. It is a tragic litany that never seems to end: the humiliation of the Jews, the destruction of Jerusalem, and the seemingly endless war for control of the Holy Lands.

Jerusalem has been broken and abused, but she is a holy city and one day she will be restored. John the Revelator declares in his mighty vision of the end times, "I saw the Holy City, the new Jerusalem, coming down out of heaven from God, prepared as a bride beautifully dressed for her husband" (Revelation 21:2). For all of the stress and strain of the last fifty years, a new day is coming when Jerusalem will experience true and lasting peace.

As the center of Israel's worship, Jerusalem was preceded by Shiloh, where Joshua placed the tabernacle and the Ark of the Law, around the thirteenth century B.C. Some three thousand years later King David made Jerusalem his capital. After David's son, Solomon, built the magnificent temple there, every aspect of Jewish life became focused around Jerusalem. It was the center of commerce and religion. Jews came to Jerusalem for Pentecost, for Passover, for the Feast of Tabernacles. Jews from all over the region thronged to Jerusalem to bring their sacrifices, to study the Torah, and to rejoice.

Even Jesus of Nazareth went to Jerusalem every year, as Luke declares: "Every year his parents went to Jerusalem for the Feast of the Passover" (Luke 2:41). He foresaw the sorrows and tragedies that would come upon Jerusalem, and he wept over the city. Indeed, for him it was a city of tears. The Romans under Titus destroyed the city in 70 A.D. and left "not one stone on top of another," just as Jesus had warned. But down through the centuries even greater indignities have been heaped on the ancient capital, and too often America has led the international pack with ruthless and unnatural demands. How terrible that so much of the world's injustice has been focused here, on this city, and on these people.

Contrary to what you may hear, when the old city was under Jordanian sovereignty, between 1948 and 1967, Muslims the world over did not bother to make pilgrimages to the Al-Aksa Mosque in Jerusalem. Today the powerbrokers say the site of the Muslim mosque is a big deal to Arabs; yet, after the Six-Day War in 1967, the traffic was one way. Israeli Arabs flocked to Egypt by the thousands, while not even a trickle of Egyptians trekked to Jerusalem. The fifteen million Egyptian Muslims felt no urge to make the pilgrimage to Jerusalem to pray at the Al-Aksa Mosque. They did *not* long to see the Dome of the

Rock, as some have said, in spite of the fact that the bus fare was a mere forty dollars.

A LACK OF OBJECTIVITY

The prophetic history of Jerusalem has been ignored or conveniently forgotten by those determined to rape her once again. The powerbrokers treat the ancient city with supreme disrespect. As but one example, American embassies are never located in any city except the accredited capital of the nation. Jerusalem is the heart and soul of Israel and its true capital, but this great city has only consular offices, a second-level American presence. For political reasons, our embassy has been located at Tel Aviv. And despite legislation by Congress to force the White House to move the embassy, the answer is still no.

America's foreign-affairs specialists have an overriding desire to placate the Arab world, assuring them that the status of Jerusalem will remain open to negotiations. But it is diplomacy more appropriate for the theater of the absurd. It is sheer hypocrisy. I was in Dhahran when America was spending billions of dollars defending Saudi Arabia, a dictatorship, and shedding American blood to restore another dictatorship in Kuwait.

While there I met an American oil worker who was imprisoned for smuggling pornography into the country. When he showed me his hands, I was startled to see that his fingernails had been pulled out. His face etched with pain, he described how his jailers had shocked his genitals with electrical current and used other unmerciful tortures. The so-called pornographic material he had smuggled into Saudi Arabia was a video called *The Love Boat*.

We gave Kuwait back to the Kuwaitis and paid billions to the

Arab world for their show of force; and our secretary of state paid homage to one of the most notorious aggressor-nations on earth, Syria, and its president, Hafez al Assad. I was shocked to see America's leaders groveling before these terrorists.

I stood near the Kuwait–Saudi border with General Khalid as he reviewed the Syrian high command, never thinking even in my wildest imagination that the money we were paying them would be used to buy missiles from North Korea for one purpose only: to mobilize for war against Israel, which they are doing today—even at the time of this writing.

More blood has been shed over the stones of Jerusalem than any spot on earth. Wars and brutal atrocities have been waged on this soil for thousands of years. But these attempts throughout history to desecrate this holy place are not coincidental. They are not mere chance events. I am convinced they are demonic acts, birthed out of hell itself. They are events that will one day consummate with the wrath of God Almighty against those who dare to lift their hand against Jerusalem and God's chosen people, the Jews. The Bible assures us that the worst battle in all of history, the Battle of Armageddon, will be waged for control of this city. But he who holds title and deed to the land *will* have the *final* word.

If it is true that Muslim countries have treated the Jews in their midst fairly and in democratic fashion, then why have the Jews in those Arab nations been forced to flee for their safety to Israel? Why have Jews been driven back to the land of Palestine throughout the centuries? Quite simply, it is because of the unspeakable persecutions they have endured throughout the years. Under Islamic law, Jews and Christians are granted slight protection under a policy called "Dhimmi." Discriminatory practices against Christians and Jews are listed in the covenant "Shurut," attributed to the Caliph Omar around 634–644 A.D. Consider the implications of just these historic restrictions listed in the *Encyclopedia Judaica*:

- The Islamic courts did not admit the sworn testimony of Jews and Christians.
- Their graves had to be leveled with the ground so that anyone could walk over them.
- Their houses and tombs were not allowed to be higher than those of Muslims. They were not to employ Muslims in their service.
- They were not to raise their voices in churches or be seen in public with a cross.
- Jews were to wear yellow cloth sashes and for Christians, the color was blue.
- The color of the shoes had to be different than that of the Muslim shoes.
- They were to accommodate Muslim travelers for three days free of charge.
- Subjects were to honor Muslims and stand in their presence.
- If struck, they must not hit back.
- The Koran was not to be taught to protected subjects.
- The building of new churches and synagogues was prohibited.
- They were not to ride on horses or camels, but only on donkeys, and without a saddle.
- Christians were forbidden to ring their church bells, a ban that remained in force for one thousand years until the mid-nineteenth century.

- The Muezzin, on the other hand, called loudly *five* times a day from the top of every minaret, that "Allah is one God, and Mohammed is his prophet."

So much for the notion of tolerance. Are these just archaic Islamic policies from centuries past? Hardly. A Christian who has that illusion should try moving his residence to any one of the twenty Arab dictatorships in the Middle East. What happens to a Christian who practices his faith with enthusiasm in one of these Muslim countries? His life will be short on this earth, for he will be imprisoned and most likely beheaded. Islam is not just a religion; it is a way of life. And it impacts every aspect of society in a Muslim nation.

The Golden Gate of Jerusalem was sealed in the year 1514 by the Muslim authorities, and it remains sealed to this day. It is believed that the reason for this was the prophecy that the Messiah would enter Jerusalem through the Golden Gate, and because Christians had used this gate for their Palm Sunday processions. In fact, a cemetery had been built just outside the gate for that reason. Later, a Muslim cemetery was built on top of Mount Calvary for a similar reason.

OPPRESSION AND INTOLERANCE

Many have witnessed the desecration of the holy city, including some who admit no love for God or his commands. The infamous Karl Marx, father of Communism, admitted in an article in the *International Herald-Tribune* published on April 15, 1854, "The sedentary population of Jerusalem numbers about fifteen thousand souls, of whom four thousand are Moslem and eight thousand are Jews. Nothing equals the misery and suffering of the Jews who are the constant object of

Moslem oppression and intolerance." Even Marx could see the truth.

But the oppression and intolerance have never stopped. Neglect and abuse of Jewish holy places continued for decades. Between 1948 and 1967, conditions were considered deplorable, even by Medieval standards. Jewish residents were expelled from the Jordanian-controlled area. Jordan transformed part of its territory into an armed camp, with guns, land mines, and snipers.

Jews were barred from worshiping at the Western Wall. The Jewish quarter in the old city was destroyed, and fifty-eight synagogues were demolished. Some were used as cowsheds, stables, or public lavatories, while others were razed to the ground. Three-fourths of the tombstones at the hallowed Mount of Olives Cemetery were ripped out and used to build a hotel and to pave a pathway leading to army latrines.

Yet the world cries out, "Let the peace process continue! Give up your lands for peace!" Until 1967, the Jews did not have the land and they certainly did not have peace. They won the land back by defending it. So how can we or anyone ask them now to give it away?

Zion's Karaite Synagogue was destroyed. The Kurdish Synagogue was destroyed. The Warsaw Synagogue was destroyed. These are just a few of the synagogues destroyed by the Jordanians. Not one Muslim mosque, however, has been destroyed by the Jews. The Arab world declared war on Israel in 1967, and the Israeli Army won a stunning victory in just six days. Things would be better for the Jews after that, but in the nineteen years of Jordanian administration of the land, according to my friend and the former mayor of Jerusalem, Teddy Kollek, municipal services were woefully inadequate. Thirty percent of households had no electricity. Twenty percent lacked running water, and few dwellings were equipped with adequate sewage disposal. An unbearable stench emanated from the complex of cisterns beneath the streets.

One of the biggest controversies of 1996 was over the resistance of Jewish settlers in Hebron; but no one speaks anymore of the horrible massacre of Jews in Hebron in 1929, or the fact that the Hebron Yeshiva had to be moved to the center of Jerusalem, where it still stands, to avoid further terrorist acts.

THE ULTIMATE REALITY

On December 11, 1996, when Beit El resident Etta Tzhur and her twelve-year-old son, Ephraim, were killed by terrorists in a drive-by shooting, and when her husband, Yoel, and their four other children aged four to seventeen were wounded, the prime minister of Israel cut short his vacation in the south to visit the family at Hadassah Hospital. The mayor of Jerusalem, Ehud Olmert, reached out his hand to them in compassion. The entire nation expressed their support and solidarity with this devastated family. Yet, not a word of compassion came from Washington or the powerbrokers who have made it their business to determine the fate of Israel. In the ultimate reality of war and death, as always in times of anguish, Jerusalem stands alone.

In Exodus, the Lord God declared, "And I will take sickness away from the midst of you" (Exodus 23:25). Many believe the time will come when the misery will depart. But there is a sinister force that works to destroy the ancient city and its people. Some call it a death angel, others say it is a demon; but they feel some sinister force hovers over the city of Jerusalem, a demon that holds the wounded soul of Israel in distress. A brutal form of terrorism that never ends, with moments of joy and days of deep heartache and despair. When will it end? What strange mysteries are yet to be uncovered on this soil? How to explain the injustices that take place on a daily basis?

More Palestinians were massacred in Kuwait after the end of the Persian Gulf War than have died in any skirmish in Israel. But, shockingly, the media never reported it. And yet, any attempt by Jewish settlers to preserve their lives and property makes headlines around the world. There is little truth and no objectivity in much of the news coverage that comes out of Israel, and on top of that a good percentage of stone-throwing incidents are actually orchestrated by media crews to make sensational footage for the evening news in New York. This is not an idle charge; it is a documented fact. Disseminating misinformation, rumors, half-truths, and lies has become common fare in Middle East coverage.

The most pointed recent example of media bias involved the outbreak of violence at the Temple Mount in mid-1996 when the media blamed Israel for inciting a mini-civil war. In fact, the Jews had nothing to do with it. Once again, Arabs began attacking Jewish worshipers and threatening more violence. If the same incidents had happened in America or any other civilized country in the world, martial law would have been declared and the national guard would have been instructed to use force to stop the hotheads. But when the Jews responded with appropriate force, the world called it excessive and brutal.

I stood in the warm sun at the White House on September 13, 1993, watching a brave Israeli prime minister with a crooked smile gritting his teeth as the president of the United States shoved his thumb into his backbone, forcing him to shake Yasser Arafat's hand for the sake of a politically expedient "photo op." For me, *that* is excessive force.

But Yitzhak Rabin was a gentleman, and he took the fateful step with his eyes open. I will never forget the words he spoke at the White House ceremony: "We have come to you from Jerusalem, ancient and eternal capital of the Jewish people. . . ."

Chairman Arafat never mentioned Jerusalem during his visit at the White House; but in his speech that same evening, beamed via satellite to the Arab world, he proclaimed, "By God's will, we shall raise our flags over the walls of Jerusalem, capital of the Palestinian State, over all minarets and churches in the city."

Thousands of jubilant Arabs draped Palestinian flags over the city walls on hearing the chairman's words. At the 1991 international peace conference in Madrid, I had challenged Secretary of State James Baker to recognize Jerusalem as Israel's capital. If America wants to be honest brokers in a genuine peace process, I said, they must first keep faith with Israel. I have made much the same challenge to every political leader I have met over the last fifteen years, at conferences and summits around the world.

When Yitzhak Rabin invited me to his office he shared with me his hopes for the restoration of his people, an end to hostilities, and the beginning of peace in the land. He dreamed of his grandchildren not having to go through what he and his generation went through. He was a great general and a fine prime minister, but he was keenly aware of the enormous economic pressure on his nation, and perhaps a little too willing to compromise because of it. I considered him a friend, and I know his motives were not small or naive. He loved Jerusalem with all his heart, and he was willing to give his life for her if it came to that. In a sense, he did.

THE "FLIGHT 800" CONNECTION

When was the last time America held a party for a terrorist responsible for the killing of diplomats, bombing of airliners, and massacre of children and heroic Olympic athletes? It has never happened before. But it was all done by the Clinton administration, with much celebration, for Yasser Arafat.

The message to the world is clear: America is willing to let Jews die to pacify terrorists. As sordid as it may sound, I believe this is the truth. Can't our diplomats face the facts? Can't they tell the truth? Why can't they see what is really happening with the terrorists of the world? Will they confess the fact they know very well that Iran is flying at least three 747 jumbo cargo jets of armaments and military supplies to Syria each month, and that a large percentage of these arms are being ferried directly to Hezbollah guerrillas for their war on Israel?

The weapons include Russian-made Sager anti-tank missiles that Hezbollah has used successfully against Israel in recent months. Israeli intelligence has informed the U.S. that each shipment contains modified long-range Katyusha rockets with a range of twenty-five miles. Any one of these missiles could strike as far south as Haifa, Israel's third largest city. They are the same Katyusha rockets that began falling on northern Israel on December 14, 1996.

In the Gaza Strip on the same day, the militant Islamic Resistance Movement, Hamas, held its first mass rally in months with a demonstration license approved by Yasser Arafat himself. During the rally the radical leaders made threats of increased suicide bombing, which they call military operations—probably the best example of "theater of the absurd" in our time. And they cheered the covert bombings conducted by their fellow guerrillas in the United States. But what follows is, if possible, even more sinister and terrible than any of the above, for it involves not only those bent on terror but those among us bent on covering it up.

Do the American people truly believe that the tragedy of TWA Flight 800 was merely an accident? Without positive confirmation of a mechanical failure, it remains likely that the explosion was an intentional act. In December 1996, I spoke confidentially with a high-level intelligence operative who gave me inside information which I believe to be true; and this information shows that the TWA airliner was downed by Iran-supported Islamic fundamentalists. According to this intelligence operative, the explosion that killed everyone on the flight was not an accident, not something done in a sudden fit of rage, but a deliberate act of terrorism carried out according to a detailed plan and in a time frame that had previously been disclosed to American authorities in a detailed warning.

The truth, as my source has detailed it to me, is that Flight 800 was not blown out of the sky as the result of mechanical difficulty. It was intentionally shot down by terrorists, then covered up rather crudely by Washington because it would have been too great an embarrassment to think that the president of the United States could not deal with terrorism on his own turf.

Furthermore, those involved in the cover-up believed that telling the truth about what really happened would have hurt commercial air travel in this country, driving up the cost of security; and it would unleash such panic and outrage among the American people that the tremors would shake the very foundations of the White House. Because of our weak-kneed policy called "Risks For Peace" and our cozying up to terrorists and murderers in the Middle East, the soft underbelly of America has been exposed. And we are vulnerable.

But if we were to seek the truth instead of the convenient lie, I wonder how many more secrets would finally come out into the open. Is it possible that the world might learn that in April 1992 the presidents of Rwanda and Burundi were killed onboard the Rwandan presidential jet, a Falcon 50, when a SAM missile struck it while the plane was on final approach to the airport in Rwanda, thus sparking Rwanda's Hutu–Tutsi Civil War?

Or would we learn about the incident in September 1993 in which an Abkhazian separatist from the former Soviet Republic of Georgia shot down three TU-134 airliners using shoulder-fired SAMs from a boat on the Black Sea? Or that in 1986 a Sudan Airline jet was shot down by a SAM missile, and that in the late 1970s two Rhodesian (now Zambian) airliners were shot down by three A-7s? The truth of our situation shatters the myths of the diplomatic community. It raises too many hard questions.

NO RETALIATION, NO RESPONSE

What motive would Iranian or any other Islamic extremists have for attacking an American airliner? The answer is simple. In June 1985 the United States began an embargo against Iran because of its sponsorship of international terrorism. These sanctions have been in place for more than a decade now, squeezing the Iranian economy, which suffers from inflation running as high as fifty percent. What better reason to direct the attention of the Iranian people toward an external enemy—in this case "the Great Satan," the United States?

Iran has been working day and night to stir up trouble throughout the Gulf region. Their militant leaders want to provoke an international incident—either with the U.S. directly or indirectly by causing trouble with their neighbors—and thus bring about a conflagration involving the United States, Bahrain, Saudi Arabia, Kuwait, and others. Hezbollah factions have been infiltrated, and the seeds of a tremendous explosion on the world scene are being sown even at this hour.

On November 13, 1995, an Iranian-backed Islamic organization known as the Movement for Islamic Change claimed responsibility for the bombing of the Saudi National Guard at Riyadh, in which five American servicemen and two Indian workers were killed. This was the first of two promised attacks. On June 3, 1996, Iran vowed to resist the embargo imposed by the U.S.; and then on June 9, Iran's spiritual leader called for Iran's military to prepare for war.

Ten days later the U.S. House of Representatives cast a unanimous vote in favor of imposing tighter sanctions on Iran. The principle was added to pending legislation. The intent of the bill was to cripple Iran's and Libya's ability to continue their support of international terrorism. A week later, on June 20–23, Teheran hosted an international terrorism conference during which it was announced that attacks against U.S. interests would be stepped up in the coming months.

Two days later, on June 25, the truck bombing of the military housing camp in Dhahran, Saudi Arabia, took place, claiming the lives of nineteen U.S. airmen and wounding hundreds of others. The Islamic Movement for Change, which had already claimed credit for the Riyadh bombing, now took credit for this attack as well.

On July 16, the United States levied its version of sanctions against Iran and Libya. On the following day, July 17, the Movement for Islamic Change sent a chilling fax to the London-based Arab newspaper, *Al-Hayat*, warning:

> The world will be astonished and amazed at the time and place chosen by the Mujahadin. The Mujahadin will deliver the harshest reply to the threats of the American president. Everyone will be surprised by the volume, choice of place, and timing of the answer. The invaders must be prepared to depart . . . dead, for their time of mourning is near.

That fax, intercepted by overseas operatives, was forwarded to U.S. agencies warning them that Iran was likely to launch an attack against a U.S. aircraft. The warning was ignored; 230 Americans died.

At 8:31 that evening, nobody could dismiss the horrendous explosion of TWA Flight 800 off the coast of Long Island. Then on July 20–21, another international Hezbollah conference was held in Teheran. Some analysts believe this was an action review of the TWA attack, possibly to assess America's response. But there was no response because, despite the early involvement of the FBI and other agencies, nobody declared the downing an act of terror. Nobody would admit that America had suffered a cruel body blow.

Despite the reluctance of our military and political leaders to tell the people the truth, just one day after the downing of Flight 800, an Iranian-backed, London-based news organization called Shanti Riv claimed that the aircraft was shot down by a missile. Up to that time nobody had ever raised the possibility of a missile. Flight 800 was a Boeing 747. Ironically, this aircraft was scheduled to be sold to the Iranian Air Force, but due to the tense situation in the Middle East the plane was never delivered.

The Boeing 747 is an extremely rugged design, but the plane had developed a slight malfunction. Flight 800 was scheduled to depart JFK at 7:00 P.M., bound for Paris, France, but the flight was held up for replacement of a faulty engine-pressure gauge. Baggage had to be removed and then reloaded. The aircraft took off from JFK at 8:19 P.M. At 8:30 the crew made its final air transmission requesting clearance to climb to fifteen thousand feet.

A few weeks later, I flew from New York to Jerusalem to meet with Israeli leaders and to reach out in compassion to victims of terrorism in that nation. As TWA flight 802 taxied down the runway at JFK and then climbed above Long Island, I thought long and hard about the possibility that something more than mechanical failure had downed flight 800.

Later, I learned another bit of shocking news. In 1982, during the Falklands War, an Argentinean AM-39 anti-ship missile struck the British destroyer, *Sheffield*. The missile was a dud, but the energy of the weapon flying at supersonic speed was enough to punch a hole through the hull and slice into the fuel lines, allowing the still-burning rocket motor to ignite a deadly fire and explosion onboard ship. Is it possible that TWA Flight 800 may have experienced an airborne version of the same fate?

The missile used to destroy Flight 800 was probably a Swedish-built RBS-90. Many experts have lumped all man-portable missiles into the heat-seeking category of the Stinger (with the exception of the RBS-70), allowing the gunner to target the widest area of the aircraft, the underside of its sentry wing box. The weapon is gyro-stabilized and can be mounted on small vessels, allowing it to be fired at sea even when the water is not calm. It also comes with an optional infrared sight for night-targeting and has virtually smokeless motors to help avoid detection. Its speed is supersonic.

As a result of what I have learned on my own, from informants and from scattered media reports, I am now convinced that Flight 800 was shot down by Iranian terrorists—the very same fanatics who are feeding terrorism in Jerusalem and throughout the land of Israel.

In light of these facts, how should America respond? First of all, we must stop negotiating with terrorists and stop rewarding them for their wicked behavior. Terrorists of the world must be held accountable for their crimes and exposed to the full scorn and judgment of an angry world. They must not be hosted by American presidents at palatial dinner parties in the White House.

Three

A Conspiracy of Silence

NEITHER I nor anyone I know is a conspiracy nut. I am not inclined to believe in organized deceptions. I do not see a demon behind every bush, and I do not look for Machiavellian plots behind every political action. It's not in my nature.

But despite my inclinations, when I look at the bizarre twists and turns taken by events in the Middle East peace process, I cannot help but see elements of collusion and duplicity on all sides. Evidence of tacit agreements between the world's superpowers, secret negotiations between the PLO and biased and outspoken Arabists within the American government—particularly the CIA and the State Department—along with the tremendous rise in influence currently enjoyed by the PLO, all these things make me realize there has to be more to it than meets the eye.

We all recognize that there are dangerous conspiracies afoot today among terrorist groups and certain Arab countries to destroy the nation of Israel. We have also seen the manipulation of American business and the U.S. government by the Oil-Producing and Exporting Countries (OPEC) through the medium of strikes, shortages, boycotts, and other forms of arm-twisting over our oil policies. And we have observed the painful effects of outright economic blackmail of Israel by the leaders of the western world, with the United States at the front of the pack.

But there is also a conspiracy of silence, whether deliberate or through ignorance, in media coverage of the Arab-Israeli conflict. This silence has contributed to public misunderstanding of the real tensions and anxieties involved. It should not be so. There are more reporters and foreign correspondents on permanent assignment in Jerusalem than in any other capital city in the world. Even the bloodiest wars, famines, and earthquakes in other parts of the world often go under-reported, while every stone thrown in Jerusalem gets a headline. But too often the news comes with a deadly backhand spin.

A WEB OF DECEPTION

Part of the problem is that little coverage is given in the English language media to what is being reported in the Arabic and Hebrew press. As a result, we get a distorted picture of reality.

For example, Yasser Arafat will conduct an interview for an American newspaper, and the reporter will accurately relay what Arafat said. But the next day Arafat will do an interview with an Arabic newspaper and say precisely the opposite, assuring his loyal followers that his words have one meaning for enemies and quite another meaning for his friends. The Arabic interview, however, is rarely translated or even mentioned in the American press.

Arabic newspapers are filled with anti-Israeli invective, and they often use anti-Semitic cartoons to drive home their hatred of the "Zionist enemy." The similarity of these drawings to the nasty caricatures of Jews that appeared in Nazi newspapers during the 1930s should make even the least sensitive observers wince. But the Islamic concept of peace is different from yours and mine. In the mind of the Shiite, the members of Hezbollah and Hamas, and the loyal supporter of the *intifada,* the concept of peace is not the absence of war, and not an end to hostilities, but a temporary cease-fire. There is no lasting peace in such a view, but only moments of strategic inaction. So when the Arab media refer to the "peace process" they speak of *insikhab,* a word that simply means temporary withdrawal.

In almost every public speech to an Arab audience, PLO Leader Yasser Arafat calls for a continuation of the *jihad,* or holy war, against Israel. PLO officials regularly state they have no intention of helping Israel to capture Islamic fundamentalist terrorists in Palestinian-controlled areas. Terrorists, suicide bombers, and assassins are accorded the highest esteem in Gaza, Ramallah, Hebron, and other Arab enclaves; those who kill Jews are treated as heroes. For a more detailed sampling of what Arafat and other PLO leaders are really saying to their own people, I have included an appendix to this book called, "In Their Own Words."

I prefer to think that if the American people ever saw the side of Yasser Arafat and the PLO visible to the Arabic media, the notion that they truly desire peace with Israel would evaporate with the morning dew.

THE TEFLON TERRORIST

Another aspect of this conspiracy of silence seems more intentional, and that is in the media's choice of what to include in their news coverage and what to leave out. Let me cite a couple of examples that should cause alarm.

Some time ago the United States Senate passed a resolution demanding that the Palestinian Authority (PA) extradite PLO terrorist Abu Abbas to the United States for prosecution in the murder of Leon Klinghoffer, the wheelchair-bound passenger killed in the 1985 *Achille Lauro* hijacking. You would think that a unanimous Senate vote targeted at a foreign leader, on the day of his meeting with the president of the United States, would be front-page news. Not so.

The fact is, Reuters, a major news-gathering agency headquartered in London, did put the story on their newswire that day, calling it "an awkward reminder of the past." But the major newspapers in the U.S. ignored the event almost completely. *The Boston Globe* ran a tiny one-paragraph blurb at the bottom of page fourteen.

In an address to an admiring and demonstrative audience at the National Press Club in Washington, D.C., Yasser Arafat repeated his outrageous accusation that fanatics in the Israeli government were actually behind the Hamas and Islamic Jihad suicide bombings. In the wake of those comments, the Zionist Organization of America did a survey of press coverage after the speech. Out of twenty major newspapers that reported on Arafat's speech, not a single one mentioned his outrageous accusation that the Israeli government was sponsoring terrorism against its own people. Not one news organization dared to show the lunacy of this celebrated public figure.

Such statements, however, are essential to a proper understanding of Yasser Arafat. His patently false allegations show that Arafat is not a credible person and that he is trying to shift the blame for increased terrorist activity away from himself and his own followers onto the victims of the terrorists he is shielding. Had he made such a statement before the U.S. Congress, one would hope, his hundred-million-dollar funding might have disappeared overnight. But unless you happened to be attending the Press Club luncheon that day, you never heard it or read about it. It was the news media's little secret.

In the 1980s the American press dubbed Ronald Reagan the

"Teflon president." The media and the president's liberal detractors could never seem to make their allegations against him stick. The world press should have a new candidate for that nonstick label—Yasser Arafat, the "Teflon terrorist." However, the charges that could and should be brought against this militant leader, and the revelations that need to be made about his belligerent words and deeds, don't stick to him because they are never reported.

By not reporting the whole truth about him, the news media have given the impression that Yasser Arafat is a reasonable man and a respectable person. He is portrayed as an important international leader. So when Israeli officials or other informed observers point out his instability, ineptitude, violent nature, and dishonesty, the charges slide off him as if he were made of Teflon. The public image of the Palestinian leader perpetuated by the American media, however, is a far cry from reality.

A WORD OF KNOWLEDGE

The United States government, while historically a staunch ally of Israel, has also been a collaborator with Israel's avowed enemies in the Arab world, both with the governments of Arab countries and with PLO terrorists. A secret CIA-PLO link was established as far back as 1969, and this dangerous liaison continued both officially and unofficially until 1988 when open negotiations with the PLO began. At that time the PLO went mainstream. Arafat was pressured into recognizing "Israel's right to exist" and he even made a public declaration that he had renounced terrorism. The covert link then became a public endorsement. But the tiger had not changed his stripes; he merely denied them.

To make these observations more cogent, let me offer one

example of the U.S. government's complicity with Arab governments. Then I will describe our covert deal with the PLO, and the results these various backroom bargains have had on America's relationship with Israel.

In 1981 I attended a White House security briefing regarding the proposed sale of Advanced Warning And Command System (AWACS) aircraft to the government of Saudi Arabia. A solid majority in Congress opposed it, but the Reagan administration was pulling out all the stops to garner support for the sale. I knew little or nothing about the AWACS planes at that time, but I knew that in the hands of Saudi Arabia such sophisticated high-altitude surveillance aircraft could pose a threat to the security of Israel.

I suspected, naturally, that there was a good possibility that our advanced technology—the most sophisticated radar equipment in the world—would find its way into the hands of other Arab countries, and perhaps even a hostile Soviet-aligned country such as Libya. Those issues were on my mind when I began my trip.

As I waited to board the commercial flight to Washington, I kept wondering why our government would be selling the most sophisticated military equipment we owned to the Saudis. Just days before, the government of Saudi Arabia had presented a check for twenty-eight million dollars to the PLO. Now we were proposing to sell high-tech aircraft to this Arab nation, a nation that was still technically at war with Israel. It didn't make sense.

So I prayed silently as I sat there in the airport lounge, and I asked the Lord to show me the reason behind these things. Within moments of that prayer, some ideas came to me out of the blue: *Israeli jets flew over Saudi airspace when they returned from blowing up the nuclear reactor in Iraq in June. The U.S. surveillance crew in the area saw this on their own radar, but they neglected to inform the Sau-*

dis, who were helping to finance the reactor. This embarrassed the Saudis, who felt they had been subjected to great indignity. They protested vigorously to the American government and demanded that these planes be sold to them as a form of compensation for their loss.

"Lord," I said, "this is incredible! Please show me if I'm really hearing from you or if this is just the fruit of my overactive imagination. In fact, if it's true, I would ask you to allow me to meet someone from the AWACS crew that was flying the plane that detected the violation of Saudi airspace."

Now, I knew that would be something only God could do. AWACS crews, as I subsequently found out, are rotated regularly, and neither the Pentagon nor the State Department would give out specific information on that. Even if I'd had time to call or write someone in authority, it wouldn't have helped.

But I did have time to write my prayer request on a piece of paper inside my Bible once I was seated on the plane. As I folded it, the passenger next to me noticed the paper and his eye caught the word AWACS. So he asked me about my interest in the AWACS planes. I told him I was headed for a briefing at the White House concerning these aircraft, but I didn't mention my specific prayer request.

Imagine, then, my astonishment when he told me that he was an AWACS crewman. As we talked, I discovered that he was the precise answer to my prayer. He had been on duty in June and had been on the flight that detected the Saudi overflight by Israeli jets! It turned out that the entire seventeen-man crew, of which he was a part, was sitting around me on that plane.

So I had the opportunity to personally question the crew about some of the things I felt God had told me. They gave few direct answers—and certainly revealed no military secrets—but with smiles and nods they confirmed some of the details. I also learned that only the most unusual circumstances had put these men on a commercial flight. Normally they would have been transported by military aircraft, but they had received urgent orders calling them back to their base to perform surveillance on Cuban flights off the Virginia coast. There was no time to make other arrangements so they wound up on this very flight with me.

At the White House briefing, the sale of AWACS planes to Saudi Arabia was presented as vital to peace and stability in the Middle East. I was able to ask questions and make statements against the sale of the AWACS, based on what the Lord had revealed—and then confirmed to me—through the testimony of those crewmen.

Afterward, one admiral actually took me by the lapel and said, "Who in the world are you, and where did you get that information? You've got the whole White House tap-dancing on the front floor!"

AND NOTHING BUT THE TRUTH

My purpose was not to give dance lessons to the Reagan administration, but to speak on behalf of Israel, one of America's most important allies. No other country in the world—not even Great Britain—has voted more consistently with the United States in the United Nations than Israel. And in spite of what you may hear about the "powerful Jewish lobby" in America, Israel needs all the friends she can get in Washington. But too often we support policies that undermine this loyal friend.

One week before the AWACS vote, a clear majority of senators was strongly opposed to the AWACS sale. But by the final Senate vote, those in favor of the sale won by a narrow fifty-two to forty-eight vote. What made the difference? Aggressive campaigning by the administration, for one thing. Two of my

Christian friends said the president himself had called them at home following the briefing. He had asked them to call their senators and suggest they vote for the sale.

Another, possibly critical, factor influencing the vote was an intense lobbying effort by pro-Arab business interests in the U.S. Unbelievable pressure was put on companies doing business with Saudi Arabia. The Saudis held up negotiations with every American company during the month before the vote: No contracts were signed, and discussions on all future contracts were stalled until the vote was taken. Saudi officials actually checked up on American companies to make sure they were lobbying for the sale of the AWACS planes and not against it.

Some executives later admitted they had the clear impression that if the sale had not gone through, their contracts would not have been negotiated or renewed. Many of them had no idea what AWACS planes were or what the sale would do to the balance of power in the Middle East; but they were told to lobby for it, so lobby they did. Among the companies awarded lucrative contracts as soon as the sale went through were Greyhound Corporation ($90 million), National Medical Enterprises ($84 million), and Westinghouse Corporation ($130 million). All of them had supported the AWACS sale.

But the most disturbing influence on the vote was the outright duplicity of the U.S. State Department. Award-winning investigative reporter Steven Emerson, who had worked on the Senate Foreign Relations Committee staff at one time, detailed the deception in his book, *The American House of Saud: The Secret Petrodollar Connection*. It is truly an eye-opening and conscience-troubling account for the people of this country.

Emerson disclosed that a classified State Department report written in December 1980 was released, without going through the process of formal declassification, as a briefing memo for

Congress during the 1981 AWACS debate. However, before its release the report had been deliberately altered to eliminate negative references to corruption in the Saudi royal family, military problems, and to potential security threats in the area.

In the original classified document, officials had been warned that, "The Shia minority could pose a major security threat over the next two to five years." But the revised version in the briefing memo offered this shocking reversal: "The Shia minority does not pose a serious threat to the regime." Nothing had changed culturally, politically, or diplomatically in the intervening six months to warrant re-evaluating the potential threat in such a manner, except that the AWACS sale had become politically expedient.

"What has emerged," Emerson said, "is a story of wrongdoing, fraud, and corruption committed by Arabists at high levels of the U.S. government." Emerson went on to say that, "Senior State Department officials participated in and sanctioned both the preparation of the deliberately inaccurate memo and the selective replication of the classified report."

This is only one example, but it is representative of the way that Arab manipulation of American businesses and government officials has been conducted over a long period of time in order to get military equipment or other financial concessions. If you ever waited in line for an hour to buy gas in the 1970s, you have had a small taste of the kind of economic terrorism most favored by the OPEC nations of the Middle East in their dealings with the West.

DANCING WITH THE DEVIL

As troubling as such revelations can be, even more disturbing is the discovery that our government made a secret agreement with the PLO in 1973, and that from 1976 to 1988 officials in the CIA and the

State Department were in continual contact with this radical Palestinian group. While our government was outwardly pretending to take a tough stand against terrorism, we were doing the very thing we said we would never do: negotiate with terrorists.

Oliver North's stellar career was destroyed when allegations of an arms-for-hostages deal with Iran surfaced in 1986. But Colonel North's deal with Teheran doesn't hold a candle to the almost two-decades-long marriage of the PLO and the CIA. The U.S. literally paid for a top PLO official—a notorious terrorist—and his new bride to take their honeymoon trip to Walt Disney World in Florida. As if blatant subversion of national policy by Arabists in the State Department weren't enough, we have pandered to the petty pleasures and amusement of marauders who would gladly destroy us.

This sinister alliance started back in 1969 when Robert C. Ames, an American CIA agent, first made contact with Ali Hassan Salameh, a senior intelligence officer in the PLO and founder of Arafat's Force 17 security guards. Ames was serving undercover in the U.S. consulate in Beirut at the time. Sympathetic to the Palestinian cause, Ames had decided that Arafat's Fatah faction was the most moderate wing of the PLO. When he initiated contact with Salameh, he did so with the approval of Henry Kissinger, National Security Council director at that time for President Nixon.

The CIA was impressed with Salameh, and in 1970 they offered to put him on the payroll, to the tune of three million dollars a year. But, lo and behold, Salameh burst into rage when approached by Ames with an offer of cash; he was a trained killer, not a spy for hire. Claiming to be insulted by the offer, he cut off contact with Ames and the CIA. But in a few short years, it seems, Salameh recovered from his bout of moral outrage and agreed to the deal; and when he married a beauty queen from Lebanon, the couple enjoyed an elegant honeymoon to

Florida and Hawaii, all expenses paid by your CIA.

The CIA had to have been aware of Salameh's terrorist activities. Over the next several years he directed several hijackings and masterminded the massacre of the Israeli athletes at the 1972 Munich Olympics. Yet the CIA reestablished their relationship with Salameh again in 1973, after Black September assassinated the U.S. ambassador to Sudan and his deputy. According to Salameh, Arafat had not approved the assassinations and was now willing to work with the CIA to prevent any harm to American officials in the future.

So on November 3, 1973, Deputy CIA Director Vernon Walters met officially with Ali Hassan Salameh to hammer out an agreement with the PLO. It would be ten years before this secret PLO-CIA agreement would become public knowledge, when it was reported by the *Wall Street Journal*.

According to the *Journal* article, American officials signed what amounted to a non-aggression pact with the PLO. The terms of the agreement stipulated that the PLO would not kill any more U.S. diplomats and, in return, the American government would eventually recognize "Palestinian rights." After the pact was signed, the PLO kept its part of the bargain. Fatalities among American diplomats due to terrorist acts declined dramatically. But the fact that America chose to combat terrorism by making a secret deal with terrorists, rather than combating terrorism openly as we might have done in an earlier age, was a sign of the dramatic weakening of America's moral sense, and an act of treachery against our closest ally in the Middle East.

THE NAKED TRUTH

As a matter of U.S. policy, substantive discussions with the PLO were banned between 1975 and 1988. The policy had little effect on reality, however. This tactic originated with Henry Kissinger in a private addendum to the 1975 agreement between Israel and Egypt, which called for withdrawal of Israeli forces from lands they had seized in the Sinai during the Yom Kippur War. Kissinger promised Israel that the U.S. would not recognize or negotiate with the PLO until the PLO recognized Israel's right to exist.

Israel had asked for this reassurance from the U.S. government for two reasons. First, Israel was relinquishing a strategic position, which subjected it to a greater security risk, and that strategic position not only included air bases, but valuable oil fields. Second, in 1974 the Arab nations had declared the PLO to be the "sole and legitimate representative" of the Palestinians. A month after that, Yasser Arafat made his famous pistol-and-olive-branch appearance before the United Nations.

The UN invitation served to legitimize Arafat in world opinion, and the Israelis needed assurance that the U.S. would do nothing to increase his stature. Their wounds were still fresh. Six months earlier the Israelis had buried sixteen school children killed by PLO terrorists in Ma'alot. Now the man responsible for that act was being touted as a hero.

President Reagan added another condition to the Kissinger policy, saying that the PLO would have to specifically renounce terrorism if they ever wanted to talk to the U.S. When Congress enacted the policy into law in 1986, the "no substantive discussions with the PLO" rule was made official policy for all government personnel.

Yet contacts between government officials and the PLO continued, most of them officially sanctioned by the administration or the State Department. And it was a private negotiating team— a group of Americans coordinated by a Swedish diplomat working directly with Secretary of State George Shultz—who finally convinced Arafat to say the magic words in Geneva, the words that would get him formal recognition by the United States government.

At that point there was no longer any need for secrecy. After the Geneva conference, the United States openly supported the PLO.

The Forty-third General Assembly of the United Nations was scheduled to take up the Palestinian issue at a session in early December 1988. Yasser Arafat requested a visa so he could come to New York and address a special session of the UN. Although Secretary of State Shultz was working with the secret team of negotiators trying to get Arafat to say the magic words—and went so far as to send documents marked "secret" and "sensitive" to Stockholm, where he knew they would be shown to Arafat—Shultz was uncertain about how to handle the visa request.

Anti-terrorist legislation specified that no waiver on visa requirements could be issued to anyone known to be actively engaged in terrorist activity. A majority of the Senate was strongly opposed to the Arafat visa. Many top administration officials, however, were in favor of granting the visa, most notably General Colin Powell, who was then national security adviser to the president. But Shultz, under the direction of President Reagan, decided to live by the letter of the law and denied the visa.

When UN leaders learned that Arafat's visa had been denied, they rescheduled the Palestinian session for Geneva one week later. I was so concerned about this special session that I decided to attend. For decades, I have watched the UN gang up on Israel and I knew that this session, where such an explosive issue would be discussed, would include few supporters from Israel's camp. As I prayed about going to the UN session, I believe the Lord told me to go and confront Yasser Arafat directly.

I didn't know how the Lord would bring this about, but I knew he was telling me to go, and I knew what he wanted me to say.

UNMASKING A MENACE

In Geneva, Arafat called a press conference for 7:00 P.M. on Wednesday, December 14. He had spoken for more than an hour to the General Assembly the day before, but he had not brought himself to say the words the United States required in order for our government to formally recognize the PLO. Under intense pressure, Arafat called his own press conference where he finally said the magic words. He recognized Israel's "right to exist," he accepted the terms of UN Resolutions 242 and 338, and he renounced the use of terrorism.

He said some other words, however, that were still cause for concern for those of us who love Israel. He said, "Let it be perfectly clear that neither Arafat nor anyone else can stop the *intifada*. The Arab uprising will stop only when practical and tangible steps are taken toward the attainment of its national goals and establishment of its Palestinian state." He called on the European Economic Community states "to play a more effective role in consolidating peace in our region." Once again, the subtext demanded, *Please put pressure on Israel to give us a state.*

Nevertheless, he did utter the required formula: "We totally and categorically reject all forms of terrorism, including individual, group, and state terrorism." Hundreds of reporters covered the press conference, eagerly recording the Teflon Terrorist's historic words.

My heart broke when I heard Arafat speak, because I knew he was lying. He has always used words as weapons. Words mean nothing to him. Arafat can tell you in one breath that you are his brother, invite you inside for dinner, then in the next breath assign someone to take you outside and stab you in the back between the main course and dessert. That's a normal day at the office for men like him.

I finally had my opportunity to confront Arafat personally at the end of his press conference at the *Palais des Nations*. It was an unforgettable encounter.

Arafat said he would recognize three people to speak. I knew he would never choose me, so before he could call on someone else I stood quickly and addressed him. "Jerusalem is Israel's capital," I said, "And the Messiah is coming back to a united Jerusalem under the authority of the Jewish people."

Arafat flew into a rage. He screamed, "Shut up! Shut up! What must I do to make you shut up? Striptease for you?"

After it was all over I wondered about this bizarre outburst. It was not unusual for Arafat to fly off the handle; his mercurial temper was legendary. But what on earth was this talk about doing a striptease?

Later I read something that made some sense of it. After his speech to the General Assembly, when he was under pressure for not having said the magic words, he spoke to Hosni Mubarak, president of Egypt. Arafat reportedly told Mubarak that he had done all he could do; he had already made so many concessions that he felt he had been stripped naked.

At that moment, however, I was more concerned about getting out of the conference room alive than figuring out what Arafat was screaming about. There must have been one hundred PLO operatives in the room, and they were all eyeing this lanky Texan who had just provoked their hero. I saw undisguised anger in their eyes. As I prayed silently, the Holy Spirit said, "Just turn and walk out of the room. I will protect you. There will be a cab waiting outside the front door."

When I turned around, to my amazement, a path had cleared

from the front of the still crowded room to the back. I walked calmly (or so I hoped) out the door. There was indeed a cab waiting in front of the building. When I got back to my room at the Hilton, the telephone was ringing. It was Dr. Reuben Hecht, senior adviser to the prime minister of Israel.

"Mike Evans, just how many bodyguards do you have?" he asked. "Did you know the entire nation of Israel was listening to you speak to Yasser Arafat?"

"I have many bodyguards," I told him. "They are angels."

OF PEACE AND APPEASEMENT

Arafat's prestige soared after the Geneva conference—for a while, that is. Saddam Hussein invaded Kuwait on August 2, 1990. Three days later Arafat flew to Baghdad to be at his crony's side. But what else could he do? Iraq had been footing the bill for the *intifada* for two years. Reportedly as much as four million dollars a month was flowing from Saddam's pockets into Arafat's.

And yet Saudi Arabia, allied with the United States against Iraq, had always underwritten a hefty portion of the PLO's annual operating budget of $350 million. One way Arafat kept the Palestinians loyal to him was through his generous handouts. With the exception of Jordan, the Arab countries have intentionally kept the Palestinian people as refugees for decades; thousands of them still live in refugee camps. Hence, the PLO has provided funding for education, healthcare, and other social services for the Palestinians, creating a welfare class totally dependent on Arafat's largesse. And Arafat himself has always had total control of the PLO purse strings.

Palestinians living in Israel have always been eligible for citizenship. But because of their long-standing hatred for the Jewish nation, most of them have refused to be assimilated into Israeli society. And where outright war by the Arab nations had not been able to push Israel back to her pre-1967 borders, it now seemed as if the Palestinians living in the territories—Judea and Samaria (called the West Bank) and Gaza—might be able to accomplish the task by continuing to throw one stone at a time.

World opinion in light of the *intifada* was turning against Israel, and the Jewish nation was becoming more and more isolated. Increasing pressure was being put upon Israel to make territorial concessions—"land for peace" as it has come to be known. The international community was determined to drag Israel to the negotiating table and to coerce them into signing a Middle East peace agreement on the basis of UN Security Council Resolutions 242 and 338.

To understand why the Israelis were reluctant, it would help to know, based on international law, what's wrong with this land-for-peace policy that has dominated the Middle East peace process for so long. It may seem complicated at first blush, but stick with me for a minute as I try to put the peace process into better focus.

UN Resolution 338 simply declared a cease-fire in the October 1973 Yom Kippur War, which had been started by Egypt and Syria, and it required the parties to work toward a "just and durable peace" on the basis of Resolution 242.

UN Resolution 242, passed after the Six-Day War in 1967, called for Israel to withdraw "from territories occupied" in that war. Israel was not opposed to negotiating a withdrawal from the territories, so long as two principles were observed: first, that Israel not be required to fully withdraw from *all* the territories, which would make her borders indefensible; and second, that Israel not be forced to negotiate with a party who was not willing to say up front that it would abide by the other provision of the resolution—that is, the recognition of Israel's sovereignty.

Just eighteen days after the Six-Day War, Robert McNamara,

then Secretary of Defense, and the Joint Chiefs of Staff issued a position paper outlining the minimum territory Israel would need to retain for security purposes. Released on June 29, 1967, the paper recommended that Israel retain eighty percent of the territories, not counting the Sinai. Under their recommendation, possession of most of the West Bank and all of the Golan Heights would be necessary for Israel's survival. The only area the Pentagon thought Israel could afford not to annex was the eastern slope of Samaria approaching the Jordan River. In 1988, twenty-one years after the Defense department recommendation, one hundred retired U.S. generals and admirals urged the government to support Israeli claims to the territories, arguing that the Pentagon's 1967 conclusion is even more valid today.

Now, the important question is this: Is Israel illegally occupying the territories? Outside of the biblical grounds for Israel's rights to the land, she holds this land as a matter of international law. International law does not recognize a legal right to possess lands gained by aggression (which is how Jordan and Egypt gained control of the West Bank and Gaza in 1948); however, when territory is gained through a defense against invasion, which is the means by which Israel gained control of the same territories in 1967, international law does not require withdrawal from those lands.

Professor of international law Louis René Beres of Purdue University elaborates on this principle: "As a non-state legal entity, Palestine ceased to exist in 1948, when Great Britain relinquished its League of Nations mandate. During the 1948–49 War of Independence, Judea/Samaria and Gaza came under the illegal control of Jordan and Egypt respectively. . . . In 1967, almost twenty years after Israel's entry into the community of nations, the Jewish State—as a result of its stunning military victory over Arab aggressor states—gained unintended control over Judea/Samaria and Gaza. Although the idea of the inadmissibility of the acquisition of territory by war is enshrined in the UN Charter, there existed no authoritative sovereign to whom the territories could be 'returned.' Israel could hardly have been expected to transfer these territories back to Jordan and Egypt."

In other words, who would Israel give the territories back to? They had not belonged to Jordan or Egypt in the first place. The territories were an unallocated portion of the British Mandate, and the sovereign entity with the best legal claim to these lands remains the nation of Israel.

THE BEST DEFENSE

This principle of international law concerning the acquisition of territory through self-defense makes a lot of sense. After all, if a bully attacks you and you manage to gain his property in the act of defending yourself, it hardly makes sense that you would just hand the bully's property back to him and say, "Oh, that's okay. You keep it." That would not be a deterrent to aggression. Quite the contrary, it would give free reign to every bully in the neighborhood to victimize the innocent with relative impunity.

But that's what the United Nations, backed to the hilt by the United States, is asking Israel to do. The suggestion is preposterous. "Look," they are effectively saying, "we know these Arab nations have attacked you, time after time, but you shouldn't have fought back and taken their land. We know it didn't belong to them to begin with, but you really ought to give it back anyway. Besides, they don't want it for themselves. They want it for these poor people you have brutally oppressed and refused to even talk to—you know, the ones who have been carrying out those silly little terrorist attacks for all these years."

"They didn't really mean any harm by it," the diplomats

seem to say, "and now they're willing to be nice to you. So why don't you just come over here to our one-big-happy-global-family negotiating table and sign on the dotted line? And don't worry about your security inside your tiny borders. We'll take care of you."

Of course, the UN would never be so plainspoken. And, yes, there are untold thousands of innocent Palestinians who have suffered terribly from decades of being caught in the middle of the conflict. But handing over these captured territories, lock, stock, and barrel, is not going to solve the problem. Instead, it will only aggravate it.

Appeasement did not stop Hitler's aggression in Europe, and it will not stop Arab aggression in the Middle East. The end result will be a weakened Israel, and as soon as the Arab world thinks the time is ripe, a new invasion will be launched—this time from a Palestinian base in Jerusalem's backyard.

Immediately after the Persian Gulf War, the United States rang the opening bell on a no-holds-barred wrestling match to get all the countries in the Middle East to participate in an international conference, in pursuit of a "just and comprehensive peace" in the region. The result was the 1991 Madrid Peace Conference, which became the basis for all subsequent peace negotiations.

During the protracted sparring that preceded the Madrid conference, the amount of pressure put on Israel to commit to the land-for-peace program was unprecedented. Moshe Arens, Israel's foreign minister during the early Bush Administration and defense minister during the Gulf War, documented the manipulation and outright economic blackmail of Israel by the Bush Administration in his 1995 book, *Broken Covenant.*

Arens relates how Secretary of State James Baker leaked false reports to the media about his diplomatic meetings in Washington. He describes how Baker deceived Israel into believing the upcoming peace discussions would be between Israel and the Arab nations, when Baker had, in fact, already made concessions to the Arabs and brought the PLO into the negotiations covertly. He shows how the Bush administration undermined the Shamir government by meeting secretly with opposition party leaders, Rabin and Peres, who were found to be more conciliatory on the land-for-peace policy. And he shows precisely how the U.S. interference in Israeli domestic affairs ultimately brought down the Likud-Labor coalition government.

But the real heavyweight in the peace-process wrestling match was George Bush, himself. Bush put a choke hold on Israel that cost Yitzhak Shamir the 1992 election, and one that may have cost Bush his own bid for reelection—it certainly cost him the Jewish/pro-Israel vote.

THE HORNS OF A DILEMMA

That presidential choke hold was a freeze on the ten billion dollars in loan guarantees pending in Congress for the Israeli government. The money—which was not outright aid as Bush had hinted, but only a series of guaranteed loans—was meant for humanitarian purposes, to help in settling the massive influx of Jewish immigrants from the former Soviet Union. Bush asked Congress to delay consideration of the loan guarantees "just for 120 days" so a debate on the issue wouldn't interfere with the peace process. But the loan guarantees had nothing to do with the peace process—at least they weren't supposed to.

Baker went to Israel to deliver the final bombshell in person. The loan guarantees were indeed being tied to the peace process. The Arab governments had told the U.S. to make Israel put a freeze on new settlements in the contested territories or they wouldn't come to the peace conference, tentatively scheduled for the following month. The Arabs opposed any more Jewish immigration, and they saw this action as a way to stop it.

But with ten thousand Soviet Jews arriving in Israel every month, the only way they could be absorbed was to build new housing in the settlements, in Judea and Samaria. And to do that, the loan guarantees were desperately needed.

According to Arens, Shamir protested to Baker. "We are not imposing our views on settlements on you," he said, "but we oppose your linking the settlements to the guarantees." Baker's quick reply was blunt: "If you want U.S. guarantees, you will have to accept our position on settlements." Baker refused to discuss the loan guarantees further. All he would say is, "We are not going to fund settlement activity."

Two weeks after Baker's visit the Israeli Air Force made a reconnaissance flight over Iraq. The United States had refused to share satellite data on Iraqi missile launcher sites with Israel during the Gulf War. Since then, the U.S. had failed to update Israel on the results of the UN inspection teams in Iraq.

So the Israelis, who were the most vulnerable to a renewed Iraqi military threat, decided to gather their own data. Israel routinely informed Washington after their reconnaissance flights. Four days later, Iraq, joined by the United States, filed a formal protest in the United Nations against Israel for violating Iraqi airspace.

Now, what's wrong with this picture? The country we just fought a war against complains because the innocent party it repeatedly hit with Scud missiles—the close ally we strong-armed into not retaliating by refusing to share our military intelligence—took aerial photographs to see if there were any missiles still pointed in their direction, and the U.S. agreed with our enemies in protesting this Israeli action?

In spite of the intense pressure brought to bear on the Israeli administration, it was almost a foregone conclusion that Israel would indeed participate in an international wrestling match sponsored by the world's superpowers. Israel wanted peace perhaps more than any other party and believed the opportunities for peace were genuine. Although there would be a Palestinian delegation included with the Jordanians, they would ostensibly not be PLO members, which satisfied the Likud government's demands.

So Israel finally said "uncle" and packed for Madrid.

Four

Illusion and Reality

In 1982 Ronald Reagan received a photograph from a PLO front group that precipitated a change in American foreign policy. It was a picture of a young Palestinian girl with no arms. The little girl, Mr. Reagan was told, had lost her arms in the Israeli bombardment of Lebanon.

On the verge of a civil war, Lebanon had been easy prey for an invasion of international terrorists in the early 1970s. Kicked out of Jordan when the guerrilla organization had fomented a near-civil war, the PLO moved its headquarters to Lebanon. There they were backed by Syrian troops and Soviet weapons, and the result was a near-takeover of Lebanon by Syria, without Syria declaring war. Terrorists from around the world poured into the PLO base in Beirut. Finally, after a dozen years of PLO occupation, the Israelis decided to invade Lebanon—not to conquer the nation, but simply to evict the terrorists who were wreaking such havoc on their northern border.

Initially the Reagan administration supported Israel's strategy of cleaning out the terrorist nest in Lebanon. But the world press excoriated Menachem Begin for bombarding the PLO base. And then Mr. Reagan received the picture of the armless Palestinian girl. The president was moved by the tragic photograph and kept it on his desk in the oval office. He was so moved, in fact, that he called the Israeli prime minister and demanded that the bombardment cease.

Begin was forced to buckle under increasing pressure from the West. At great risk to Israeli troops stationed deep inside Lebanon, not to mention the risk to Israeli citizens living in Galilee who had been the target of frequent attacks from across the border, Begin halted the bombardment. The people of Israel watched in frustration as ten thousand PLO gunmen were escorted out of Beirut, weapons in hand, to the safety of PLO bases in Tunisia and other Arab states.

There was just one problem with the photograph that influenced President Reagan to abandon his support of the Israeli campaign: The photo was a public relations illusion, the propaganda equivalent of a magic trick using smoke and mirrors. The little Palestinian girl had indeed lost her arms, but it had happened years earlier during the Lebanese civil war—and she had been a victim of Arab, not Israeli, gunfire. The smoke-and-mirrors trick, however, worked all too well. An image of Israeli brutality had been indelibly burned into the minds of the American public and most of the world.

Over the next few years the PLO public relations campaign succeeded almost beyond belief. To read some press accounts, it sounded as if the PLO were promoting tourism, not terrorism. Suddenly Yasser Arafat was transformed from a terrorist to a diplomat.

But had Arafat really changed, or was it all a cleverly-crafted illusion? For decades Arafat had pursued two political goals: an independent Palestinian state and the elimination of Israel. He adopted terrorism as the means of achieving those goals. Arafat gave up all semblance of a normal life and devoted his every waking moment to this cause. For years he never slept in the same place two nights in a row, always keeping on the move, always one step ahead of his enemies.

Some fifty years after Arab nationalists adamantly rejected the UN plan for Palestine and instead launched a war against the new nation of Israel, Arafat finally appeared to realize his mentors had been wrong. The Jews were never leaving their homeland, and the Palestinian Arabs should have accepted partition all those years ago. Some of the land would have been better than none of the land after all. Despite decades of insurrection and bloodshed, Arafat had never succeeded in creating a Palestinian state. He was a leader without a land, his followers reduced to throwing stones and slashing tires, instead of fighting the all-out war against the Jews they had long sought.

So in 1988, at the UN General Assembly in Geneva, Arafat reluctantly declared that he had abandoned his second goal, the elimination of Israel, in order to realize his first goal, an independent Palestinian state. The United States believed him, and on his word alone the world's greatest superpower became Arafat's biggest supporter in pressuring Israel to negotiate with the PLO and accept a "two-state solution" to the Middle East conflict.

The Israelis did not believe Arafat had really given up his goal of eliminating them or, as the Egyptians and Palestinians had once proclaimed, of driving the Jews into the sea. Although they had accepted the idea of partition back in 1947, the Jews certainly were not interested in going back to that idea, as Arafat was now proposing.

After five wars launched by their Arab neighbors, and after thousands of terrorist attacks launched by the PLO, why should they now carve a Palestinian state out of their land and hand it over to Yasser Arafat? Given the history of Arafat and the Palestine Liberation Organization, who could blame Israelis for refusing to take Arafat's 1988 proposal seriously?

A COVENANT OF DESTRUCTION

The Palestine Liberation Organization was actually the brainchild of Gamal Abdel Nasser of Egypt. The late Egyptian president created the armed guerrilla organization as a useful political tool—a way to keep the unruly Palestinian refugees living in Egypt under his control—and to use them to help fight the Israelis. The PLO was first organized in Cairo in 1964. Its founding document is the Palestine National Covenant. This declaration rejects the Balfour Declaration of 1917, the UN Partition Agreement of 1948, the Jews' biblical claims to the land, and it denies the right of the Jewish people to have a nation.

The Covenant has been revised several times over the years, but it still contains the vehement anti-Jewish sentiment of the original document. It insists that all the territory of the nation of Israel properly belongs to the Palestinian Arabs, and only those Jews living in Palestine prior to the "Zionist invasion" can be regarded as legitimate Palestinians and thus allowed to stay in the land.

The Covenant doesn't say it, but if you ask any PLO spokesman or leader when the Zionist invasion began, he will tell you that it started in 1917 with the British Mandate. Despite the lengthy rhetoric, the Covenant essentially calls for the physical eradication of Jewry and the state of Israel, and the establishment of a Palestinian state in place of both Israel and Jordan.

Some six years before Nasser created the PLO, Yasser Arafat had started his own group dedicated to an armed struggle to "liberate Palestine." Then living in Kuwait, where he made quite a bit of money as an engineer, Arafat and a handful of revolutionaries created a military organization. They called it the Palestinian National Liberation Movement. In Arabic the initials spelled out HATAF, which was the word for death. So they turned the letters around to spell FATAH.

Fatah members were provoked when Nasser started up the PLO, seeing it only as a pawn of the Egyptian government. But in spite of their disdain for the origins of the PLO, Fatah members had joined it under the theory of "the enemy of my enemy is my friend." By 1969 Fatah had become the largest guerrilla group affiliated with the PLO. At that year's meeting of the PLO's executive body, the Palestine National Council, Yasser Arafat won complete control of the PLO. He has remained its chairman ever since.

Under the Oslo Accords signed with Israel, Arafat was obligated to amend the Palestinian National Covenant, which explicitly calls for the eradication of Israel and the Jewish people by May 7, 1996. In late April, the Palestinian National Council finally voted to amend the Covenant; however, it was a vote to change the Covenant in principle only: "The Covenant shall be amended by repealing all that contravenes the mutual letters of recognition between the PLO and the state of Israel."

No actual changes were made to the Covenant, nor was it specified which Covenant provisions (about half of the Covenant's thirty-three provisions call for the destruction of Israel) would be amended, or when the actual amendment might take place. This is perhaps the single most significant fact affecting the outcome of the current peace process. Yet it is a fact that is glossed over in media coverage. Over and over the media decry Israel for not living up to the Oslo Accords; almost never is it noted that the Palestinians have totally failed to meet their most basic obligation under the accord: the elimination of their Covenant pledge to destroy the nation of Israel.

Under the 1993 Declaration of Principles, Israel granted the PLO diplomatic recognition in exchange for a promise that the PLO would amend its Covenant. Israel kept the agreement; the PLO didn't. Under the 1994 agreement signed in Cairo, Israel gave control of Gaza and Jericho to the PLO in exchange for the same promise. Again, the PLO did not keep their end of the bargain. The 1995 Interim Agreement gave the PLO six major cities in Judea and Samaria, plus civilian control of over four hundred smaller towns and villages, in exchange for yet another promise to amend the PLO Covenant. Another agreement, another broken promise. Woven into the 1997 Hebron Agreement is the same threadbare promise. Why is there no outrage from the international negotiators, no public exposure by the media?

Here is Yasser Arafat, holding an olive branch in one hand and a declaration of war in the other—yet it is Israel who is blamed for failure to abide by the Oslo Accords. This simple truth is not being told: The PLO has not kept the promise to amend its Covenant.

A TIDAL WAVE OF TERROR

No wonder, then, that so many Israelis have been skeptical about the land-for-peace process. With the Palestinian Covenant still calling for their destruction, it gives them little confidence that they will actually receive peace in exchange for giving up more land. And Israel continues to face a barrage of terrorist activity from PLO splinter groups and Islamic fundamentalist groups operating from Palestinian-controlled areas.

It is difficult to describe the effects of decades of terrorism on the people of Israel. A catalogue of terrorist operations, with a description of all the death and carnage, would still not convey what it is like to know that you are never safe from violence.

On a trip to Israel during the heyday of PLO terrorism, I visited the port city of Eilat. While there, I was delighted to see an attractive young school teacher taking her class on an outing. It seemed to be a normal excursion, until I noticed the one small detail that let me know I was still in Israel: The teacher was carrying an automatic weapon. Thomas Jefferson once said that the price of liberty is eternal vigilance. This young teacher had discovered the truth of his words.

Terrorism is so frightening precisely because it is a purposeful attack against the innocent—school children and teachers were a favorite target of the PLO from the start. In his recent book, *Fighting Terrorism: How Democracies Can Defeat Domestic and International Terrorists,* Benjamin Netanyahu defines it this way: "Terrorism is the deliberate and systematic assault on civilians to inspire fear for political ends."

PLO terrorists sought to victimize children as one of their most devastating weapons of fear against Israel. Perhaps these two examples will indicate how these people operate. In April 1974 three terrorists entered a school in Kiryat Shmonah, a town in northern Israel. Unknown to the terrorists, the schoolchildren were away on a trip. So the terrorists used the weapons intended for the massacre of the schoolchildren on nearby residents, killing eight adults and eight children in an apartment building close to the school. Israeli soldiers trapped the terrorists inside the building, but the Palestinians were killed when their own explosives were detonated.

In May of that year, Palestinian terrorists struck another northern town, Ma'alot. During the early morning hours the terrorists fired on motorists, killing an Arab woman; then they murdered an entire family asleep in their home. This time, when they reached the school building, the terrorists found one hundred children and took them and their four teachers hostage.

The terrorists demanded the release of more Palestinian prisoners, other terrorists who had been captured in Israel. The government agreed to exchange the prisoners for the school children, but refused to allow the terrorists to hold the children until the prisoners could be transferred to Damascus. In a standoff, the terrorists refused to release the children, so Israeli troops surrounded the school building. Eventually the soldiers killed all of the terrorists, but not before the Palestinians had killed sixteen children and injured sixty-eight others.

That's why, in Israel, school teachers on field trips carried automatic weapons.

But Israel's terrorist threat did not come from the PLO alone. In the 1970s a tidal wave of international terrorism was unleashed, not just against Israel, but against all the western democracies. It was not until the collapse of Communism and the breakup of the Soviet Union that the world discovered just how deeply the Soviets had been involved in this conspiracy of international terrorism.

THE SOVIET CONNECTION

"Most of the international terror that plagued the world from the late 1960s through the mid-1980s was the product of an *ad hoc* alliance between the Soviet bloc and dictatorial Arab regimes," Benjamin Netanyahu says in *Fighting Terrorism*. "The centrality of terrorism to Soviet foreign policy emerged in the 1960s, with the stalemate in the Cold War and the emergence of independent Arab states willing to hitch their oil revenues and their war against Israel to the terrorist internationale.

"Since a direct assault on the democracies had become unthinkable, the Soviets developed international terror as one of the weapons in the arsenal for carrying on the Communist struggle in many western strongholds, while maintaining plausible deniability about their complicity. Even less able than the Soviets to take on the West directly, these Arab regimes embarked on a covert terrorist campaign against American and western targets."

In the 1970s, the PLO camp in Lebanon became a training center for terrorists worldwide, housing at one time or another the IRA, the Sandinistas, the Japanese Red Army, the German Baader-Meinhof, and other notorious groups. Some of these militant cells assisted the PLO in attacks against Israeli targets, and the PLO assisted the other groups in operations around the world.

A new terrorist group was initiated by the PLO, Black September, named after their 1970 revolt in Jordan. One of this group's most famous operations was the 1972 massacre of Israeli athletes at the Munich Olympics. A year before that the group had assassinated the prime minister of Jordan, who was attending a meeting of the Arab League in Cairo. The hit was made in retaliation for their eviction from Hussein's kingdom.

In 1973 Black September took an American ambassador and his deputy, along with a Belgian diplomat, hostage in Khartoum. The terrorists demanded the release of Abu Daoud, a military leader who had been captured by Hussein's forces, and Sirhan Sirhan, the Palestinian who had assassinated Robert Kennedy during a 1968 campaign stop in California. When their demands were not met, Black September executed the diplomatic hostages.

Several Arab countries, most notably Syria, Libya, and Iraq, became state sponsors of terrorist groups like Black September, allowing them to set up headquarters in their countries and providing them with financial support and refuge from their pursuers. All these governments asked in return was that the terrorists carry out a few attacks on their designated enemies. According to

Netanyahu, this kind of state-sponsored terrorism is used "to fight a proxy war as an alternative to conventional war."

THE VIEW FROM THE INSIDE

During the period of the PLO stronghold in Lebanon, I visited with Major Saad Haddad, commander of the Lebanese Christian Army in Southern Lebanon. Haddad and his troops tangled frequently with PLO terrorists moving from camps in his area toward the Israeli border. I met with Haddad in the town of Metullah, inside the Israeli border.

His courage astonished me. Haddad brought no bodyguards with him. As we sat in a public restaurant drinking tea, I had to remind myself from time to time that the PLO hated him and had probably targeted him for assassination. At any moment a Jeep could have roared by and a terrorist could have hurled a bomb into our midst.

I asked Haddad if his forces had captured many of the PLO Arabs. "Do you think I'm fighting Arabs on the front line? Far from it," he said. "I'm fighting terrorists from all over the world. North Korea, Cuba, South America—and just a month ago, two Czechs got killed in a fight. The PLO has people from almost all the communist countries. And from all the Islamic countries too—Libya, Iran, Egypt."

"What about the UN forces north of you?" I asked Haddad. "Are they helping to keep peace?"

"The UN is doing nothing. They are just there for show. Worse than that, sometimes they are covering for the PLO. The PLO has moved in and they have camps inside the UN area from which the PLO makes terrorist actions."

"What about Israel?" I asked him.

"That's the only country which cares for us. Without Israel we would have been exterminated a long time ago. They are supposed to be our enemy, but they are helping us."

Haddad told me how his troops had first come into contact with the Israelis at the fence strung up at the border between Lebanon and Israel. The PLO had isolated Haddad's forces in an area close to the border. These southern villages were cut off from doctors or hospitals in the rest of Lebanon. One day a woman brought her sick baby to the fence and got the soldiers' attention. They couldn't understand her language, but they could tell she was distressed because her baby was so sick.

The Israelis got the woman to hand her baby over the fence and they took it to a hospital. The next day the soldiers cut a hole in the fence so the woman could come into Israel and visit her child. When the woman later took her healthy baby back to the village and told what had happened, the Lebanese realized the Israelis were not their enemy.

"When someone is dying of thirst and you give him even a drop of water, it gives hope," Haddad said. "Pretty soon they started calling that fence the 'Good Fence.' Now they've even let some of our people have jobs down there during the day. Today it is like regular relations between two countries who have a common enemy."

But the common enemy, Haddad said, was not the Lebanese Muslims or even another nation. The common enemy was the Soviet-backed international terrorists operating from the safe haven of the PLO base.

THE PISTOL OR THE OLIVE BRANCH?

In November 1974 Yasser Arafat became the first and only speaker to address the United Nations General Assembly wearing a pistol strapped to his waist. Holding up an olive branch, he told the delegates: "In one hand I carry an olive branch, while the other grasps the gun of revolt. Do not let the olive branch fall from my hand." His ninety-minute speech was punctuated by frequent applause and concluded to wild acclamation.

But there was at least one person in the audience who did not applaud. British writer John Laffin could not help recalling the last time he had seen Arafat's hands held high in triumph. It was just a year earlier, when he had accompanied Arafat on a visit one August afternoon to a PLO military training camp in Lebanon.

In one of the training exercises he witnessed, a young Palestinian plunged a hand into a basket of live chickens, plucked one out, and briskly wrung its neck.

"No, no!" Arafat said angrily, as Laffin recorded in his book, *The PLO Connections.*

Then Arafat reached into the basket, dragged out a squirming chicken, and proceeded to pull it apart, limb by limb. "*This* is how we teach the boys to deal with the Israelis," he told Laffin.

The year 1974 was an important one for Arafat and his PLO. That year has become a code word for the formulation arrived at by the Palestine National Council in their annual meeting, the "Phased Plan," which calls for the gradual destruction of the nation of Israel. Arafat's words and his celebrity status notwithstanding, nothing has happened to modify this plan during the "peace process" of the past several years.

Following the 1967 war, two different schools of thought developed among the Arabs concerning their dilemma of what to do with Israel. With the increased territory Israel gained as a result of the war, it was believed impossible to defeat Israel by conventional means. Where the east-west borders of Israel had been a mere nine miles wide at its narrowest point, after 1967 Israel was considerably larger. Israel's borders were no longer vulnerable to quick penetration.

The first school of thought held that since it was no longer possible to defeat Israel by conventional means, then there was no choice but to make formal peace with the Jewish nation. This view was held by Anwar Sadat of Egypt, who accepted Mehachem Begin's invitation to help negotiate a settlement with Israel. The peace treaty, called the Camp David Accords, was drafted in late 1978 and signed in early 1979.

Eventually King Hussein of Jordan, who had probably held this view the longest but had been prevented from acting on it by intense political pressure, did the same, signing a formal peace agreement with Israel in 1994.

The second school of thought held that since it was no longer possible to defeat Israel within her existing boundaries, then the course of action should be to first reduce Israel to the pre-1967 borders and *then* destroy it. The means of reducing Israel's borders would be a combination of a continued campaign of terrorism by the PLO, and political pressure on America and Europe by the Arab states.

This view was officially adopted by the PLO at their 1974 conference in Cairo. It was formalized in a document known as the Phased Plan. Dr. Aaron Lerner, a Middle East analyst, summarizes the goals of the PLO's Phased Plan as follows: "First, to establish a combatant national authority over every part of Palestinian territory that is liberated (article 2); second, to use that territory to continue the fight against Israel (article 4); finally, to start a pan-Arab war to complete the liberation of all the Palestinian territory [i.e., eliminate Israel] (article 8)."

The bottom line is that the PLO finally decided it would be acceptable to get rid of Israel in stages, if it couldn't be done all at once. They have yet to renounce this view. Instead, Arafat has publicly told his followers, on numerous occasions, that the Declaration of Principles signed with Israel in 1993 is actually a part of the PLO's Phased Plan.

For example, in November 1994, in a speech marking the celebration of Palestine National Day, Arafat said: "What has been a dream has become a reality. In 1974 the PNC decided on establishing a Palestinian Authority on the first piece of land from which the enemy has withdrawn or that we have liberated."

Much has been made of Arafat's reference to Israel as "the enemy," an expression hardly compatible with the PLO's peace agreement with Israel. But far more worrisome is the reference to 1974 and the Phased Plan, which still remains the blueprint for Israel's destruction.

MAPS AND ROLE MODELS

Other PLO leaders have made similar references to 1974's Phased Plan. A media watchdog group in Israel, Independent Media Review and Analysis, reported on a 1996 interview conducted in Damascus with a Palestinian official. Their report states, "In an appearance on Syrian television on the English-language interview program "Focus" at 9:30 P.M. on Monday, September 9, Faisal Husseini, who holds the Jerusalem portfolio for the Palestinian Authority, was asked what the boundaries of Palestine are.

"In response, Husseini replied that all Palestinians agree that the just boundaries of Palestine are the Jordan River and the Mediterranean Sea. He explained that, realistically, whatever can be obtained now should be accepted and that subsequent events perhaps in the next fifteen or twenty years would present an opportunity to realize the just boundaries of Palestine."

Another clue that the PLO has not totally renounced its idea of eliminating Israel, but has merely postponed it, is the fact that the official PLO letterhead still has for its logo a map of the nation of Israel labeled "Palestine." When a PLO representative testified, in March 1996, before a United States congressional committee reviewing PLO compliance with the Oslo Accords (required to renew annual funding for the Palestinians), he submitted his written testimony with a cover sheet on the PLO letterhead.

The PLO letterhead isn't the only item with a mislabeled map of Israel. Faisal Husseini, a PLO leader in Jerusalem and head of the Arab Studies Institute, published a map showing Tel Aviv and Haifa as "Jewish settlements." Textbooks in Egyptian and Jordanian schools, as well as those used in Palestinian schools, do not even show the nation of Israel on their maps. Is it any wonder then that a recent poll by the Center for Palestine Research showed that only 26 percent of Palestinians believe Israel has a right to exist?

Arafat's role models tell you a lot about the kind of man he is. The PLO was furious with Egyptian President Anwar Sadat for offering to make peace with Israel. After Sadat courageously went to Jerusalem in late 1977, in a genuine overture toward peace, the PLO struck with a vengeance. The next year was to be one of Israel's bloodiest in terms of vicious murder and assault by terrorists.

On March 11, 1978, a band of PLO terrorists plied their way toward a beach fifteen miles south of Haifa. They had numbered thirteen when they started out. Their numbers were reduced when two drowned in the Mediterranean.

Finally reaching the beach, they surprised an American tourist with a camera. By the time she realized who and what they were, it was too late. One blast of automatic weapon fire and she was dead. The murderers stepped over her body and onto the highway where they commandeered two busloads of Israelis returning from a holiday. The terrorists then crammed everybody into one bus and ordered the driver to head south toward Tel Aviv.

The overloaded bus became a moving vehicle of death. The trigger-happy terrorists fired on passing cars at will. When word of the crisis reached authorities, security men quickly erected an emergency roadblock seven miles north of Tel Aviv. When the bus came into sight, the terrorists opened fire. This was obviously no hostages-for-ransom situation.

Steeled for the worst, the Israelis tried to return fire without riddling the bus with bullets. Even through the thunderous gunfire, the screams and sobbing of women and children reached their tortured ears.

Then it happened: One earsplitting blast and the whole bus burst into flames. The PLO had detonated an incendiary bomb. By some miracle, seventy people survived. But thirty-seven innocent people died in the inferno. Security men rushed in and took two terrorists prisoner. In the burnt-out rubble, nine others lay dead.

The Coastal Road Massacre, as it became known, was one of the most horrific incidents in recent history. Imagine the Israelis' surprise, then, when they heard Yasser Arafat call Dalal Magribi, who led the raid, "the star among the heroes who carried out the landing operation on the coast." Speaking to the Islamic Women's Association in Gaza on June 18, 1995, he said, "She was the commander of the squad that pioneered the first Palestinian republic on that bus. This is the Palestinian woman with all its meanings and implications, the woman we are proud of and take pride in and compete with her glory."

To the Israelis, Magribi was not a heroine, but a monster. A scene from the Coastal Road Massacre was permanently etched in the memories of the survivors: One of the women passengers tried to save her baby by throwing him out of the burning bus; Magribi picked the child up and threw him back into the flames. This is the role model Arafat also held up to the Fatah Girls School in Gaza at their opening ceremonies. "Follow in the footsteps of Dalal," he told the young girls.

"PRETTY GOOD RESULTS"

In his new-and-improved public relations image, Yasser Arafat now appears to be a moderate. With the establishment of the Palestinian Authority (PA) and its control over Gaza, Jericho, and numerous other areas, Arafat has had to at least appear to have renounced terrorism. But is it another trick with smoke and mirrors?

While Arafat may not be directly involved in terrorist attacks any more, he allows groups that are even *more* radical than the PLO to continue waging the battle against Israel and the Jewish people. The two most prominent terrorist groups these days are Hamas (the Arabic acronym for the Islamic Resistance Movement) and Islamic Jihad. These two groups have been responsible for the wave of suicide bombings since the Oslo Accords were signed in 1993, and the deaths of well over two hundred people in Israel since that time.

Israel and the United States have repeatedly called for Arafat and the PA to crack down on Hamas and Islamic Jihad terrorism. A few arrests will be made—"small fry," never the real leaders— then the terrorists will be released in short order. Virtually all of the terrorists arrested by the PLO after the rash of suicide bombings in early 1996 had been released by September.

And yet President Clinton, when asked about PLO compliance with the requirement to deal with terrorism said, "We have found pretty good results when we've worked closely with the Palestinians in getting increased compliance." If these results are "pretty good," I'd hate to see "abysmal."

Arafat has not eliminated terrorism in his government. Instead, he has elevated it to official status. In May 1996 Arafat set aside four cabinet seats in the Palestinian Authority for representatives of the most active terrorist groups: Hamas, Islamic Jihad, and two PLO rejectionist groups, the Popular Front for the Liberation of Palestine (PFLP), and the Democratic Front for the Liberation of Palestine (DFLP). The U.S. law that provides financial aid to the PA specifically says that aid will be cut off if the PLO allows terrorists to be included in the governing agencies. But to date, Congress has made no move to terminate the annual one hundred million in financial aid to the Palestinians.

Hamas and Islamic Jihad are part of the "war by other means" still being fought by an international conspiracy of terrorists against Israel and the western democracies. These two Islamic fundamentalist groups are funded, trained, and armed by Iran and Syria. The Hezbollah, or Party of Allah, which operates against Israel primarily out of Syrian-controlled southern Lebanon, is also sponsored by Iran. These groups are adamantly opposed to peace with Israel and, in fact, they are fanatically dedicated to waging continual "war by other means" against *all* non-Muslim countries.

In *Fighting Terrorism*, Benjamin Netanyahu says, "Iran, Hezbollah, and their satellite organizations have rapidly replaced both Communism and Pan-Arab fascism as the driving force behind international terror. . . . A hint of the potential power of this [new kind of militant Islamic] policy was provided by the convening of a special Islamic conference called by Iran and held in Teheran in October 1991, on the eve of the Madrid Peace Conference between Israel and its Arab neighbors; the Teheran conference was attended by radical Islamic movements and terrorist groups from forty countries, and declared itself to be against making any kind of peace with the Jewish state."

Because the media so often focus on Israel as the target of these groups, we tend to think it is strictly an Arab-Israeli problem. But radical Muslim groups were anti-American long before Israel ever existed. And remember, it was the Islamic fundamentalist movement that was behind the World Trade Center bombing in New York a few years ago. So we are still fighting state-sponsored terrorism today, although the western countries seem to be weakening their position considerably.

Since the 1980s the United States has taken the lead, passing tough anti-terrorist legislation and using economic sanctions against the sponsoring countries. In 1996 Congress passed legislation that would penalize foreign companies who invest heavily in Iran and Libya, and President Clinton called on our European allies "to join with us in increasing the pressure on Iran and Libya to stop their support for terrorism."

But the European Union nations want to trade with countries like Iran, and are trying to get around or eliminate any sanctions against the state sponsors of terrorism. A *Jerusalem Post* report published just after the U.S. sanctions were passed detailed the trade activities of the EU countries in the last few years. "The French, Germans, Italians, Japanese and other U.S. 'allies' have given the imams of Teheran a staggering thirty billion of credit," the report said.

"The Iranians have paid the Russians to build a nuclear reactor as the first step to creating atomic weapons. German, French and Italian industrialists, faced with millions of restless unemployed, are supplying Teheran with vast amounts of raw materials and the tools to create chemical and biological weapons. . . . Germany, for instance, sells $1.6 billion of its products, much of it of military use, to Iran. French sales total over half a billion dollars of equipment."

According to this investigative report, Germany, who is Iran's largest trading partner, claims it will be able to "influence the Iranians" by continuing to do business with them. France openly defied the U.S. economic sanctions, warning President Clinton that he had set a "dangerous precedent." The dangerous precedent, however, is actually being set by world leaders who are willing to wink at global terrorism in order to line their coffers with precious petro-dollars from the oil-rich sponsors of genocidal madness.

THE WISDOM OF HISTORY

There is an old saying that those who ignore history are condemned to repeat it. Perhaps we can explain Yasser Arafat's current reluctance to deal with the terrorism of Hamas and Islamic Jihad by looking to the past. During his youth in Cairo, Arafat's family had close ties to a group called the Muslim Brotherhood, an Islamic fundamentalist group active in Egypt and the Middle East.

As a teenager Arafat fought with the Muslim Brothers in Jerusalem in 1948 and, during his university days, he often went on secret missions with the Brothers when they were fighting the British at the Suez Canal. Many of the early Fatah members were tied to the Muslim Brotherhood, which once tried to assassinate Egyptian president Gamal Abdel Nasser.

The Islamic Resistance Movement (Hamas) Charter, released to the public in 1988, states that "Hamas is one of the links in the Chain of Jihad in the confrontation with the Zionist invasion. It links up with . . . the Muslim Brotherhood who fought the Holy War in 1936; it further relates to another link of the Palestinian Jihad and the efforts of the Muslim Brothers during the 1948 War, and to the Jihad operations of the Muslim Brothers in 1968 and thereafter. . . ." So the current masters of terrorism affirm their historic link to the Muslim Brotherhood. And it's a link that joins them directly to Yasser Arafat.

In their biography of the PLO leader, *Arafat: In the Eyes of the Beholder*, Janet and John Wallach say that "the Muslim fundamentalists [of the Brotherhood] sought an independent state in which Islamic law, called Sha'ria, would prevail, and they did not hesitate to use violent and brutal means to their end." According to the Wallachs, Yasser Arafat's "nationalist and religious sympathies lay with the Islamic fundamentalists."

So perhaps we should not be surprised today when Arafat praises suicide bombers, acclaims terrorists as "heroes and stars," arrests them for show and then releases them, allows them to serve in his police force, and even appoints them to positions in his cabinet. Perhaps it simply means that Yasser Arafat is still one of the Brothers after all.

Five

The Focal Point of Faith

For Christmas 1995, Bill Clinton and Yitzhak Rabin chipped in to get Yasser Arafat a nice gift—Bethlehem. Under the agreement signed with the PLO in 1995, Bethlehem, the birthplace of the Messiah, and 460 other towns and villages in Israel were transferred to the Palestinian Authority. The transfer took place just hours before Christmas.

Each year tourists flock to the traditional site of the Christ child's manger. As pilgrims arrive at Manger Square, however, their mental images of a lean-to stable with a straw-covered floor are shattered. This large, open plaza with its massive stone walls is the center of town. And tucked inside the walls is the ornate Church of the Nativity—an elaborate shrine far removed from the simple backdrops of our Christmas pageants with bathrobe-clad shepherds and cardboard-winged angels.

After the 1995 holiday, one Bethlehem shopkeeper was quoted as saying, "What kind of Christmas is *this?* Bethlehem isn't celebrating the birth of Jesus this year. It's celebrating Arafat and the birth of the Palestinian state."

Twelve hundred Jews and Christians were prevented from entering Bethlehem on Christmas Eve, but Yasser Arafat delivered a speech to his PLO flock assembled for the occasion in

Manger Square. "We pray this year in Palestinian Bethlehem," he said. "We will yet pray in Jerusalem, the capital of the Palestinian state. . . .Today we embrace in the Church of the Nativity and tomorrow we shall embrace in the Church of the Holy Sepulcher in Jerusalem."

From Jerusalem's back porch (Bethlehem is only five miles southwest) Arafat was making clear what his position would be during final status negotiations. He intends to split the city in half and make East Jerusalem his capital.

In his Christmas Eve speech, Arafat made the outrageous claim that Jesus Christ was a Palestinian. The arrogance of such a preposterous lie reminded me of a heated exchange I had with Dr. Hanan Ashrawi, a Palestinian delegate to the Madrid Peace Conference in 1991. She had given a strong speech in support of Arafat and the PLO, and she mentioned that she was a Christian. So during the question time afterwards, I stood up to challenge her position. Our exchange was as follows:

> *Mike Evans:* "Dr. Ashrawi, I am an American evangelical Christian. What is the logic in the term 'land for peace' as a guarantee for peace, when the Arab world started three wars against Israel when the Arab world had Judea and Samaria?"

> *Dr. Hanan Ashrawi:* "First of all, I find the reference to Judea and Samaria as being in extreme bias and therefore offensive. I am a Palestinian Christian . . . and I am a descendant of the first Christians in the world. Jesus Christ was born in my country, in my town. Bethlehem was a Palestinian town. . . ."

> *Mike Evans:* "A Jewish town . . ."

> *Dr. Ashrawi:* ". . . so I will not accept this offensive implication on Christianity . . . nor will I accept a distortion

of my religion, which, once adopted by the West, has become in a sense, a Western religion. But please let me explain to you again, that Christianity is an Eastern religion and that we as Palestinians claim our right to our continuous existence in the land of Christianity, in the land of the birth of Christ and the resurrection of Christ, and we are legitimately there. You cannot make it any better, and you cannot divorce us from the land."

Ashrawi was merely repeating an assertion Palestinians have used in recent years to bolster their claim to the land. These Christian Arabs say they are different from all the other Arabs, and they trace their roots back to the Canaanites who were in the land before the Hebrews.

HISTORY WITH A BIAS

I once enjoyed a good laugh with prime minister Menachem Begin over the claims of these people. I had just come across a state information service publication printed in Cairo, Egypt, titled "Jerusalem, an Arab City." This state publication established its first major argument with the declaration that "Jerusalem was invaded by Christian Arabs in the year 90 B.C. and remained under their domination until it was occupied by the Romans in the first century A.D." In other words, the Arabs now had a right to Jerusalem because *Christian* Arabs had invaded Jerusalem ninety years *before* the birth of Christ.

We laughed because the nation of Israel is forced to deal with misinformation like this daily. There is no biblical evidence and no historical evidence for the Palestinians' claim. For years Prime Minister Begin hosted a Saturday night Bible study group in his home, and he was often criticized for quoting the Bible in public. When I asked him about it, he told me he made no apologies for it.

"When we face our various problems," he said, "we should always strive to live by the Bible. That is true for all of humanity. This is the book which has kept the Jewish people alive—that is my belief. And I am proud to quote the Bible in substantiation of our rights. If anyone brings it up, I tell them I plead guilty of quoting the Bible on matters of public policy, but I don't apologize.

"Ben-Gurion had a wonderful saying," he told me. "He was my opponent, of course, but it was a wonderful saying anyway. When he addressed the British Royal Commission he said, 'Some people say that the Mandate is our Bible, but it is not. The Bible is our mandate.'" When I read my Bible, I find that the Jews do indeed have a mandate over the land that came to be called, erroneously, Palestine. But Yasser Arafat and the PLO have no such mandate.

The 1991 Madrid Peace Conference became the framework for all subsequent peace negotiations in the Middle East. Madrid initiated bilateral talks between Israel and Syria, Israel and Lebanon, and Israel and Jordan (which is the only dialogue that has resulted in a formal peace treaty, signed in October 1994). It also initiated bilateral talks between Israel and the Palestinians, aiming at a two-stage settlement: an interim arrangement for self-government (signed in 1995), and final status negotiations for a permanent settlement (begun in May 1996).

As I had done in Geneva, I went to Madrid to stand by my friends in Israel. Perhaps the most important press conference I attended was held by Secretary of State James Baker. Although there were thousands of press representatives from across the globe there, the Lord granted me favor and I was able to field the first question to Secretary Baker.

I first asked him why America continued to refuse to recognize Jerusalem as Israel's capital and suggested that recognition would be a gesture toward peace. "That is a matter that we think should be determined by negotiations," Baker said. "That has long been the policy position of the United States. . . . I'm not going to engage in a debate with you or anybody else about specific policy issues or specific U.S. positions. . . . That is not really the issue here. The issue is can Arabs and Israelis get together and . . . begin talking in a way that can resolve these very, very difficult and fundamental differences."

The second part of my question to Baker had been about offering military assistance to Israel because of the security threats and the dear price Israel paid during the Persian Gulf War. Baker conveniently ignored that one.

Over the next two days I attended dozens of meetings at the Middle East Peace Conference. At the Israeli meetings, my questions were directed to Benjamin Netanyahu, who was then deputy foreign minister. Some of his comments are worth repeating at length, and as I review them, it becomes obvious why this man was destined to become the prime minister of Israel at such a critical time in her existence.

I first asked this question about human rights, which had been an important issue at the Madrid Conference. "For human rights not to be biased," I said, "Jews would have to have the same freedom as Arabs regarding settling in territories if they chose to do so, be it Riyadh or Amman, etc. Has there been any discussion on that?"

Netanyahu replied, "On the question of individual rights of Arabs and Jews, there is no symmetry now. That is, if Arabs desire to live among Jews, as they do and they have a right to, Jews should have the right to live among Arabs. The fact is that no Jews are allowed to live in Jordan or Saudi Arabia, and that is the kind of conception—an apartheid peace, if you will—that we cannot tolerate and that no one should tolerate in the closing part of this century."

"On the territories for peace issue," I asked him, "the aggressors throughout history have given up territory such as Germany, Poland, and France. What territories have the Arabs been willing to give up for peace?"

"As far as the question of territories for peace," Netanyahu said, "that is a subject that without preconditions should be left to negotiations. But I think when we talk about the conception of compromise, Israel—that has already ceded a full 91 percent of the territories it took in the war of self-defense; Israel—that has made enormous sacrifices, including all the oil in its possession, handing it to the Egyptians—I think that we should think of a conception of compromise that is different from the idea that one side gives 100 percent and the other side gives zero."

At the following conference I asked this question: "Since this is a peace conference, how many of the Arab countries have made commitments to rescind the UN Resolution equating Zionism with racism?"

Netanyahu replied, "The UN lost much, not all, but much of its valuable moral capital as a result of the relentless Arab campaign against Israel that adopted all these resolutions. One of my predecessors in the UN, Mr. Eban, said that if the Arabs had wanted to pass resolutions declaring that the earth was flat, they would have passed that.

"But that's effectively what they have done. They've adopted thirty-five resolutions in the UN which effectively call for the annihilation of Israel, and they now call these resolutions the basis of international law. And the crystallization of this negative attitude is the idea that Zionism is racism. Zionism—that has just transported thousands of Ethiopian Jews, black-skinned people, from the soil of Africa; Zionism—which is the only movement in history that has transported blacks out of Africa, not to enslave them but to liberate them—this Zionism is presented as racism. The important thing, I think, is this: the Arabs have a choice now—to cling to the rhetoric of the past, or move to the future. I hope they choose the future."

AN INTERNATIONAL MUGGING

Throughout the Madrid Conference, the words of Scripture were rolling in my spirit, especially the prophecies which indicate that in the last days Israel will become the center of world attention, her problems unable to be solved by various attempts at peace. I thought of Zechariah's prophecy about Jerusalem being an "immovable rock" when besieged by all the nations of the world in the final moments of history. Surely I was seeing the precursor of these events.

That week I had many opportunities to ask questions at press conferences, and to address world leaders. They kept saying over and over, "Israel is not the Promised Land and the Bible has nothing to do with this issue." I kept responding, "You are wrong. God will have the final word."

The foreign minister of Egypt told me, "I don't accept Israel as the Promised Land."

I replied, "May I refer you, Mr. Foreign Minister, to the greatest foreign minister who has ever served your nation. He turned your economy around. He balanced your budget. He believed God's promises and knew that, indeed, God had given precious land to the Jewish people. His name was Joseph."

During the meetings, I prayed silently as I gazed at the ceiling in the grand Hall of Columns, where the nations of the world were gathered to make their version of peace. The magnificent hall was ornamented with the likenesses of false gods: Apollo, Aurora, Zephyrus, Ceres, Bacchus, Diana, and Panngalatea. From their lofty perch these false gods looked down on these official proceedings for a false peace. Like the apostle Paul at Mars Hill, I found myself praying to the one True God while under this canopy of idolatry.

How ironic, I thought, *that Israel had been forced to come here, of all places, for an international peace conference—to Spain, where one-third of the Jewish population of the day was massacred in the Inquisition.* I watched as nation after nation mounted the podium to insult and accuse Israel, and to demand that she give up the majority of her land.

Their voices reverberated in the marbled hall as they said, "We will accept your land in exchange for peace." And what they were really saying was: "This is a stick-up. Give me all your money and you won't get hurt." The Madrid Conference, by any measure, was an international mugging. And the world was the silent witness too intimidated to report it to the police. Most of them pretended they didn't even see the "gun" pointed at Israel's head.

Watching these international muggers at work reminded me of a conversation I had in Jerusalem once with a prominent Israeli official. He said he had a very deep conviction that we were reliving the 1930s. "We are viewing the rise of a new Nazism," he said. "In the 1930s the strength and might of Nazi Germany was its steel and coal. Now we have the Arabs with their oil. But their thrust is anti-Semitic now, just as it was then. And the attitude of the Western democracies is one of appeasement now, as it was then.

"It was a fashionable intellectual mood in the West to appease the Nazis and say, 'What do you know, they are making the trains run on time. And basically we need to make sure that we have steel and coal for our economy, so we mustn't rock the boat. If they want to gobble up Czechoslovakia, why make a fuss?'"

The Israeli official talked about how English Prime Minister Neville Chamberlain was willing to sacrifice Czechoslovakia to avoid confrontation, and how America just didn't want to get involved. "So an entire nation was lost to the Nazis without interference. Well, Israel is jut trying to get across to the world today that the message from Jerusalem is, 'We're not Czechoslovakia.' We will not permit a sellout."

Prime Minister Begin had made a similar statement to me about appeasement. I was privileged to develop a wonderful relationship with him, meeting with him on more than a dozen occasions over the years. We talked more about Jerusalem and the Bible than anything else in our meetings.

But on this particular day, we had talked about the prospects for peace. Begin told me that at the Camp David meetings, President Carter had promised he would oppose an independent Palestinian state. "But some European countries are so thirsty for oil and petro-dollars that they would rather surrender," he said. "And it would not be the first time they surrendered to pressure. It happened in the thirties. And it brought disaster on the world.

"A Palestinian state is a mortal danger to Israel," Begin said, "and a great peril to the free world. And we never agreed to a Palestinian state at Camp David. What we agreed to was autonomy as a way to solve the problem of the Palestinian Arabs. With autonomy they can elect their own ministers of council to deal with daily affairs. This would be a great historic change for them. Under Turkish, British, and Jordanian occupation they lived under the whip. The only thing we want to retain is the matter of security. If we do not, the PLO will come in."

JERUSALEM BETRAYED

How sad Menachem Begin and Anwar Sadat would be to see how the Camp David Accords—forged in the friendship of two courageous peacemakers, one Jewish and one Arab—have been turned upside down. These two great leaders left a legacy that has been squandered. Now, just as Mr. Begin feared, "the PLO" has "come in." The responsibility for security in many of the Bible lands Mr. Begin loved so much has been turned over to the PLO. And the next item up for discussion is the biggest prize of all: Jerusalem.

AN EMBASSY IN JERUSALEM

But just consider the irony of their situation. Paris is the capital of France and we have a U.S. embassy there. Moscow is the capital of Russia and we have an embassy there, too. Jerusalem is the capital of Israel, but we have our embassy in Tel Aviv.

The United States maintains diplomatic relations with more than 160 countries, and in each of those countries our state department maintains a U.S. embassy in the capital city. Each of those countries, that is, except Israel. Under pressure from the Arab world, the U.S. has maintained its embassy in Tel Aviv since 1948.

Jerusalem has never been the capital of any other country, and under international law every country has the right to choose its own capital. For forty-eight years, though, we have ignored Israel's choice, for fear we might antagonize one or more of the Arab countries who don't recognize Israel's right to exist, let alone to choose her own capital.

One of the oldest capital cities in the world, Jerusalem celebrated its 3,000th anniversary as the capital of Israel in 1996. Yet no other world capital has been subjected to the indignity that the United States has bestowed on the capital of Israel, a country which has always been our ally, never our enemy.

To rectify this injustice, the U.S. Congress finally enacted The Jerusalem Embassy Act of 1995, which calls for the embassy to be moved to Jerusalem by May 31, 1999. The bill provides funds for construction, targeted to begin in 1997. There was broad bipartisan support in both the House and the Senate, and the measure was passed by over 90 percent majorities.

Moving the embassy is not a new issue. It has, at various times, been a plank in both the Democratic and Republican party platforms, something the American people have supported for years. Campaigning for president in 1992, Bill Clinton said, "I do recognize Jerusalem as Israel's capital, and Jerusalem ought to remain an undivided city." He even put it in writing. In a June 1992 letter to the Rabbinical Council of America he wrote, "I recognize Jerusalem as an undivided city and the eternal capital of Israel."

But by 1995 the president had changed his tune. His administration opposed the Jerusalem Embassy Act, and he refused to sign it when it was passed. Clinton could not veto the bill, with a 90 percent majority supporting its passage. His veto would have been overridden easily, so he allowed it to become law without his signature.

However, nothing has been done about moving the U.S. Embassy to Jerusalem. A waiver was written into the bill allowing the president to put the new embassy construction on hold for six-month intervals if he deems vital national security interests to be at risk and so reports to Congress. Most foreign-policy bills contain a similar waiver, but this one was more tightly written than usual. The bill's sponsor warned that "no president should or could make a decision to exercise this waiver lightly."

But the Clinton administration immediately moved to take advantage of the waiver, claiming national security interests would be jeopardized by moving the embassy, because it might disrupt the Middle East peace process. But will this turn out to be another costly compromise for the American president?

Since the embassy is to be built in western Jerusalem, in an area never contested by the Palestinians, there is no threat to U.S. security or the peace process. Yet that was the claim of the Clinton administration, as delivered by White House spokesman Mike McCurry, who said that Congress "ought to butt out for the sake of the peace process."

Bob Dole, Senate majority leader at the time and chief sponsor of the bill, replied, "This legislation is not about the peace process, it's about recognizing Israel's capital." And, despite candidate Clinton's recognition of Jerusalem as Israel's capital, Clinton as president has taken a completely different position. He is now unwilling to recognize Jerusalem as Israel's capital, and for that reason he will not allow the Jerusalem Embassy Act to go into effect.

In March 1996 President Clinton visited Israel, but refused to have his official welcome take place in Jerusalem, causing the president of Israel and the mayor of Jerusalem to boycott his arrival at the Tel Aviv airport. Media spokesmen for the president admitted that the decision not to allow the welcome to take place in Jerusalem was calculated to avoid giving the impression that the U.S. recognizes Jerusalem as the capital of Israel.

For almost five decades now we have officially refused to recognize Jerusalem as Israel's capital. Israel, of course, does not recognize our non-recognition. Jerusalem, their "ancient and eternal capital" has always been the seat of government, both for the ancient nation of Israel under King David and for the modern nation of Israel.

PRINCIPLES WORTH FIGHTING FOR

In the early twentieth century, during the long negotiations for the establishment of the Jewish National Homeland, a friendship grew up between Dr. Chaim Weizmann, the Jewish statesman, and Lord Balfour, the British foreign secretary. Balfour was unable to understand why the Jews were insisting they would accept only Palestine as their permanent homeland. Turning one day to Dr. Weizmann, he asked for an explanation.

"Well, Lord Balfour," replied Dr. Weizmann, "if I were to offer you Paris instead of London, would you accept?"

"But," answered Balfour in some surprise, "London is ours."

"Lord Balfour," said Weizmann, "Jerusalem was ours when London was a swamp."

Indeed. For three thousand years the Jewish people have regarded Jerusalem as their capital, even when most of them were exiled from the city.

When the Jews were driven at various times from their land, wherever they found themselves, they faced toward Jerusalem when praying. Their synagogues were oriented toward the city, and when a Jew built himself a house he left part of a wall unfinished, to symbolize that it was only a temporary dwelling until he could return to his permanent home, Jerusalem.

It was never that big as far as major cities go: Until modern times just over two-and-one-half square miles inside the city walls, with most of the holy sites confined to a half-square-mile enclave in the Old City. But without doubt it is the most coveted—and contested—piece of real estate in the world.

What is it about Jerusalem that has made it a prize worth fighting for almost since time began? Compared with the great cities of Europe, Jerusalem is very small. It stands on no great river, as do London, Paris, or Rome. It has no port, no great industries, no mineral wealth, or adequate water supply. Nor did the city stand on a great highway of the ancient world, or command a strategic crossroads. It was even off the main trade routes. Why then did it not remain merely an unimportant village, which, like so many others in the course of time, have vanished?

What accounts for its hold on the minds and hearts of adherents of the world's three monotheistic faiths? The moral grandeur and spiritual wisdom which the biblical prophets who spoke from Jerusalem gave to the world has gained for the city its unique place in the minds and hearts of men.

The spiritual stature of Jerusalem is echoed in its physical situation; the city stands upon hills high above the surrounding countryside. Coming to Jerusalem is always spoken of among the Jews as "going up to Jerusalem." Those who leave her, having once lived in Israel, are considered ones that "go down," in more than just the physical sense.

Jerusalem is a city of many names, so many, in fact, that there is no exact record. Some of them include: City of David, City of God, City of Peace, City of Truth, Joyful City, Faithful City, Lion of God, Paragon of Beauty, Dwelling of Righteousness, Ariel, Zion, Moriah. But only one name—Jerusalem—has prevailed through the centuries.

In Hebrew the city is *Yerushalayim*. The name literally means "city of peace," from the words *yerah* (city) and *shalom* (peace)—a rather ironic designation given the amount of violence and bloodshed it has seen through the centuries.

Although its origins are lost in the mists of antiquity, archaeologists have found evidence of human habitation which goes back four thousand years. The Israelites first occupied Jerusalem in the days of the Judges, but the Jebusites persisted there in the face of assaults by the tribes of Judah and Benjamin.

It was the great King David who wrested the city once and

for all from the Jebusites, making it his capital. From that time, roughly three thousand years ago, Jerusalem has been the capital city of the Jewish people.

THE CRUCIBLE OF FAITH

To help understand the unique circumstances of the City of God, let's look briefly at Jerusalem's place in, and meaning for, the three monotheistic religions of mankind. What does the city mean to them? What place does it occupy in their thinking and in their faith?

For Christians, Jerusalem is the place in which the great final drama in the ministry of Jesus took place, his crucifixion and resurrection. It is revered as a place of pilgrimage, but in no sense does it occupy a central position in the life of the Christian. The pilgrim goes, not so much to Jerusalem, as to the holy places he will find in and about the city.

The old song which says "I walked today where Jesus walked" expresses the sentiment of the Christian pilgrim; he longs to set foot in all the places where Jesus of Nazareth lived and ministered, especially the city where he paid the ultimate price for our salvation. The Christian treasures Jerusalem, and all the land of Israel, because he treasures God's word. But the city is not the focal point of his worship.

For Islam, Jerusalem has a different, and lesser, significance. In the Jewish Scriptures (the Old Testament for the Christian), Jerusalem is mentioned more than seven hundred times, but it is not referred to once by name in the Koran, the holy book of Islam.

To support their claims to the city, Muslims point to the fact that for thirteen years Muhammad and his followers turned their faces, when praying, to Jerusalem. However, this episode was of short duration; after the Jews fell from favor with

Muhammad, it was changed, and pious Muslims from that time on have prayed with their faces toward Mecca.

So for Muslims, Mecca and Medina are their two holy cities. In their hierarchy Jerusalem ranks third. While thousands of pious Muslim make the pilgrimage to Mecca each year, Jerusalem is not a place of such pilgrimage, and the Islamic connection with Jerusalem did not commence until the seventh century A.D.

The story of the Jews in Jerusalem, however, began over three thousand years ago—and the final chapter has yet to be written. Jerusalem is the focal point of Jewish history. It is Judaism's birthplace and the central shrine of the faith. Its people have always revered it as home. The statement, "Next year in Jerusalem," is always used to mark the end of Passover, the festival of national redemption, and closes the Yom Kippur service, the festival of personal redemption.

Unlike the Christian and Islamic connections with the city, the Jewish people's link with Jerusalem has been historical, religious, cultural, physical, and fundamental. It has never been voluntarily broken; any absence of Jews from the city has been the result of foreign persecution and eviction.

"Without Jerusalem, we are a body without a soul," said the great hero David Ben-Gurion, the first prime minister of modern Israel. Jerusalem remained alive in the hearts of Jews, even when they were not allowed to live or worship there. No amount of oppression could erase the longing of the Jewish people for *Eretz Yisrael*, the land of Israel, and *Yerushalayim*, the City of Peace.

Once you have heard the haunting strains of the *Hatikvah*, Israel's national anthem, you can never forget it. The simple, poignant lyrics express what has been the heart's desire of millions of Jews—from every corner of earth, through the millennia of time:

As long as deep in the heart,
The soul of a Jew yearns,
And towards the East
An eye looks to Zion,
Our hope is not yet lost,
The hope of two thousand years,
To be a free people in our land,
The land of Zion and Jerusalem.

That dream, "to be a free people in our land, the land of Zion and Jerusalem," finally became a reality, after two thousand years of suffering, when Israel regained her independence and then restored her sovereignty over the City of Peace. For all those years, Jerusalem remained the symbol of a people who were reviled, humiliated, enslaved and even massacred. But as a people they never despaired of God's promise of restoration.

THE FINAL STATUS

Final status talks between Israel and the Palestinians began on May 5, 1996. Nothing substantive was discussed at that meeting, but an agreement was reached regarding what items would be negotiated in the permanent settlement. The status of Jerusalem, and the exact borders of Palestinian autonomy are the two biggest issues to be decided.

At this moment, the future of Jerusalem hangs in the balance. Israel now stands alone—*completely alone*—in defending her historical, biblical, and legal right to the Holy City. America has betrayed Jerusalem.

In spite of the overwhelming support in our Congress for recognizing Jerusalem as Israel's capital, President Clinton resolutely toes the new world order line and refuses to let legislation go into effect that would acknowledge that simple fact. He not only has subverted the will of the people on the issue of moving our embassy to Jerusalem, his ambassador to the United Nations refused to stand with Israel when the rest of the world—literally—said that Israel has no legal right to Jerusalem.

Just two months after the exciting Congressional vote to finally recognize Jerusalem as Israel's capital, the Fiftieth General Assembly of the United Nations passed a resolution chastising Israel for her claims on all of Jerusalem. The resolution passed by a vote of 133 to one—Israel was the only nation to vote against it. The United States, once Israel's staunch ally, abstained from voting.

The UN Resolution called Israel the "Occupying Power" in Jerusalem and said that Israel's claim to Jerusalem as the capital of Israel was "null and void and must be rescinded forthwith." The resolution went on to say that, "the decision of Israel to impose laws, jurisdiction and administration on the Holy City of Jerusalem is illegal, and therefore null and void and has no validity whatsoever."

The UN has made it clear that the only acceptable action for Israel is to relinquish her claim on the Old City, where all the holy sites, including the Temple Mount and the Western Wall, are located. The UN and the world order crowd will push Israel relentlessly until the barbed wire is stretched through the heart of *Yerushalayim*, the City of Peace.

Prime Minister Natanyahu has forcefully stated that he will never allow a Berlin Wall to be erected in Jerusalem. But Yasser Arafat is waiting in the wings, ready to wave his Palestinian flag over the mosques and churches of the Holy City, as he has so frequently promised those who answered his call for *jihad*.

Unless America wakes up, Jerusalem is destined to become a bitterly divided city, and the Jewish people will once again be severed from their biblical heritage.

Part II:
Dispersion &
Discord

Six

City of Stones, Immovable Rock

VIEWED from the Mount of Olives, the sweeping pan-
orama of Jerusalem is breathtaking. The multi-towered
landscape is a splendid drama written in stone, a drama that
has received rave reviews from countless pilgrims to the Holy
Land.

You can see it all from up here: the ancient ruins of the City
of David, the gilded dome of the monument on the *Haram esh-
Sharif*, the Dome of the Rock, the tombstones that dot the hillside beneath the crenellated walls of the ancient city. These
massive stone walls, with their battlements intact, have proudly
survived the sieges of invading armies. The parapets of these
walls once sheltered archers; today soldiers patrol the same
parapets with automatic rifles.

The Olivet view entices you to descend into the city itself.
Jerusalem is a city of stones, and to visit the Old City with its
Jewish Quarter is to lose yourself among the stones. As you
wander through the tangled labyrinth of narrow alleyways, you
can almost touch the stone walls on either side of you. There
are stone arches above your head and paving stones beneath
your feet. Stones, stones, stones. From the ancient ruins to the

medieval ramparts, these stones that have baked in the warmth of a million sunrises have a story to tell.

The stones most beloved by the people of Israel are those of the Western Wall, the holiest shrine of the Jewish faith today. This fifty-foot-high wall is all that remains of the Temple Mount as it existed in the first century. The stones stacked together to build this wall are so massive that it's hard to imagine how they were chiseled out and carried up the hills of Jerusalem.

To grasp the perspective, it is helpful to look backward across the centuries and then to follow the course of events that have led to today's impasse. Consider the view from the temple when its stones were still new and the city of Jerusalem shone like alabaster in the morning sun. Herod the Great began rebuilding Solomon's temple in 20 B.C. and the project occupied the rest of his administration. The fifteen-story-high temple was constructed during Herod's reign, but the outer courts and walls were not fully completed until 64 A.D., some sixty-eight years after his death.

One day, after Jesus had been teaching in the temple precincts, he called his disciples' attention to the temple buildings as they departed into the hillside. "'Do you see all these things?' he asked. 'I tell you the truth, not one stone here will be left on another, every one will be thrown down'" (Matthew 24:2).

The words of Jesus were precisely fulfilled in 70 A.D. when the Roman armies swept through Jerusalem and reduced Herod's magnificent temple to a pile of blackened rubble. All that remains of Herod's decades of construction is a section of the retaining wall that once supported the western portion of the Temple Mount. The stones of the temple itself are buried in the garbage pile of history, somewhere deep beneath the Old City.

The remaining stones of this wall, called the Western Wall

because of its location in relation to the original Temple Mount, have become a symbol of the enduring hope of the Jewish people. Even non-religious Jews venerate the Wall as a national monument. The plaza in front of the Western Wall can accommodate 100,000 congregants. It is the gathering place of the nation of Israel, the scene of both joyous celebration and solemn memorial. For a city that has changed ownership twenty-six times and been leveled to the ground five times, the Wall remains a testimony of God's all-encompassing providence.

THE PRAISES OF HIS PEOPLE

I feel at home among the stones of Jerusalem. For one thing, the stone here is quite similar to the native limestone of my home state, Texas. It is one of our most popular building materials, although not required by construction codes as it is in Jerusalem. But it's more than that. These stones speak to my soul. They call me back again and again to this eternal city. They sing a song to me, an ancient song in a minor key. A song of the long millennia of anguish and suffering.

The Western Wall is also known as the Wailing Wall, because worshipers who have come here to pray over the centuries have washed these stones with rivers of tears. Tears of mourning, tears of joy, tears of intercession. Visible in the cracks and in the spaces between the huge stones are tiny pieces of paper, freshly crinkled and wedged in the nooks and crannies of the Wall. It's a tradition here to write your prayer on a slip of paper and place it among the stones, "turning the wall," as Israeli writer Amos Elon describes it, "into the mailbox of God." Once a month the caretakers of the Western Wall carefully remove the scraps of paper and bury them ceremonially.

When I stand in front of these ponderous stones, I feel a

connection with the other worshipers offering their prayers and praises to God. Like those around me, I reach out and touch the ancient, weathered stones. The sound of the muezzin calling the Muslims to prayer at the mosque above mingles with the chanting of the black-coated Hassidic Jews beside me at the Wall, and I think of the many Jews who were killed for daring to stand in this very spot.

This Wailing Wall has long been a silent witness to the sufferings of God's chosen people. But what wails our ears would hear if these weathered stones could speak.

AN INALIENABLE RIGHT

The very fact that the Jewish people and the nation of Israel exist today is a miracle. No other group of people has been so systematically targeted for destruction throughout the ages. Most Jews were exiled from their homeland, and even in exile they were hunted down and humiliated, and massacred by the millions. There would be no trace of the Jews as a people were it not that the sovereign Lord of the universe has ordained their preservation.

Throughout history some twenty-three nations that lifted their hand against Israel have ceased to exist. But the people of the Book live on. Their perseverance, based upon faith in God and in his Word, has outlasted all persecution.

That God has ordained the preservation of his chosen people is written throughout the pages of Scripture.

Almighty God made a covenant with Abraham, the father of the Jewish people. He promised to protect them and prosper them, and through them, to bless the whole world. The first expression of God's promise is found in Genesis 12: "I will make you into a great nation and I will bless you; I will make your name great, and you will be a blessing. I will bless those who bless you, and whoever curses you I will curse; and all peoples on earth will be blessed through you" (vv. 2–3).

Along with this covenant the Lord gave Abraham and his descendants, Isaac and Jacob, the title deed to the land of Israel, and he specifically said it would be their possession perpetually.

"He also said to [Abraham], 'I am the Lord who brought you out of Ur of the Chaldeans to give you this land to take possession of it.' But Abram said, 'O Sovereign Lord, how can I know that I will gain possession of it?'" (Genesis 15: 7–8).

The Lord then made a covenant with Abraham, as a guarantee of the promise of the land. "On that day the Lord made a covenant with Abram and said, 'To your descendants I give this land, from the river of Egypt to the great river, the Euphrates—the land of the Kenites, Kenizzites, Kadmonites, Hittites, Perizzites, Rephaites, Amorites, Canaanites, Girgashites and Jebusites'" (Genesis 15:18–21).

In non-biblical terms, this would be called a royal land grant. This type of grant, common in antiquity, was perpetual and unconditional. The king, or sovereign, possessed all the land and he granted parcels of land to loyal subjects as rewards for faithful service. In biblical terms, God is sovereign over all the earth—he created it, and you can't get better ownership rights than that—so the land is certainly his to dispose of as he wishes.

Years after God made his original covenant with Abraham, God confirmed it, and Abraham accepted the terms of the covenant by the rite of circumcision. The Lord said, "As for me, this is my covenant with you: You will be the father of many nations. . . . I will make you very fruitful; I will make nations of you, and kings will come from you. I will establish my covenant as an everlasting covenant between me and you and your descendants after you for the generations to come, to be your God and the God of your descendants after you. The whole land of Canaan, where you are now an alien, I will give as an everlasting possession to you and your descendants after you; and I will be their God" (Genesis 17:4–9).

This covenant with Abraham is said to be an everlasting or eternal covenant, and the title deed to the "whole land" has no expiration date or conditions; it is given "as an everlasting possession" to Abraham's descendants. This covenant is everlasting from God's viewpoint, although it is capable of being broken by man.

In other words, the possession of the land might be lost temporarily through disobedience, but God's everlasting, unconditional promises are never rescinded. God reconfirmed the Abrahamic covenant with Isaac: "For to you and your descendants I will give all these lands and will confirm the oath I swore to your father Abraham. I will make your descendants as numerous as the stars in the sky and will give them all these lands, and through your offspring all nations on earth will be blessed" (Genesis 26:3b–4).

He also reconfirmed it with Jacob: "I am the Lord, the God of your father Abraham and the God of Isaac. I will give you and your descendants the land . . ." (Genesis 28:13); and with every one of Jacob's descendants: "The land I gave to Abraham and Isaac I also give to you, and I will give this land to your descendants after you" (Genesis 35:12).

Why should this ancient covenant matter to us several thousand years after the fact? It's simple. God never revoked Abraham's title deed to the land and gave it to someone else. God is still sovereign over the land, and as far as he's concerned it still belongs to Abraham, Isaac and Jacob's descendants.

Yet the place where God made and confirmed his covenant, in an area north of Jerusalem between Bethel and Ai, is in the heart of what is today called the West Bank (it's really Judea and Samaria)—land the United Nations says Israel is occupying illegally and must give up for the sake of an elusive peace.

Because of God's Word, the people of Israel have an inalienable right to their land. Yet the governments of the world, especially the United States, are pressuring Israel to give up her right to the land. We Americans love rights, especially inalienable ones, even though most Americans today don't understand what that means. We think we do, because our Declaration of Independence uses the term: "We hold these truths to be self-evident, that all men are created equal, that they are endowed by their Creator with certain unalienable rights. . . ."

We have the mistaken idea that an inalienable right is one that cannot be taken away from you. It means the opposite: An inalienable right is one you cannot give away. When something is said to be inalienable, it means that the possessor of that thing cannot give it away, sell it, surrender it, or legally transfer it to someone else.

The Jewish people have a God-given, inalienable right to possess the land of Israel. The all-time best-selling historical Book says so. Since it is an inalienable right, it means Israel does not have the right to give away her land or transfer it to another party. Even among themselves, the people of Israel were forbidden to sell the land permanently, "because the land is mine," God said, "and you are but aliens and my tenants" (Leviticus 25:23).

Giving away any of the land violates the covenant God made with Abraham, Isaac, and Jacob and puts the nation of Israel outside of God's covenant blessings—and puts the nations who are coercing Israel into giving up the land under the curse of God.

THE CITY THAT BELONGS TO GOD

God's sovereignty over the land of Israel extends in a special way to the city of Jerusalem. It is the only city he ever claimed as his own, and it is called in Scripture "the City of God" and the "Holy City." And for that reason alone, Christians should be concerned about the fate of Jerusalem. If Jerusalem is dear to God's heart, it ought to be dear to our hearts as well.

King David, who conquered Jerusalem and made it his capital city, is described in Scripture as a man "after God's own heart." And the desire of David's heart was to build a temple in Jerusalem as the dwelling place of God. But because David's kingdom was so associated with warfare and bloodshed in the conquest of Israel's enemies, the Lord would not allow David to build the temple. He promised David, though, that his successor would fulfill the dream.

He made an unconditional promise, another "everlasting covenant," with David. This covenant promised that the line of David would endure forever. In fact, the Messiah would come from the Davidic line.

Solomon, David's son and successor, built the temple his father had planned as the dwelling place of the Lord. Solomon's temple was one of the wonders of the ancient world, attracting visitors from kingdoms far and near. More than just a tourist attraction, however, it represented God's earthly palace. His earthly throne, the ark of the covenant in the Holy of Holies of the temple, was the symbol of the abiding presence of God.

Because he had designated the temple as his earthly dwelling place, and because it was located in David's capital, Jerusalem, God chose to be permanently identified with the city. A number of Bible passages speak of God choosing Jerusalem as his city. For example, "In this temple and in Jerusalem, which I have chosen out of all the tribes of Israel, I will put my Name forever" (2 Chronicles 33:7).

Another passage, from 1 Kings, shows not only that God chose Jerusalem but that he would be faithful to his promise to continue the Davidic line·

The Lord became angry with Solomon because his heart had turned away from the Lord, the God of Israel, who had appeared to him twice. Although he had forbidden Solomon to follow other gods, Solomon did not keep the Lord's command. So the Lord said to Solomon, "Since this is your attitude and you have not kept my covenant and my decrees, which I commanded you, I will most certainly tear the kingdom away from you and give it to one of your subordinates. Nevertheless, for the sake of David your father, I will not do it during your lifetime. I will tear it out of the hand of your son. Yet I will not tear the whole kingdom from him, but will give him one tribe for the sake of David my servant and for the sake of Jerusalem, which I have chosen" (11:9–13).

Solomon's disobedience precluded his participation in the covenant blessing. But because God had made an unconditional promise to continue the Davidic line, and for the sake of Jerusalem, Solomon was not totally cut off. God is faithful to his covenant and he always keeps his promises. Not only did God choose Jerusalem as his city, the symbol of his intent to dwell among his people, but he continued to exercise control over his chosen city. God's sovereignty over Jerusalem is demonstrated by the fact that he decreed both its destruction and its rebuilding.

The Lord is "slow to anger," says Psalm 103:8. What an un derstatement!

Decade after decade—even century after century—God's heart was broken because of the idolatry of his people. As he had promised Abraham, he had brought the Israelites out of slavery in Egypt and into the Promised Land. He had established them in the land promised unconditionally to Abraham,

Isaac, and Jacob, and their descendants, in the royal land grant.

But time after time the people left the worship of the one true God and followed after the pagan gods of the nations around them. A righteous king, of the line of David, would bring reform and revival, tearing down the groves and "high places" where Baal and Ahserah (Ishtar) and other idols were worshiped. Then the next king would be more wicked than ever and would reintroduce pagan beliefs—even child sacrifice—to God's chosen people.

Prophet after prophet warned the people to return to God or face the consequences. And yet this "stiff-necked" people would not obey his commandments. If you read world history, you may get the idea that Nebuchadnezzar, the great Babylonian conqueror of the sixth century B.C., simply got it in his head that Israel would be a nice little piece of real estate to add to his collection. That's only one side of the story.

Read the Bible and you'll find God specifically telling Jeremiah that *he* was behind Babylon's expansion of Nebuchadnezzar's empire into Israel. God said he would use the Babylonians as his tool to destroy Jerusalem, his own city, because the people would not repent of their continued idolatry.

Why wouldn't the people listen to Jeremiah? They didn't like his message of gloom and doom. They preferred the other prophets, who were saying not to worry because there would be peace. So they ignored the armies coming against them and chanted, "the temple of the Lord, the temple of the Lord," as if it were a magical incantation that would protect them from harm. They couldn't imagine that God would let the temple, the place where he had chosen to place his Name, be destroyed. But while they attended temple activities, it was nothing but an outward ritual; their hearts were far from the Lord.

Jeremiah warned that the temple would face destruction just

like the tabernacle at Shiloh earlier. "Go now to the place in Shiloh where I first made a dwelling for my Name, and see what I did to it because of the wickedness of my people Israel. While you were doing all these things, declares the Lord, I spoke to you again and again, but you did not listen; I called you, but you did not answer. Therefore, what I did to Shiloh I will now do to the house that bears my Name, the temple you trust in, the place I gave to you and your fathers" (Jeremiah 7:12–14).

For forty years Jeremiah faithfully delivered God's word to the people. They never repented. So in 586 B.C. God allowed Nebuchadnezzar to destroy the city and raze the temple. God's own people were exiled from the City of God. Most of them were taken as captives to Babylon, where they would be free to worship their pagan gods all they wanted. But even then, God did not abandon them altogether.

Along with the prophecy of judgment God gave Jeremiah, he also gave a promise of restoration. Just as God had brought the Israelites out of Egypt, there would be a second exodus when God would bring his people out of Babylon, after they had endured seventy years of captivity. Jeremiah said that, in time, even legal documents would be sealed with the saying, "As surely as the Lord lives, who brought the Israelites up out of the land of the north [Babylon] and out of all the countries where he had banished them" (Jeremiah 16:15).

As promised, the exiles came home, and they rebuilt the temple and rebuilt the walls of their beloved city.

THIS ROCK CANNOT BE MOVED

The seventy-year period the exiles spent in Babylon is not the only time the Jewish people temporarily lost possession of the land of Israel. Actually, the city of Jerusalem has changed hands twenty-six different times and been leveled to the ground five times. But God has always brought his people back, just as it was prophesied. We can be confident, then, that any Bible prophecies which remain to be fulfilled will come to pass.

I happen to come from a branch of the Protestant church that believes Bible prophecy will be fulfilled literally, and that the nation of Israel is a fulfillment of prophecy. By the early twentieth century, many of the historical Protestant churches had branched off into a liberal theology with little respect for the Bible as God's Word, period, let alone any hope that there was prophecy yet to be fulfilled.

Other Christian groups had veered off into replacement theology—a theology that says that the church is "spiritual Israel" and has replaced the actual nation of Israel in prophecy, so that all of the promises originally made to Abraham, Isaac, and Jacob, or to national Israel, now apply to the church. You have to render a lot of Bible passages meaningless to accept such a notion.

But millions of Bible-believing Christians have steadfastly held to the notion that God really meant what he said when he promised the land of Israel, in perpetuity, to the physical descendants of Abraham, Isaac, and Jacob. Before 1948 many dispensational prophecy teachers were ridiculed for making statements like that. There had been no nation of Israel for almost two thousand years, so how could it play a role in the last days?

Most of the critics were silenced on May 14, 1948, when the modern state of Israel was declared. One day there was no nation of Israel, the next day there was. It happened just as the prophet Isaiah described it: "Who has ever heard of such a thing? Who has ever seen such things? Can a country be born in a day or a nation be brought forth in a moment? Yet no sooner is Zion in labor than she gives birth to her children" (Isaiah 66:8).

The sovereign Lord of the universe ordained the nation of Israel. He is the one who set her borders. The Bible says that God does not lie or change his mind like man does. His Word is unchanging and his promises are non-negotiable. He has promised to bless those who bless Israel, and curse those who curse her. The kings and powerbrokers of the world, therefore, would be well-advised to quit trying to manipulate the rooks and pawns on God's Middle East chessboard or they will wind up checkmated—permanently.

The same goes for the City of God. Pursuers of the Middle East peace process can hold all the "final status" negotiations they want, but Jerusalem is not a piece of pie to be divvied up or gobbled up. Almighty God decreed the final status of Jerusalem thousands of years ago. As far as he is concerned, it's not on the bargaining table, and he will have the final say on the matter. Jerusalem, this city of stones, is God's immovable rock.

The prophet Zechariah describes a coming siege of Jerusalem by the nations surrounding Israel. The Lord gave his prophet this word: "I am going to make Jerusalem a cup that sends all the surrounding peoples reeling. Judah will be besieged as well as Jerusalem. On that day, when all the nations of the earth are gathered against her, I will make Jerusalem an immovable rock for all the nations. All who try to move it will injure themselves" (12:2–3).

God says he will use the leaders of Judah as a torch to ignite the other nations like a burning woodpile. "They will consume right and left all the surrounding peoples, but Jerusalem will remain intact in her place. . . . On that day I will set out to destroy all the nations that attack Jerusalem" (vv. 6, 9).

That will be a divine payday. Nations will be judged by whether they helped Jerusalem, or tried to destroy her, and rewarded or punished accordingly. At that point the nations of the world will finally quit trying to push Jerusalem around—because when you run up against God's "immovable rock," you will only get hurt.

ISRAEL'S HOPE

The Gospels relate the marvelous story of the birth of the Savior who will come to restore hope to the people of God. There is no other story like it. The Nativity—the story of God reaching out to man, a story of the splendor and glory of heaven touching the dirt and dust of a stable floor, a story of a humble manger where a tiny baby born of a virgin was cradled, a story of stars and angels and shepherds and wise men and of peace on earth.

The story of Jesus is unique. It is not like the myths of the ancient Near East, whose gods were condemned to perpetual cycles of death and rebirth, and whose origins could not be pinpointed in time or place. The Living God, the God of Abraham, Isaac, and Jacob, intervened in time and space and made himself known to a particular people, at a particular time, in a particular place.

While Matthew offers a uniquely Jewish perspective on those events, Luke anchors the narrative of the birth of Christ squarely in history. It happened, he says, when Quirinius was governor of Syria, at a time when Caesar Augustus had called for a census of the empire. The Messiah was born in Bethlehem, into a historic lineage, the house and line of David, from which it was prophesied that the Savior, the Messiah, would be born.

Most of Jesus' early life was spent in Galilee, in the rough-neck town of Nazareth. But each year his parents took him and the rest of their family to Jerusalem to observe the Passover. His early ministry also took place outside Jerusalem, primarily in Galilee. Jesus made no attempt to gain entrance to the ranks of the religious establishment, instead reaching out to sinners and despised tax collectors. His disciples were mostly fishermen, not scribes or scholars. But for his inner circle of twelve, and a somewhat larger group who closely followed his ministry, he had established his credentials as Messiah.

All along Jesus knew that Jerusalem was his destiny. After preaching, teaching, healing and working miracles throughout Galilee, and then Samaria, Judea, and Perea, he "resolutely" set out for Jerusalem (Luke 9:51). The scripture literally says that he "set his face to go to Jerusalem," emphasizing that Jesus was determined to accomplish his mission.

As Isaiah had prophesied centuries earlier, he would be "despised and rejected" by the religious leaders. Knowing that would be his fate, Jesus went up to Jerusalem—to be humiliated, to die at the hands of the Romans, and to rise again on the third day.

God had a bigger plan in mind than most people were thinking about when it came to what the Messiah would accomplish. At the dawn of time God was faced with his creatures' rebellion. The first eleven chapters of Genesis are a story of mankind's unrelenting decline. Finally, after the episode with the Tower of Babel, God focused his attention away from all men and turned to one particular man, Abraham. And from that one man he fashioned the nation of Israel to be his chosen people—those who would bear witness to the truth about God in the midst of all the races of man which had turned their backs on their Creator.

But even Israel's story was a story of decline marked by backsliding, apostasy, and idolatry. They became a people, as Jeremiah described them, "uncircumcised in heart." But the Lord also gave a promise to Jeremiah: he would make a new covenant with his people. Where the old covenant was written on tablets of stone, the new covenant would be written on human hearts.

Yet centuries of darkness and oppression were endured before this new covenant was inaugurated. Then, like a fresh shoot out of a rotten stump, came Jesus, the righteous Branch. He purchased the forgiveness of sins and opened the door for the entry of the Gentiles—the nations—into the kingdom of God.

Shortly before he ascended to heaven, Jesus told his disciples not to leave Jerusalem, but to wait there for the gift the Father had promised, the gift of the Holy Spirit. "You will receive power when the Holy Spirit comes on you; and you will be my witnesses in Jerusalem, and in all Judea and Samaria, and to the ends of the earth" (Acts 1:8). That's the way it happened. The Christian church was born, in Jerusalem, on the Day of Pentecost, and the Good News of the Gospel of Jesus Christ has spread ever since—almost "to the ends of the earth" in our time.

Jerusalem served both as the birthplace of Christianity, around 30 A.D., and as the site of the preaching and miracles of the first apostles.

PERSECUTION AND DESTRUCTION

As the early church faced a bitter persecution, the city's political problems were also increasing. After Herod the Great's death, the kingdom was divided between his sons. There was so much squabbling over Herod's will, and such incompetence in his successors, that in short order Rome had to intercede. Archelaeus, who succeeded to the throne when Herod died, proved so ineffective that the Romans demoted him from king and made a direct colony of Judea. Herod Antipas, whom Jesus once called "that fox," was made tetrarch over Galilee and Perea, and Herod Philip was tetrarch over the northern province bordering Galilee and Syria.

Jewish resistance to the Roman administration smoldered quietly most of the time among its chief proponents: the Zealots, the Hassidim, and the Essenes. However, a good deal of trouble was stirred up when the Emperor Caligula attempted to install a statue of himself in the temple in Jerusalem and to have sacrifices made to it. Herod Agrippa, who had been given the kingdom of his uncle Philip by Caligula, persuaded his patron to drop the idea of the temple sacrifices.

Agrippa had made another powerful friend in Rome, Claudius. When the mad Caligula was assassinated, Claudius succeeded him as emperor and Agrippa reaped a great reward. Claudius reestablished the entire kingdom of Herod the Great and gave it to Herod Agrippa, Herod's grandson. Agrippa was part Jewish and while in Judea he was particular to observe Jewish law. Under his supervision things in Jerusalem proceeded much more quietly.

But after Agrippa came a particularly unfortunate succession of governors. Their graft and corruption rekindled the fires of Jewish revolt. Finally the Pharisees joined forces with the Zealots, and war broke out in the summer of 66 A.D. Caught off guard, the Roman forces in Judea quickly lost control of the Masada and Antonia fortresses and were slaughtered by the rebels. At Masada the rebels gained a vast armory Herod the Great had stockpiled in preparation for a possible war with Cleopatra over one hundred years earlier, along with enough dried food supplies to sustain them for years. Jerusalem was soon in Jewish hands.

In Jerusalem the rebellion's leaders coined money, collected taxes, and organized the entire country for defense. From Rome, Nero dispatched Vespasian with several legions to crush this, the most stubborn and desperate revolt Rome had ever faced. Bloody fighting for the next three years resulted in the isolation of the revolt in Jerusalem and Masada.

Vespasian became emperor in 70 A.D. and returned to Rome, leaving his son Titus in charge of the Judean campaign. Titus laid siege to Jerusalem with eighty thousand veteran troops. Fewer than a third that many Jews defended the city. But in the face of incredible shortages and starvation, they clung tenaciously to their city.

By late July, Titus had the Antonia fortress; but the defenders, hollow-eyed with hunger, regrouped in the temple platform. From the roof of the portico around the edge of the platform they rained down stones, arrows, and fiery brands against the legionnaires. The Romans then burned the roofs out from beneath them. After that the attackers gained access to the platform itself and the defenders retreated behind the walls of the temple proper into the Court of the Women and the court of Israel. More flaming projectiles set the sanctuary itself ablaze, and the rest was slaughter.

The Jewish historian, Josephus, who had been defeated earlier in the rebellion and gone over to the Romans, was an eyewitness to the event. He claimed that the streams of blood pouring from the corpses of the defenders were more copious than the streams of fire that were engulfing everything flammable in the vicinity.

Before the Roman legions were finished, all of the city lay in ruins with the exception of Herod's palace, where the Tenth Legion was stationed as a permanent force of occupation. But it would be three more years before the imperial armies recaptured Masada, the last stand of the Jewish revolt. Nearly one thousand men, women and children had been hiding in this isolated mountaintop fortress.

When the Roman armies finally scaled the awesome heights and reached the fortress, they were met with an eerie silence. All of the Jews at Masada had committed suicide, preferring to die at their own hands than be slaughtered by the armies of Rome.

NAMED FOR THEIR ENEMY

Judea was prostrate from the war, and life revived slowly. Early in the second century a new emperor came to the throne, Hadrian. He was a great administrator. He organized Roman law under a uniform code, sought ways to improve government efficiency, started an empire-wide communications system not unlike the pony express, and fortified the frontiers. Wanting to unify and strengthen the empire, Hadrian invoked laws to eliminate regional peculiarities. One of these, which prohibited "mutilations," was aimed at the Jewish practice of circumcision.

Hadrian was also a great builder. There was a wall that ran across northern England named after him; remnants of it are apparent to this day. But he also drew up a plan to rebuild Jerusalem as a center of pagan worship in honor of Jupiter, Juno, Venus, and himself. The city's name would be changed to Aelia Capitolina in honor of the Aelian clan, Hadrian's family. Work had not progressed far on this new plan before it began to get a response from the Jewish population. The leader of that response was named Simon Bar-Kochba. He united the Jews and managed to draw recruits from all over the Diaspora.

Even Samaritans and Gentiles were drawn into the ranks of this charismatic leader. His troops totaled nearly four hundred thousand when the new rebellion burst into the open in 132 A.D. It took three years for five legions of battle-hardened Roman troops to retake Jerusalem. Bar-Kochba himself was not captured and killed until 136 A.D.

The revenge of the Roman Army after its victory was terrible. Some of the leaders of the rebellion were skinned alive prior to their execution. Massacres during the fighting had been common. Now the survivors were either sold into slavery or allowed to starve. Burial was not permitted, so heaps of corpses decomposed in the streets and fields.

The Temple Mount was literally plowed under and an entirely New City was constructed north of the old. It contained two buildings together with pagan temples. The temple platform was used as a public square on the south side of the city. It was decked with statues of Hadrian and other Roman notables. It became an offense punishable by death for Jews to enter Jerusalem. Nor were they allowed to observe the Sabbath, read or teach the Law, circumcise, or otherwise follow God's law.

Hadrian changed the name of Judea to Syria Palaestina and made its capital Caesarea. Jerusalem, no longer a capital city, was renamed Aelia. And, apparently, over the years, its old name was all but forgotten—at least among those who didn't read the Bible. And that Book had not yet attained the status of being the world's bestseller.

Syria Palaestina, Hadrian's new name for Judea, is the origin of the name Palestine, in modern times applied to the area that would become the national homeland of the regathered Diaspora Jews. It was said that Hadrian renamed Judea after the ancient enemy of the Jews, the Philistines. Romans in general, and Hadrian in particular, hated the Jews.

Of all the nations the Romans had conquered, the Jewish people were the only group who would never quite submit to the Roman yoke. For that reason, Hadrian was determined to wipe the memory of Judea and the Jewish people from the pages of history. For the next five hundred years, no Jews would be allowed in the city of Jerusalem—now known as Aelia—except for one day each year, the anniversary of the burning of their temple.

With the Jewish population thoroughly subdued, Rome turned its attention to another foe that threatened its cultural survival: Christianity. Christians, who refused to sacrifice to the emperor and believed in none of the pantheon of Roman gods, were said to be atheists. Persecution against the early church continued off and on for over two centuries. Although Jews were forbidden in Jerusalem, Gentile Christians were not. Consequently the church, which had disappeared from the city after 70 A.D., began to reappear there. Sometime in the second century, the first church building was erected on Mount Zion. Early in the fourth century, the Emperor Constantine underwent a conversion to Christianity. He moved the capital of the empire from Rome to Byzantium, which he renamed Constantinople, partly as a consequence of the conversion.

Suddenly Jerusalem began to regain prestige. Constantine sent funds to Jerusalem, to be used to excavate and preserve Christian relics and sites. Later, Constantine's mother, Helena, an elderly and pious woman, went to Jerusalem to supervise and pay for the erection of various churches. In addition, she also saw to the demolition of the temple of Aphrodite. It was on the site of this pagan temple that, tradition held, Jesus had been buried after his crucifixion; thus, the origin of the Church of the Holy Sepulcher, which was first built in 335 A.D.

THE CENTER OF WORSHIP

Jerusalem quickly became the site of frequent pilgrimages. Churches, monasteries, and hospices for pilgrims became more and more plentiful. Gradually the evidence of Rome's paganizing of the city disappeared. Under the Emperor Theodosius, Christianity became the official religion of the Roman Empire in the late fourth century. This meant simply more boon and prosperity for Jerusalem, which became one of the four most important cities in Christianity, together with Alexandria, Rome, and Antioch.

In the fifth and sixth centuries, the Roman colonies suffered an economic recession which weakened the empire considerably. Taking advantage of this, the Persians started moving west, seizing lands that had formerly belonged to the Romans. In 614 A.D. they besieged Jerusalem. The patriarch refused to surrender and the city was taken with an awful slaughter. In addition, the Persians put as many of the churches and monasteries to the torch as they could.

But the Persian occupation was short-lived. In 628 A.D. the emperor invaded Persia to reclaim the empire's lost holdings. He retrieved the cross thought to have been the one on which Jesus had been crucified and returned it to Jerusalem. In the following years the Christians sought to rebuild what the Persians had destroyed, but they never had time to restore the previous splendor. Events in Arabia, where a new religion had blossomed, would see to that.

Seven

Jerusalem Under Siege

Most of us in America do not face life-or-death issues every day. We take our daily routines for granted: We get up in the morning, rush around fixing breakfast and getting the children ready for school, kiss them good-bye and put them on the bus, and dash off to work—without thinking twice. It's a difference scenario in Jerusalem, where life has never been quite that simple or easy.

Journalist David Grossman describes what it is like to live in a city vulnerable to violence and terror: "This morning, when I woke up my eleven-year-old son, he asked: 'Has today's bombing happened already?' My son is frightened, as are most Israelis. We have witnessed horrifying sights of civilian slaughter, of a type we did not see in our worst wars."

In the wake of a rash of suicide bombings, what should be routine becomes a critical decision, Grossman says. "Fear masters everything: When you walk down the street you inspect all those who pass you with, as we say in Hebrew, seven eyes. Any one of them could be your murderer. . . . Every decision is a fateful one. Should I send both boys to school in the same bus? And if not, which one will get on the 7:10 and which one on the next bus?

"We Israelis are accustomed to living in the vicinity of death. I will never forget the young couple who once told me of their plans for the future. They would get married and have three children. Three—so that if one died, there would still be two left."

Jerusalemites have always lived "in the vicinity of death," where everyday decisions are magnified into fateful moments. Their city has been ransacked, captured, or under major siege at least fifty times in the last thirty centuries—three times so far in this century.

As you consider the perils and the complexities of this tour of Jerusalem's stormy past and the threats today to her security, I hope you will keep in mind that this is not just a story of kings and soldiers and armies. It is the ordinary civilians, men like David Grossman and his eleven-year-old son, who are the ones who pay the heaviest price for living in this city under siege.

A NEW CONQUEROR

Muhammad never actually set foot in Jerusalem. He was living the last years of his life in Mecca and Medina during the time of the Persian occupation of Jerusalem. Just four years after his death, however, his followers would be storming the gates of the Holy City.

Few non-Muslims realize that Jerusalem is not mentioned by name in the Koran. The tenuous connection of the Holy City with Islam is based on a single line in the Koran describing Muhammad's famous "flight to heaven," or *Isra'*. "Praise be to Allah who brought his servant at night from the Holy Mosque to the Far-Away Mosque the precincts of which we have blessed." The unspecified "Far-Away Mosque" was later (probably not until the eighth century) said to be Jerusalem, perhaps for political reasons.

The *Isra'*, or nighttime visit to heaven, was an ecstatic experience or dream. The legend of the *Isra'* says that Muhammad was carried to Jerusalem on al-Burak, a winged horse with the face of a woman and tail of a peacock. Arriving at the temple platform, Muhammad dismounted and the angel Gabriel hitched al-Burak (or "Lightning") to a ring in a gate of the Western Wall. Muhammad then proceeded up to the outcropping of rock on the platform. There, assembled around the rock, were a group of the old prophets; among them were Abraham, Moses, and Jesus. They all joined Muhammad in prayer.

Then the prophet climbed a ladder of light from atop the sacred rock, through the seven heavens and into the very presence of Allah, who gave him a teaching about prayer. After that, Muhammad descended by the same ladder back to the rock. Then al-Burak carried him back to Mecca and his bed before the night was over.

In his early years, when he still expected both Jews and Christians to receive him as a prophet, Muhammad had designated Jerusalem as the direction one ought to face in prayer. Angered when he was rejected by the orthodox of both faiths, Muhammad changed his instructions and directed his followers to face Mecca in their daily prayers.

But the heart of Muhammad's religious lore had biblical roots. His concept of Islam, for example, was derived from Abraham, who submitted (Islam means "submission") his son as a sacrifice to God. But it was through Ishmael that the true faith was descended. In fact, it was Ishmael—not Isaac—that Allah told Abraham to sacrifice to him, according to Muhammad.

During the last ten years of his life Muhammad enjoyed phenomenal success. He built an empire that covered all of Arabia, and he found competent men to carry on his work after him. Those men were called caliphs, and by 700 A.D. they had extended the empire to include Palestine, Syria, Mesopotamia, Egypt, all of North Africa, Spain, and Asia Minor.

Islam arrived at Jerusalem's doorstep in 636 A.D., four years after Muhammad's death, when the army of Caliph Omar began a two-year siege of the city. When Patriarch Sophronius decided it was time to surrender, he remembered the bloodshed that had accompanied the Persian conquest twenty-four years earlier. So he sent out a request that the caliph himself would come to Jerusalem to receive the surrender.

Omar and Sophronius met at the Muslim encampment on the Mount of Olives. Omar was disposed to be generous. The Christians would be permitted complete freedom to practice their religion and retain their sites. The main change would be that they would now pay their taxes to the Muslims instead of to the Byzantines. Omar's tolerance extended to the Jews. For the first time in five hundred years they were allowed to live in Jerusalem.

As the city's new conqueror, Omar wanted to see the Temple Mount and the sacred rock from which Muhammad had ascended to heaven that celebrated night. When they got there, however, he and his men discovered that the area had been turned into a garbage dump—probably as a gesture of disdain by the Christian community against the infidel Jews.

Appalled, Omar started to work on the spot to clean the area. The thousand men with him pitched in as well so that the job was completed in reasonably short order. They went down to the southern end of the platform to face Mecca and pray. Sophronius must have looked on in horror.

By default the Muslims had taken over the Temple Mount. They rededicated it as a Muslim place of worship, which they called Haram esh-Sharif, "Noble Sanctuary."

THE DOME OF THE ROCK

Oddly, though, the Muslims did not use Jerusalem as their district capital, but ruled from various other locations. Under Caliph Abd al-Malik, who ruled from Damascus, the Dome of the Rock—still perhaps the most famous landmark in Jerusalem—was built on the Temple Mount, where Solomon's temple had originally stood. Al-Malik had a peculiar stake in Jerusalem because a rival caliph controlled Mecca and Medina.

So, in order to attract pilgrims to Jerusalem and, the story goes, to erect a structure that would rival churches in the city, he built the dome. Begun in 687 A.D., the Dome of the Rock required four years to complete. History would show that Abd al-Malik succeeded in producing a building that would outshine the city's churches. But he failed to draw Muslims away from their principal devotion to Mecca and Medina.

The Dome of the Rock is a mosque, but it serves primarily as a shrine for the sacred rock beneath. It is an octagon on a square base reached by six stairways. By any standards it is magnificently beautiful. In the intervening years, time and earthquakes have taken their tolls and made repairs necessary. But what stands today is still very much like what stood there in 691 A.D.

The sacred rock enshrined beneath the cupola is roughly two hundred feet in perimeter. During the centuries following the dome's construction, the rock was surrounded by rich brocade curtains. Daily it was anointed by lovely mixtures of incense. More than one hundred and fifty chains suspended overhead held scores of candelabra for illumination. A staff of over three hundred people was employed to maintain the building and its grounds.

Gradually the administration of Jerusalem became more repressive toward Christians and Jews. Muhammad had declared there could be no other religion in Arabia than Islam.

His followers extended that dictum to varying degrees throughout the rapidly-expanding empire.

Even today Muslims see the world as divided into two parts: *Dar el-Islam,* or the world of Islam; and *Dar el-Harb* (literally, "the world of the sword" or "the world of war"), those non-Islamic nations that have not yet been conquered by Muslim armies. Muslims regard both Jews and Christians as "people of the Book."

But all non-Muslims living in Muslim countries are regarded as *dhimmis,* "protected ones," or "tolerated ones," second-class people in every sense inferior to themselves. And the Koran commands imposing *jizya,* or a poll tax, on non-Muslims.

Eventually the various ruling dynasties of the Islamic empire began to rely heavily on Turkish mercenaries called Seljuks. By the middle of the eleventh century the Seljuks had gained political and military ascendancy in the empire. The caliphates were effectively reduced to centers of purely religious affairs. The Seljuk rulers called themselves *sultan,* which meant "master."

A strong and vigorous group, the Seljuks brought new life into the old sagging empire. They captured Jerusalem in 1070 and tales of their maliciousness and persecution (against both Christians and Jews) reached Europe in short order.

Gregory VII was the first pope to urge Christendom to launch a crusade against the Turkish expansion into Europe and Islamic oppression of Christians in Palestine. But it was his successor, Urban II, who gathered a great assembly of churchmen and nobles in Clermont, France, in 1095.

In a stirring sermon he urged the knights of Europe to stop their feuds and to rescue their fellow Christians and the Holy Land from the Turks. The response was thunderous as the hall was filled with shouts of *"Deus vult!"* (God wills it!) Soon thousands had enlisted in the holy cause. Jerusalem was about to be liberated from the Muslim infidels.

THE CRUSADER KINGDOM

The Frankish knights of Godfrey de Bouillon gazed at last on Jerusalem on June 7, 1099. They had already endured hard battles with the Saracens (their term for the Muslims) at Nicea and Antioch. Traveling over two thousand miles, with most of them walking, it had taken three years to arrive at this, their true goal.

Jerusalem was the great prize of the Crusades. The knights had come to rescue their fellow Christians, to halt the Muslim expansion into Europe, and to liberate the sacred shrines of their faith from the heathen. So at the first sight of the walled city, many of them raised their hands to heaven and gave thanks; others removed their shoes and bent down to kiss the holy ground on which they were standing.

Inside the walls of Jerusalem were a thousand men beseeching the assistance of Allah against the great host of the enemy arrayed on the surrounding hillsides. The city's defenders had reason to be uneasy. The Crusaders outnumbered them nearly twelve to one.

During the first few weeks, however, the Muslims resisted the Christians stoutly and it was beginning to look to the Europeans as though it would be another long siege. Before the Crusaders' arrival the Muslims had poisoned or stopped up all the wells outside the city. Now the soldiers were parched from the fierce summer heat. Food had also become scarce. There were more desertions. One entire company held a baptismal service in the Jordan River, and then left for the coast to find a ship sailing for Europe.

But the Crusaders were not just short of food and water; they were short of weapons. The initial assault on the city had failed because they did not have enough ladders to scale the walls in sufficient numbers to overtake the enemy soldiers; they were forced to retreat.

Time was critical, as additional troops from Egypt were headed their way to reinforce the Muslims. The Crusaders still vastly outnumbered the city's defenders, but they would need to build catapults and siege towers to successfully take the city before their enemy's reinforcements arrived. They still lacked the supplies, however, needed to build their siege equipment.

Just when it appeared that hope was lost, six ships sailed into Jaffa carrying food and supplies for the Christians. Now all they lacked was wood. The hills around Jerusalem were bare, so the soldiers traveled as far as Samaria to bring sufficient timber, loaded on camels and the backs of captives, to the army.

A priest who had accompanied the army had a vision and related it to the military leaders. He exhorted the Crusaders to stop feuding among themselves, to fast, pray and repent, and then to march barefooted around the city, praying to God. He said he had received this message: "If you do this and then make a great attack on the city on the ninth day, it will be captured. If you do not, all the evils that you have suffered will be multiplied by the Lord."

In response to the vision, the soldiers did repent and stop their quarreling. On Friday, July 8, they marched with bare feet around the city in a solemn procession. The Muslims gathered on the walls to watch, mocking them and blaspheming.

By Sunday the Crusaders had finished building their siege towers and put them in place against the walls of the city. On Wednesday they renewed the attack, charging the walls of the city. The bombardment lasted through Thursday, until an uneasy quiet settled in that evening. And on Friday morning, one week after they had marched around the city, the Crusader armies shouted "God wills it"—and stormed over the walls. The Muslims fled to take refuge in the Al-Aksa mosque, but were quickly overtaken.

THE HORROR OF CONQUEST

What followed after that is horrible to recount. The Crusaders launched into a rampage of looting and carnage as bloody as any episode in Jerusalem's history. Many of the city's defenders were beheaded, shot with arrows, or forced to jump from towers. Piles of heads and hands and feet littered the streets. Corpses were everywhere.

Nor was the massacre limited to soldiers. All infidels were in jeopardy of their lives, regardless of sex or age. Even infants were slaughtered. What Jews the Crusaders could find were accused of having aided in the defense of the city, rounded up, and taken to a synagogue where they were incinerated. Estimates of the total number of people killed in this sack of Jerusalem hover around forty thousand men, women, and children—most of whom were civilians.

Without excusing the barbarism of the Crusaders, we must understand something about medieval laws of warfare: If a city surrendered, it was not sacked; if the city resisted, then it was sacked once it was taken. Jerusalem had resisted, and the Crusaders felt justified in sacking the city. They were also avenging the horrors of the Muslim persecution against the Christians. It is repulsive to us, but was not uncommon at the time.

For battle-weary soldiers, who had spent three years traveling over two thousand miles and then endured the stress of weeks of siege combat, discipline—even if attempted—would have been impossible to maintain. The knights of the Middle Ages were nurtured on a revenge mentality; to them, bloodshed was simply a part of evening the score.

Now, not quite one thousand years after Hadrian had dubbed his rebuilt city Aelia, the city was officially renamed Jerusalem—

although Christians had never called the Holy City by any other name.

Godfrey de Bouillon became the king of Jerusalem and took for himself the title, "Defender of the Holy Sepulcher." He and his associates imposed a feudal system on the city and the surrounding territory. The land was parceled out to various barons to whom the people became serfs. The mosques were converted into churches and chapels.

A steady stream of up to ten thousand Christian pilgrims began journeying to Jerusalem each year. The Crusader kings of Jerusalem built or rebuilt almost forty churches in the city. The Church of the Holy Sepulcher received the highest priority. It was dedicated, after elaborate restoration and refurbishing, in 1149.

The Kingdom of Jerusalem continued to expand until it stretched from Lebanon all the way to Egypt. Muslim attempts to regain lost territory aroused a Second Crusade, but it ended in complete failure. But then a new Muslim leader arose by the name of Saladin. He quickly unified Syria and Egypt under his rule, and within a few years his kingdom stretched up into Mesopotamia.

Then Saladin turned his attention to Jerusalem. He marshaled one hundred thousand troops and soundly defeated the forces of the king of Jerusalem, then Guy of Lusignan, in a pitched battle north of the Sea of Galilee. Saladin actually captured the king. He also captured a large wooden cross which the knights were convinced was the true cross on which Jesus had died, and sent it to the caliph of Baghdad.

After a series of battles, Saladin reached the city of Jerusalem itself in 1187. A delegation sued for peace. Saladin said he would prefer not to besiege the city because he, too, regarded it as holy. He realized the city's Christian garrison was small and said he would allow them a few months' breathing spell to strengthen their defenses and replenish their supplies. If, at the end of that time, they still had hopes of rescue, they would be in a position to fight honorably. Otherwise, they ought to surrender now, he said, because he was willing to spare their lives and their property.

The Europeans couldn't tolerate the idea of giving up the city without a fight, nor would they accept the breathing spell offered. So the siege commenced the next day, and within a few weeks the city had fallen. Saladin's terms were unusually humane. Because the city surrendered, he permitted no slaughter by his troops. From those who had any means he exacted a ransom of ten gold pieces per man, five per woman, and one per child. Those who could not pay the ransom—some fifteen thousand Christians—were sold into slavery.

Under his administration Jerusalem, which he renamed al-Quds (the Holy One), was once again opened to the Jews. The Crusader period was the last time the Jews would be prohibited from free access to the city until 1947. In addition, Saladin opened the city to Christian pilgrims, so long as they were unarmed.

Saladin restored the temple platform—the Haram esh-Sharif—to Islamic status. The Crusaders had used both the Dome of the Rock and the Al-Aksa Mosque as their headquarters. Both places had been turned into churches and a gold cross had replaced the crescent that had stood atop the Dome. Now the cross came down, and the crescent was restored.

THE FALL OF JERUSALEM

The fall of Jerusalem sent a shock wave through Europe. The pope issued a call for still another Crusade, and Richard the Lionhearted answered the call. In 1191 Richard retook Acre on the Mediterranean coast of Palestine, and in several other battles with Saladin, proved himself a worthy opponent for the Saracen.

However, Richard was unable to wrest Jerusalem away from

the Muslims. But in the process of all this, something of a respect and friendship grew between Richard and Saladin so that they were able to effect a truce. Under its terms the Muslims kept Jerusalem, while the Christians controlled the seacoast between Acre and Jaffa. And citizens and merchants of whatever persuasion were permitted to pass between the two zones unmolested.

After Saladin's death, his empire disintegrated. More Crusades followed. But by 1291 the Crusader era was ended and the Christian presence in the Holy Land was extinguished. Jerusalem would remain under the firm hand of Muslim landlords for a long time to come.

At the end of the fifteenth century Ferdinand and Isabella succeeded in driving the Moors (Muslim North Africans) out of Spain. And in their zeal to procure a purely Catholic state, they expelled the country's large, highly-educated and cultured Jewish community in 1492—the same year they dispatched Columbus across the Atlantic for different reasons.

It was a disastrous blow to the Jews, most of whom had to content themselves with much humbler quarters in the less habitable climes of the Middle East—many came to Jerusalem. But for Spain, it constituted a self-inflicted wound from which the nation has not recovered to this day.

Then in 1516 a new group of conquerors headed for the Holy City. While Martin Luther was expounding Pauline doctrine to his students at Wittenberg University, the Ottomans, Turkish tribesmen, were coming to Jerusalem. A vigorous and unusually warlike group, the Ottoman Turks subdued one district after another throughout the Middle East. Eventually their empire would be one of the most vast in the history of man.

By the next year, 1517, Jerusalem had a new landlord. The Ottoman conqueror of Jerusalem was Selim I. During his reign, heavy poll taxes *(jizya)* were imposed on all non-Muslims. Selim's son was the famous Suleiman the Magnificent, whose reign marked the strongest and most robust period of the Ottoman Empire. Suleiman restored Islamic shrines throughout the empire and provided the Dome of the Rock with the exterior mosaic of glazed Persian tiles that still bedeck it.

In fact, the shape of things on the Haram esh-Sharif as they exist today is largely Suleiman's responsibility. He rebuilt the walls of the city and, again, today we can still see his handiwork. And it was Suleiman, according to legend, who ordered the sealing of the Golden Gate on the east side of the Haram to prevent the entry of the Messiah, who was supposed to enter the city through that gate.

During the Ottoman period the Jewish population of Jerusalem grew slowly but persistently. But the Ottoman landlords let the city fall to pieces through inattention and corruption. The city's total population shriveled to around ten thousand (about a thousand Jews, three thousand Christians, and six thousand Muslims).

And so, through the seventeenth and eighteenth centuries, Jerusalem sat idly in the backwaters of the Ottoman Empire— still trodden down by the Gentiles in spite of all the changes.

But one year short of the nineteenth century, something would happen to put the Holy City back in the headlines. As his troops came ashore at Alexandria, Napoleon eyed them confidently. He had come here to Egypt, where the Ottoman sultan's rule was most vulnerable, to establish a European colony. But the French general had more in mind than military conquest alone. This colony would be a tribute to the ability of modern France to resurrect the splendor that had once stretched along the shores of the Nile when the pharaohs had reigned.

To accomplish this he had brought with him some of France's most prestigious scientists, engineers, naturalists, orientalists, and antiquarians. And, in so doing, he planted a seed that would grow and bear fruit long after he and his commission were gone from the scene. His team of experts started the work of large-scale archaeological activity that has persisted in the Middle East to this day.

On the night of August 1, 1798, Admiral Horatio Nelson's squadron appeared off Alexandria. By daybreak the British had destroyed Napoleon's massive fleet. With the combined threat of an Ottoman army amassing against him and the British openly mobilizing to invade Egypt, officials in London were confident Napoleon would relinquish Egypt and go back to France. But they were wrong. Napoleon was not easily intimidated.

THE SECRET STRUGGLE

In January 1799, Napoleon took thirteen thousand men and headed north into Palestine to meet and smash the Ottoman army. He moved steadily across the Sinai and took al-Arish and Gaza with ease. At Jaffa the Turks put up stiff resistance. After defeating them, Napoleon loosed his troops in a spree of bloodshed and looting that alerted the land and its people to the true face of this new invader. Many of them saw it as divine retribution when, not much later, Napoleon's army suffered an epidemic of bubonic plague.

Napoleon was finally stopped at Acre, the old Crusader stronghold. After the battle, something happened that illustrates the real point of all this. The Ottoman sultan announced that he intended to massacre the native Christians of Palestine whom he suspected of having aided Napoleon. But Commodore Smith of Britain's offshore fleet let the sultan know that the guns of his men-of-war would protect the Christians, just as they had protected the Turks from Napoleon.

To underscore his point, Smith dispatched a detachment of sailors to make a showy march up to Jerusalem where many of the native Christians lived. The Catholic and Orthodox churchmen greeted them thankfully and uttered nervous appeals for protection. It was the beginning of a British involvement with the Holy City that would last nearly 150 years.

Napoleon's adventure in the Middle East served notice that the Ottoman Empire was no longer the impregnable bastion it had once been. It also made clear the strategic importance of the area of Palestine in the quest for empire that would dominate nineteenth-century politics in Europe. The major nations of Western Europe began maneuvering for position, knowing that when the Ottoman Empire eventually fell, Palestine would be ripe for the plucking.

Spurred by Napoleon, a secret struggle was launched among the Europeans for control of this vital area—but it was a struggle not carried out with armies or navies. Its primary agents would be curiosity-seekers, explorers, missionaries, archaeologists, and diplomats.

News of open doors of access to the land of the Bible was nothing less than electrifying in England and the United States. Both nations were freshly imbued with Christian zeal as a result of the Wesleyan revivals of the eighteenth century and the consequent spread of Methodism. As news of the dramatic Battle of Acre and the accompanying reports about the Holy Land reached the ears of Americans and Englishmen, they instantly wanted to know more about this "land of milk and honey" they had read of in their Bibles.

But the first wave of explorers and curiosity-seekers found the land much less romantic and idealized than they had imagined. The terrain was desolate, the shrines spurious, and the inhabitants uncouth. It would require hardier resolve than could be mustered by mere curiosity to surmount these obstacles.

The zeal of American evangelical Christians, however, was more than adequate for the task. The people of the Levant, the countries on the eastern Meditteranean, were not ripe for revival in the usual sense of that word. But a handful of hardy Christians paved the way for others to come to this forbidding land. And the groundwork for the field of scientific biblical archaeology was laid.

In the 1840s an American naval expedition explored the nature of the passage down the Jordan from the Sea of Galilee to the Dead Sea. By the middle of the century, however, the British, French, and Germans began to be more plentiful in the region. Consular offices were established in Jerusalem. And the maneuvering for position in Palestine grew more intense.

A critical moment in the secret struggle came in 1865 with the formation in London of the Palestine Exploration Fund. Gathered for the event were some very notable Victorians. The archbishop of York outlined the goals of the new society in his address. "This country of Palestine," he said, "belongs to you and me. It is essentially ours. It was given to the father of Israel in the words, 'Walk through the land in the length of it and the breadth of it, for I will give unto ye.'

"*We* mean to walk through Palestine, in the length and breadth of it, because that land has been given unto us. It is the land from which comes news of our redemption. It is the land to which we turn as the fountain of all our hopes; it is the land to which we look with as true a patriotism as we do to this dear old England."

Queen Victoria, the archbishop announced, had consented to be the official patron of the society and had sent her contribution of 150 pounds to help it get started. One of the other speakers addressed the need of the Fund to counteract the efforts of the French to stake their claim of the land.

That same year the official Ordnance Survey of Jerusalem was published in London. Conducted by the Royal Engineers, the survey contained two accurately drawn plans of the city, together with precise architectural plans of the Church of the Holy Sepulcher, the Dome of the Rock, and other monuments in the city.

A short while after its publication, a second party of Royal Engineers were sent off, this time under the sponsorship of the Palestine Exploration Fund, to commence a survey of the entire country of Palestine. It marked the commencement of a project that T. E. Lawrence, the legendary Lawrence of Arabia, would help complete in 1914.

THE WESTERNIZATION OF JERUSALEM

Charles Warren became the first agent of the Palestine Exploration Fund to engage in serious archaeological excavations. He also was an officer of the Royal Engineers, and highly experienced in the work of digging mines and tunnels for military purposes.

Because of the nervousness of the Turkish officials as well as the townspeople in Jerusalem about excavations of holy sites, Warren's techniques proved invaluable. To explore the walls of the Haram and the like, he simply sank shafts into the ground and then tunneled to whatever it was he wanted to examine. All that was seen of his work above ground was an innocuous opening of the shaft. That allayed fears that he would tear the place apart.

At the same time Warren was working in Jerusalem, the terrain was being torn apart to the southwest in a project that would affect Jerusalem more deeply than anything Warren was doing. The French had been busy digging the Suez Canal for ten years. On November 17, 1869, it was finally open for business.

Oddly, the British, who had the most to gain from the canal, had nothing to do with its construction or management at first. But then the Franco-Prussian War (1870–71) destroyed the empire of Napoleon III and left Britain virtually unobstructed in its efforts to gain control of the canal. Egypt was in the process of becoming a British colony.

However, the secret struggle for Palestine would continue much longer. Europe was aware that the Ottoman Empire was crumbling and that when it did at last fall apart, there would be a scramble to divide it up, particularly among Britain, France, Germany, and Russia. The situation was fraught with risks, and the consensus was that Istanbul's domain should be left intact as long as possible until other matters were settled.

Meanwhile, Jerusalem was blossoming. The influx of Europeans and Americans was changing the face of the city. Signs like *Deutsche Palaestina Bank* and *Barclays* began to appear on its streets. The Turks did what they could to hold the line, but the tide of westernization seemed irresistible. Besides all the diplomatic and archaeological activity, the French even found time to construct a railroad from the coast up to Jerusalem in the 1880s.

New forces were at work, too, that increased the Jewish population of the city. By the middle of the century Jews constituted nearly half its population. Many of the new immigrants still fell into the pattern of the scholars and sages who had lived in the city supported by the charity of Jews in Europe and the United States. It would take a while before the idea of reclaiming the desolate countryside would seriously seize the Jewish imagination.

Sir Moses Montefiore, a wealthy English banker, contributed a good deal of his money and energy to expanding the concept of what it meant for Jews to live again in their own land. He even convinced some of the Jews in Jerusalem to live outside the city walls in a housing project he constructed there.

Called *Mishkenot Sha'ananim* ("Dwellings of Tranquility"), it is used today by the Israeli government to house honored guests of the country.

The constant influx of westerners increased with the opening of the Suez Canal. Almost one million Europeans visited Jerusalem in the nineteenth century. It was no longer a tourist attraction solely for the wealthy or the religious. After the opening of the canal, a Baptist lay preacher by the name of Thomas Cook opened a travel agency that made it affordable for middle-class Europeans to tour Jerusalem.

Travelogues about the Holy Land, and especially Jerusalem, became best-selling books, with famous authors such as Benjamin Disraeli, Gustave Flaubert, Herman Melville, and Mark Twain contributing to the genre. Twain's *Innocents Abroad* was a biting satire on the prolific accounts of devoted pilgrims.

THE ROOTS OF ZIONISM

In the years between 1860 and 1890 the concept of Zionism began to take shape as books on the subject began to appear. Many Orthodox Jews had long insisted that any return to the Holy Land would be carried out by the Messiah, and that to take matters into one's own hands would be blasphemous. However, the new Zionists vigorously denied this and urged a serious program of immigration and settlement.

Theodor Herzl, a Viennese playwright and journalist, regarded himself as a largely assimilated Jew (meaning he was assimilated into the Gentile culture and no longer clung with any great tenacity to his Jewish heritage) until he began to be confronted by persistent anti-Semitism in Europe.

He was working in Paris during the Dreyfus Affair, and when he heard the crowds taunt the unfortunate French Jewish army captain with shouts of "à la mort les juifs" (death to the Jews), it became his own critical moment of recognition—nothing would do but a Jewish state, a sovereign nation. For the first time in his life Herzl began attending Jewish religious services.

Less than two years later, in 1896, he published *Der Judenstaat*—the classic testament of Zionism. The title is usually translated *The Jewish State*, but is more correctly rendered *The Jew-State*. Herzl chose the title to fling his concept into the teeth of anti-Semites and of acculturated Western Jews who preferred euphemisms like "Israelite" or "Hebrew."

Shortly after the book's publication, Herzl was placed at the helm of the burgeoning World Zionist Organization. In 1897 the organization held its first Congress in Basel, Switzerland. The immediate goal was to gain the sponsorship and support of one of the great European powers. Finally, in 1903, the British offered them territory in East Africa. Herzl thought the offer attractive, but he died before a decision could be made.

In 1905 the Zionist Congress rejected the offer and resolved instead that the Jewish national home had to be in Palestine. The Jewish National Fund was established for the purchase of property in Palestine wherever it could be found for sale. Real estate prices in Galilee, Samaria, and Judea inflated with awful suddenness, but the Jews were not deterred. The Jewish population of Jerusalem was growing impressively. Of the city's sixty-eight thousand inhabitants in 1910, fully fifty thousand were Jewish. But no longer were they primarily Talmudic scholars.

Now, in addition to the scholars, there were workers, craftsmen, professionals, technicians, merchants—a broader spectrum of occupations within the Jewish population. Public libraries, art schools, trade unions, and light industry began increasingly to find their places in the streets of Jerusalem.

In the meantime the maneuvering among the European

powers for control of the Holy Land was becoming more and more open. Russia had moved against the Ottomans in 1877 and delivered them a humiliating defeat. The status quo was becoming more precarious as Britain, France, and Russia grew more eager to get their hands on more of the Ottoman territory. Germany alone among the Europeans seemed to hold out a helping hand to the sultan. Kaiser Wilhelm sent a number of German military and economic missions to Istanbul. In 1889 he traveled there in person to further cement relations. These gestures served to help hold the other nations, particularly Great Britain and France, in check.

To further bolster his plans for an expanded German empire, Wilhelm traveled to Jerusalem in 1898. At the port of Haifa, a Turkish military band greeted him with appropriate martial music as he was welcomed by Ottoman officials and German colonists. At Jerusalem a special "imperial campground" awaited him. Heavily guarded by Turkish soldiers, its tents were furnished with fine Persian carpets and ivory inlaid beds, tables, and chairs. The city itself was festooned with flags and lanterns—even the Dome of the Rock had been cleaned and refurbished for the occasion.

On October 29, 1898, Kaiser Wilhelm II entered Jerusalem's Jaffa Gate astride a white stallion, his spiked helmet glistening in the sun, escorted by Prussian and Turkish cavalry. That evening his visit was saluted by a gigantic fireworks display. During the next two days, he and the kaiserin, Augusta Victoria (a daughter of Queen Victoria), visited the city's shrines and sites, dedicated an orphanage in Bethlehem and an impressive Protestant church near the Holy Sepulcher, and presented the city's German Catholics with a plot of ground on Mount Zion for the erection of a new church of their own.

In one of his speeches Wilhelm announced, "From Jerusalem a light has arisen upon the world—the blessed light in whose splendor our German people have become great and glorious." After his visit, the Augusta Victoria Hospice was built on Mount Scopus. The kaiser had staked his claim as firmly as he could.

A year later the German-Turkish alliance began to take formal shape. The die was cast. England and France knew that if they were going to have Palestine, they would have to fight both the Germans and the Turks to get it.

Eight

The Conquest of Palestine

T. E. Lawrence looked up from his notes and studied the landscape that stretched before him. He was in the Negev Desert, known to Bible readers as the Wilderness of Zin, to do archaeological research with his companion, Leonard Wooley. They were employed by a church-sponsored organization in London called the Palestine Exploration Fund which had been active since the middle of the nineteenth century. But now it was 1913. War was coming and everyone knew it.

Lawrence and Wooley stood atop the lofty site of an ancient Nabatean city called Nizzana, roughly thirty-five miles southwest of Beersheba. Their job was to prepare notes about the site which would help prepare the way for full-scale excavation at a later time. But as much as he loved archaeology—he had studied it at Oxford—Lawrence was even more fascinated by military strategy.

And so the Turkish fortifications and camp that stretched out below him on the desert floor competed successfully for his attention. He had seen the likes of it before around Gaza and Beersheba, both behind him to the north.

He and Wooley were participating in the end of a project

that had been going on for some time, a thorough survey and mapping of western Palestine. The Palestine Exploration Fund had been doing this with the help of the Royal Engineers who had been loaned to them from time to time by the British government, almost since its inception. By 1913 everything west of the Jordan River valley from Galilee to Beersheba had been mapped with the precision and attention to detail for which the Royal Engineers were justly famous.

What remained to be done was the Negev. Consequently, Lawrence and Wooley were becoming unusually familiar with its barren countryside. In this sort of country, where one could pretty much roam at will, fortifications like the ones he was seeing through his binocular lenses were virtually useless.

Lawrence and Wooley, in conjunction with a small contingent of Royal Engineers headed by Captain Steward Newcombe, continued their work all through the winter of 1913–14. Once the surveying was done, however, Lawrence and Newcombe left the others to finish the job while they went south to Aqaba at the lower tip of the Negev. But the exploratory warrant issued to the Palestine Exploration Fund by the authorities in Istanbul had not included this region.

Nevertheless, the two men were curious to know more about this strategic point. The Ottoman governor there was not inclined to be charitable to two snoopy Englishmen. His government was in league with Germany and Austria-Hungary, and the British, together with the French and Russians, were on the other side. Lacking proper documentation, the scientists had to satisfy themselves with a brief moonlit reconnaissance before they beat a hasty retreat back to the north.

In June 1914 the word was conveyed to London that the survey of western Palestine was complete. The war, which had been imminent for some time, broke out within days. Shortly before noon on Sunday, June 28, crowds gathered in Sarajevo, the capital of the Austro-Hungarian province of Bosnia. They had come to see Archduke Franz Ferdinand, heir to the Hapsburg throne, and his controversial wife, Sophie.

As the open touring car drove the royal couple through the cheering crowds, a young man leaped onto the car's runningboard and began firing a pistol at point-blank range. Franz Ferdinand was struck by two bullets and his wife caught a third when she tried to shield his body. They were dead within minutes, but the aftermath of that assassination would endure through the four bloody and barbaric years of the Great War.

When Austrian authorities investigated the assassination, they discovered that its perpetrator, Gavrilo Princip, had lived in Serbia for several years, even though he was a Bosnian. Serbia had been at odds with Austria-Hungary and its Hapsburg monarchy since it had broken away from the Ottoman Empire. They concluded that Princip had acted as an agent of the Serbian government in murdering the crown prince, and on July 28, 1914, Austria declared war on Serbia. By the end of October the Central Powers—Austria-Hungary, Germany, and the Ottoman Empire—were at war with the Allies—Belgium, France, Great Britain, Russia, and Serbia.

Back in the Middle East, Lawrence, Newcombe, and Wooley were quickly called to Cairo and commissioned to serve in the intelligence division of the British forces stationed in Egypt. Britain had maintained a military presence in Egypt in the interests of protecting the Suez Canal. The trio's first assignment was to complete the execution of the maps of the Negev. The army knew the maps would be vital.

The Turkish VIII Corps set up headquarters in Jerusalem where a German-Turkish High Command was making plans to attack and seize the canal. By mid-January 1915, nearly one-hundred thousand Turkish troops had been assembled in and around Beersheba. They were sent across the Sinai in a human-wave assault against well-entrenched and heavily-armed British and Indian troops east of the canal. British machine guns and artillery decimated the Turkish ranks, and the survivors limped back to Palestine in utter humiliation.

THE WAR IN PALESTINE

Meanwhile, on the Western Front in Flanders, the blood of England's manhood was being spilled in places such as Ypres and the Somme. If the government had not been able to hide the nature of the fighting and the unbelievable percentage of casualties, surely the war would have been halted by the public outcry.

But it could not be hidden from everyone, and one man, Field Marshal Horatio Kitchener, offered a plan to break the stalemate in the trenches of France. Years before, as a young officer, Kitchener had worked in Palestine for the Palestine Exploration Fund. He knew the Middle East better than most, and as Secretary of State for War he proposed the creation of a full-fledged expeditionary force into Egypt for the purpose of achieving a stunning victory against the Turks.

Lord Kitchener died during the summer of 1916, but the newly elected prime minister, David Lloyd George, saw merit in Kitchener's plan and took steps to implement it. If it didn't break the stalemate in France, it would at least make the Suez Canal secure. That, in itself, was a worthy goal. So the Egyptian Expeditionary Force (EEF) of the Royal Army struck out across the Sinai in December 1916. They moved along the coast, much as Napoleon had done in 1799, and took al-Arish and Rafah with little opposition. From there they moved up into southern Palestine.

At Gaza they found the Turks heavily entrenched. The commander, Sir Archibald Murray, hurled his men at the lines, but the fighting was tougher than he had expected. The Brits took heavy casualties and were driven back. Murray regrouped and assaulted the fortress at Gaza a second time, in April 1917. But the Turks were even more prepared this time, with reinforcements and soldiers from the German Asienkorps. Back in London, Lloyd George was furious. His plan was being dashed to pieces, he was convinced, by an incompetent commander. But something happened that month to give the British prime minister new optimism—the United States declared war on the Central Powers. The stalemate would be broken after all.

Lloyd George relieved Murray of the command of the EEF and replaced him with General Edmund Allenby, a dogged and tenacious fighter who had earned the nickname "the Bull" in the trenches of the Western Front. Before he embarked for the Middle East, the prime minister summoned the Bull to No. 10 Downing Street. The British government had no intentions, Lloyd George made it very clear, of suffering a third defeat in Palestine. Allenby was ordered to marshal his wisdom during the coming months and to prepare a Christmas gift for the British people—Jerusalem.

The British Commander arrived in Egypt in June 1917 and went directly to the front near Gaza. Another frontal assault, he quickly recognized, would be folly. He had to come up with a better plan. While he was reviewing his options, unexpected news arrived seemingly out of nowhere. T. E. Lawrence and a handful of Bedouins had managed to cross an impassable desert and drive the Turks out of Aqaba on the coast. The capture of that strategic port would provide protection for the rear and right flank of Bull Allenby's planned assault on the Ottoman lines at Beersheba.

On October 31, British artillery began shelling Gaza intensively. The same day a British scout was spotted by Turkish sentries. When they gave chase, the British officer fled, but he had dropped his courier pouch which contained what appeared to be secret British plans for a massive assault on Gaza.

The Turks swallowed the bait. To prepare for the attack, they pulled back most of their strongest units from Beersheba to man the trenches at Gaza. Only a small garrison remained at Beersheba. As the two sides manuevered into place, a large body of British troops moved up across the desert and set up within easy striking distance of Beersheba. They were guided in their task by the precise topographical maps compiled four years earlier by Captain Newcombe and his partners, and by up-to-date intelligence supplied by a network of Jewish spies in Palestine.

When the British officers received the signal to attack, the soldiers swarmed Beersheba with lightning speed. The Turkish garrison was stunned and retreated frantically to Gaza. This was the moment Allenby had waited for. In addition to the demoralizing effect of his capture of Beersheba, Allenby had a few other things on his side. One was the superb support of the British navy and its seaborne artillery. Another was aircraft for reconnaissance and support, a first for the EEF.

Finally, and perhaps most decisively, he had tanks. This would be the first time tanks had ever been deployed in the Holy Land. Clearly Allenby had the resources he needed to storm the fortified trenches and drive out the German and Austrian machine-gun units defending the city. After nine days of relentless pressure, Gaza fell to the Allies.

THE BALFOUR DECLARATION

On November 2, 1917, in the middle of that momentous battle, something even more momentous was taking place in London.

Lloyd George had for some months been wrestling with his plans for Palestine. He regarded Palestine as the strategic buffer to Egypt. He meant for Britain to control Egypt and the Suez Canal after the war was over. To make that control workable, he had to have Palestine as well, otherwise the whole arrangement would be in jeopardy. But he had to offer a loftier rationale than that to get the postwar allies to endorse his plan.

Both Woodrow Wilson and the provisional government in Russia had said that, as a matter of principle, the acquisition of new territory by means of war was wrong. But Lloyd George had a loftier ideal in the form of the Jewish people. He turned to an Anglo-Zionist alliance that had been taking shape increasingly over the previous several years. The designer and the true backbone of that alliance was a man named Chaim Weizmann. In 1914 Weizmann was forty years old and a chemistry professor at the University of Manchester. Born in Russia, he was educated in Germany and Switzerland. In addition, he had already shown himself to be a lucid and convincing propagandist for the Zionist movement. And he had begun to win a hearing in the highest echelons of British society.

Two newspaper editors introduced him to, among others, Lloyd George, Winston Churchill, and Lord Robert Cecil. Weizmann's prestige in the eyes of these important men was increased by a vital service he was rendering to the British Admiralty. A shortage of acetone was slowing down the production of cordite, an important naval explosive. Between March 1916 and the spring of 1918, Weizmann successfully developed a process of fermentation which guaranteed plentiful supplies of acetone for the Admiralty.

But there was more. Weizmann was a man of unusual charm and charisma. He had a striking profile. The brow of his massive bald pate was etched with veins, his eyes were penetrating, his moustache and goatee were distinguished, and his garments were finely tailored. Though his command of English was perfect, it was laced by an exotic Russian accent. And he managed to adapt his arguments to his listener with unusual skill.

With Britons and Americans he could use biblical language to awaken deep emotions, but he shifted away from this approach with other nationalities whose biblical background was not so rich. When talking with a Welshman like Lloyd George, he emphasized Palestine's hilly topography which made it seem so much like Wales; with Balfour he could explore the philosophy of Zionism; with Lord Cecil, he spoke of Zionism in terms of a new world organization; and with Lord Milner, he stressed the extension of British imperial power inherent in the plan.

The evangelical heritage of many of Weizmann's listeners worked mightily on his behalf. These men had read the Old Testament and were familiar with it to a degree unparalleled by their Catholic allies in France and Italy. To them, the children of Israel and the land of Canaan were things to be venerated.

Lloyd George later wrote about his first meeting with Weizmann in 1914. Historic sites in Palestine were mentioned that were, he said, more familiar to him than those of the Western Front. Balfour came from a decidedly evangelical background, as did Jan Christiaan Smuts, the South African member of the War Cabinet. Each of these men recognized deeply Christianity's historic obligation to the Jews. They felt that debt compounded by what Weizmann was doing for the war effort.

And they knew of Weizmann's uncompromising loyalty to Britain and the Allied war effort. Scotland Yard's files contained a copy of a letter written by Weizmann in 1916 terminating relations with the "neutralist" Zionist Bureau in Denmark. In that letter Weizmann had repeated his insistence that the fate of Zionism and that of the Allies were unalterably linked.

So Weizmann's talk of a "British protectorate over a Jewish

homeland" began to interest Lloyd George's government more and more. Several high-ranking officials in particular began to advocate a partnership with the Zionists.

Other factors continued to move the British government steadily toward the fateful step they would take on November 2, 1917. In spite of the entry of the United States into the war, France's strength was all but spent; its troops were even in mutiny in some places. No American troops had yet reached the trenches; Italy had suffered a major setback; German submarine warfare was taking an enormous toll on Allied shipping.

The prime minister's two greatest needs, as he perceived them, were to get the Americans fully involved and committed, and to keep Russia from dropping out altogether. And he believed that in each of those countries Jewish public opinion "might make a considerable difference." He was wrong in both instances, but since he didn't know that, it made no difference.

Meanwhile, Weizmann kept up his pressure for a statement from the government. Finally, on June 17, 1917, Balfour urged the Zionists themselves to draw up an appropriate declaration. He would, he promised, submit it to the cabinet with his endorsement. But critics claimed the original draft of the declaration made too great a commitment to the Zionists, so a milder version was suggested by the government. Weizmann and his friends didn't like it, but they decided it was the best they could get.

Finally, on October 31, the War Cabinet gave the Balfour Declaration, as it would become known, a solid majority vote. Arthur Balfour's niece later wrote that, near the end of his days, her uncle had looked back on his career and reflected that what he had been able to do for the Jews had been the most worth doing. On November 2, 1917, Balfour addressed a personal letter to Lord Rothschild, president of the British Zionist Federation, which said:

> I have much pleasure in conveying to you, on behalf of His Majesty's Government, the following declaration of sympathy with Jewish Zionist aspirations which has been submitted to, and approved by, the Cabinet: "His Majesty's Government view with favour the establishment in Palestine of a national home for the Jewish people, and will use their best endeavours to facilitate the achievement of this object, it being clearly understood that nothing shall be done which may prejudice the civil and religious rights of existing non-Jewish communities in Palestine, or the rights and political status enjoyed by Jews in any other country." I should be grateful if you would bring this declaration to the knowledge of the Zionist Federation.

This was a momentous occasion for the Jewish people and the first solid support they would have for establishing their claim upon Jerusalem. In Palestine, Allenby's troops were now pursuing Turks and Germans northward along the Mediterranean coast. By late November they had taken Jaffa. And from there they turned east and began to concentrate on their primary objective—Jerusalem itself.

BRITAIN TAKES JERUSALEM

The Turkish-German High Command in Jerusalem was in a state of near panic. Prisoners of war and wounded soldiers from both sides crowded the city, which was already threatened with starvation. Finally, when the Ottoman commander realized that

British forces were approaching the city not only from the west, but also from the north and south, he ordered evacuation of the city.

Headquarters staff officers, both Germans and Turks, grabbed whatever they could find—autos, wagons, carts, camels, horses—and loaded them with furniture, records, gold and silver, and frantically retreated to Damascus. What was valuable but couldn't be transported they destroyed or put into hiding. The Turkish barracks, the stone buildings near the Jaffa Gate which had been the center of Ottoman authority in Jerusalem since 1516, were abandoned.

By December 9, the Turks and Germans were gone, and the citizens of Jerusalem were left to fend for themselves in the face of the impending British attack. Little did they know that Allenby, himself a pious man and unwilling to do damage to the Holy City, had consulted the Imperial War Office and then the King himself about how to take Jerusalem. His sovereign had counseled him to make it a matter of prayer. Presumably he did just that and thereafter decided to drop leaflets on the city from an airplane. They addressed the now-absent Turkish authorities and invited them to surrender.

Jerusalem's civilian mayor, Haj Amin Nashashibi, decided to take Allenby up on the offer. He borrowed a white bedsheet from an American missionary and walked out of the city by way of the Jaffa Gate toward the southwest, the direction from which he understood the main body of the British troops were coming. Besides his associates, a small group of boys from the city trooped along behind and ahead of him.

They had not gone far down the road when they encountered two startled British scouts, Sergeants Hurcomb and Sedgewick of the London Regiment. By pointing to their flag and employing the few words of broken English the mayor had at his disposal, he managed to make his intentions clear to them.

Within hours the first British troops marched into the city. Everybody seemed glad to see them. The Jews, the largest single population in the city, had heard about the Balfour Declaration. To them, the arrival of these troops signaled the seriousness of the promise the declaration had given them of a national home. And, of course, the Christians cheered. No longer would the holy sites be under Muslim domination.

Two days later, Allenby himself arrived at Jaffa Gate to mark the arrival of the new regime. His troops had fought hard to bring him this far. A fierce Turkish counterattack in late November had halted their advance into the Judean Hills from Jaffa on the coast. Only three days ago had they renewed their forward movement.

Now, at the Jaffa Gate, as Allenby dismounted, he reached for the visor of his cap and removed it from his head. Unlike the German kaiser, the British conqueror humbly entered the Holy City as the bells of the various churches and the clock tower rang a joyous welcome. Once inside he mounted the steps of the Turkish citadel and read a proclamation which assured the city's inhabitants that the rights of their religious communities would be upheld and their various shrines scrupulously protected. He also gave formal greetings to the chief rabbis, the mufti, the Latin and Orthodox patriarchs, and the other religious leaders.

Winter rains held up further advances by Allenby's troops, so the Turks remained in control of Palestine above a line running just north of Jaffa and Jerusalem. Consequently, Jewish residents of Galilee suffered bitterly because the Turks perceived them to be firmly aligned with the Allied cause.

Ottoman troops confiscated Jewish farms, and Turkish army

deserters, numbering in the thousands by this time, terrorized Jewish settlements, looting and killing. In addition, hunger, illness, and exposure took their toll, so that by September 1918 the population of the Yishuv (the Jewish settlers in Palestine) was reduced from eighty-five thousand to fifty-five thousand. But by then, Allenby had reached Megiddo and scored another striking victory. Great Britain's conquest of the Holy Land was complete. The Bull had succeeded where Richard the Lionhearted had failed.

THE BEGINNING OF TERRORS

Allenby had succeeded, but the Arab nationalists living in Palestine were enraged by the Balfour Declaration and its call for a national home for the Jewish people. When their protests were not heard—the League of Nations endorsed both the Declaration and the Jewish homeland—they resorted to violence, determined to run out both the Jews and the British, and set up an Arab state encompassing the whole of Palestine.

The first high commissioner sent by England to govern in Jerusalem was Sir Herbert Samuel. Because he was Jewish, the Arabs felt betrayed. Because Samuel bent over backward to appear impartial, he wound up appeasing the Arabs—and the Jews felt betrayed. Even then, it might have been possible for the two groups to live together in peace, had it not been for a disastrous political appointment Samuel made—a fatal appointment from which the Middle East has not recovered to this day. It was the appointment of Haj Amin al-Husseini as the grand mufti of Jerusalem, the highest Muslim office in Palestine.

One faction of Arabs, led by Abdullah of the Hashemite clan (soon to become King Abdullah and given the kingdom of Transjordan by the British) were willing to accept a portion of

Palestine rather than lose the entire area. Allied with Abdullah was the Nashashibi clan in Palestine. But their bitter enemies, the Husseini clan, were adamantly opposed to sharing the land with the Jews and opposed to British rule altogether. Nothing less than full independence and complete Arab control of Palestine would satisfy the Husseinis.

In 1919 the leader of the Husseini clan, Haj Amin al-Husseini, formed the Palestinian Society, with a military arm to carry out actions against both the British and the Jews. Haj Amin immediately began leading demonstrations and protests, demanding an end to the British Mandate and repudiation of the Balfour Declaration.

The first major riot was sparked in April 1920 when the religious holidays of Easter, Passover and Nabi Musa all fell in the same week. Thousands of Muslims convened at the Al-Aksa Mosque while Jews were worshiping at the Western Wall. It didn't take long for agitators, spurred by Haj Amin, to whip up the crowds against the Zionist intruders. The police stood by while the crowds got unruly and began to attack the Jews in three hours of bloody rioting.

When British troops finally arrived, they only jailed the instigators for a night. When they were released the next morning, the rioting resumed, and it took three more days to quell it. By then a number of Jews and Arabs were dead, and hundreds had been injured. Whole families were massacred in the Jewish quarters of Jerusalem and Hebron.

What happened afterwards was as appalling as the violence of the rioting. British authorities dismissed the Arab mayor of Jerusalem and gave stiff sentences to two of the leading Arab agitators, to be sure. But most of the rioters got off with light sentences, while Vladimir Jabotinsky and several other Jews who had organized the Jewish self-defense were all given fifteen-year jail terms.

This obvious favoritism toward the Arabs produced such an uproar in England that the government decided to set up a court in Jerusalem to inquire into the matter. During the hearings the British officers defended themselves by saying the Jews had started the whole thing. The Jews accused the British officers of encouraging Muslim unrest. At that point the chief intelligence officer in Cairo took the stand and certified, very convincingly, that the Jews were telling the truth. He was able to show that the military administration of Palestine clearly favored the Arabs to the detriment of the Jews and in violation of the Balfour Declaration.

WITH THE STROKE OF A PEN

London announced that it would dismantle the military government in Palestine and replace it with a civil administration. That is when Lloyd George appointed former cabinet member Herbert Samuel to be civil high commissioner. Samuel arrived in Jerusalem on June 30, 1920, under heavy guard.

After the April rioting, Haj Amin al-Husseini, the chief instigator, had slipped across the border into Transjordan. He was sentenced in absentia by a British military court to ten years' imprisonment. But Samuel, hoping to calm the embittered Arabs and gain Haj Amin's loyalty to the Mandate, pardoned him.

Then, a few months after his release, Haj Amin was appointed by Samuel as grand mufti of Jerusalem. Samuel had recently appointed a member of the rival Nashashibi clan as the civilian mayor of Jerusalem. By appointing Haj Amin to the supreme religious post, he hoped to balance the power between the two clans.

But Haj Amin was not a man to be balanced by anyone.

Historian Paul Johnson describes him in this way: "He had innocent blue eyes and a quiet, almost cringing manner, but he was a dedicated killer who devoted his entire adult life to race-murder. . . . The Mufti outrivalled Hitler in his hatred for Jews. But he did something even more destructive than killing Jewish settlers. He organized the systematic destruction of Arab moderates."

During the 1920s more and more Jews began to arrive in Palestine to escape growing anti-Semitism in Europe. The Arab population grew more uneasy with the increasing Jewish population. Before the end of the decade, Haj Amin would emerge as the strongest Arab leader in Palestine. And he would subject the Holy Land to another bloodbath.

The early days of Samuel's administration demonstrated his desire to strengthen the Palestinian economy, to encourage Jewish immigration, and to be utterly impartial in his administration of the government. It was the latter, his appeasement of the Arabs in his desire to be impartial, that continued to cause problems. In order not to offend the Arabs, he eventually put restrictions on Jewish immigration and imposed other measures that impeded Zionist progress. The effect, he hoped, would be to placate the Arabs; instead, it served to encourage the Arabs to want more and to compromise less.

Winston Churchill was then serving as colonial secretary in the British Cabinet. And Britain's colonies and mandates in the Middle East presented him with some of his most taxing problems. One solution Churchill reached, influenced by Samuel, was to carve out a kingdom for Abdullah, leader of the Hashemite clan, by creating the Transjordan.

With one stroke of Churchill's pen, 78 percent of the territory under the British Mandate was severed from Palestine to create an exclusively Arab state. Balfour had envisioned a boundary for Palestine well east of the Jordan to accommodate further Zionist agricultural development. And the terms of that mandate, as finally approved by the League of Nations, had included the exact words of the Balfour Declaration. But Sir Herbert traveled to London, hoping to secure a definitive interpretation of the Balfour Declaration that would dispel Arab fears once and for all. Churchill accepted Samuel's arguments and told him to draft such an interpretation for his signature.

Known as the Churchill White Paper, it said that the Jewish national home was restricted to the area west of the Jordan, that the Balfour Declaration had not meant to envision a predominately Jewish state, and that Jewish immigration should be limited to the economic capacity of the now much smaller country.

The Zionist Organization examined the draft in June 1922 and signed it with great reluctance, and only because they didn't want to lose British support altogether. The Arabs rejected it flatly, establishing a pattern that would be repeated again and again.

Sir Herbert Samuel completed his term of office as high commissioner in June 1925. Also that month dignitaries arrived in Jerusalem from around the world to mark the opening of the Hebrew University on Mount Scopus. Bull Allenby came from Cairo. Arthur Balfour came from London and was moved to tears by the evidence of progress he found all around.

In the eight years since the Balfour Declaration, the Jewish population had doubled from 55,000 to 103,000. From 1924 to 1928, Jerusalem's Jewish population would again double. Zionism had finally caught the imagination of the Jewish people, and as oppression increased in Europe, thousands of Jews fled to Palestine and the sanctuary of a Jewish national homeland during the decade of the 1920s. In a few years, the doors would close completely, and one man who foresaw that was Vladimir Jabotinsky.

Frustrated with the mainstream Zionists' accommodation to the continual hammering away of the Balfour Declaration, Jabotinsky created the World Union of Zionist Revisionists. Jabotinsky, who had been sentenced to fifteen years of hard labor for organizing a Jewish defense to the Arab riots of 1920, was released after a public outcry. It was widely considered outrageous that self-defense had earned Jabotinsky a stiffer sentence than the instigators of the riots—stiffer even than Haj Amin who was sentenced to ten years and then released a few weeks later and rewarded with the position of grand mufti.

It was Jabotinsky, a Russian Jew who had organized a self-defense movement against czarist pogroms in his native land, who came up with the idea of a Jewish Legion to fight alongside the Allies in World War I. The British grudgingly allowed him to organize a Jewish transport corps, called the Zion Mule Corps. The corps participated in the 1915 action at Gallipolli.

In 1917 he convinced the British to allow him to form three battalions to fight Turkish troops in Palestine. Enlisting as a private, Jabotinsky was promoted to lieutenant under General Bull Allenby. After the war, Jabotinsky wanted the Jewish Legion to remain armed, in order to protect the Jewish community in Palestine. But the British would not allow it, and disbanded the Legion.

For several years Jabotinsky traveled to the United States and across Europe promoting the Zionist cause. He returned to Palestine in 1928 to edit a daily Hebrew newspaper. While there, amid the growing Arab-Jewish tension fueled by British appeasement of Arab demands, Jabotinsky again tried to organize an underground Jewish military force. His self-defense effort was discovered by the British, and in 1929 they expelled him from the country. He never saw Palestine again. Had Jabotinsky been successful in organizing the Jewish resistance, it might have prevented the bloodbath unleashed by Arab radicals the year he was exiled.

ORCHESTRATED VIOLENCE

Haj Amin had been working quietly and steadily for several years to build his power base. His most significant achievement in that vein was his rise to the presidency of the Supreme Muslim Council. With that post went unrestricted control of all Muslim religious funds in Palestine.

He also controlled the schools, courts, mosques, and cemeteries, so that no teacher or official could be appointed who had not demonstrated his undying loyalty to Haj Amin. And the mufti, who distrusted intellectuals, made sure his most loyal following was among the illiterate residents of the villages and farms of Palestine. Finally, Haj Amin was ready to make his move. And he found a pretext for violence at the Western Wall.

After the riots of 1920, the Muslims had declared that the Western Wall was not sacred to the Jews, but was strictly a Muslim shrine. Although a long tradition had granted the Jewish community access to and the right of prayer at the southern end of the Western Wall, roughly adjacent to the Al-Aksa Mosque, the Arabs began to intimidate Jewish worshipers.

They drove sheep through the narrow alley where the Jews prayed at the wall, dumped garbage and human excrement there, and beat drums to disrupt the prayers. They protested when the Jews wanted to sound the shofar, or ram's horn, to announce Rosh Hashanah, the Jewish New Year. One day the British administrators would side with the Jews, and the next day with the Muslims.

As Yom Kippur approached in 1928, the Jewish sexton, who

kept the area of pavement in front of the wall, set up a portable screen running perpendicular to the wall in order to separate the women from the men during this holy day, when unusually large crowds would be in attendance. It was a minor change in the status quo, but in Jerusalem any change in the status quo can quickly achieve major significance.

With the mufti's careful orchestration, a series of protests and counter protests built over the ensuing year. The mufti steadily fed the fears of his followers that the Jews were trying to take over their property—their sacred property. The British tried vainly to keep everybody happy.

Finally, on August 23, 1929, Haj Amin struck a deadly blow during the weekly Muslim prayer service. It was also the Day of Atonement, the most holy day in the year for Jews. At noon Haj Amin mounted his pulpit in the Dome of the Rock to preach a commonplace sermon to the faithful gathered there. Actually his audience had been carefully chosen by Haj Amin's deputies to carry out their mission after the service. They were armed and ready to go.

Later in the afternoon, the Jews began to congregate at the Western Wall to begin observance of the Sabbath that would commence at sundown. Haj Amin went to his little garden just above the Western Wall on the Haram esh-Sharif. From there he could watch the Jews writhe and scream in the early twilight under the pounding fists and clubs of Allah's servants.

That night the rioting spread into the Jewish Quarter and from there it spread out across nearly every part of Palestine. The Arab policemen were of no use, and a contingent of the Royal Air Force stationed in Amman could not restore order. By the time troops arrived from Cairo and managed to bring things under control five days later, 133 Jews had died, 399 were injured. The Arabs' casualties were somewhat lighter: 87 dead, 91 injured.

A turning point had been passed in Arab-Jewish relations; it was now evident there would be no peaceful coexistence. Haj Amin emerged as the undisputed leader of the Palestinian Arabs. There were no longer any Arab moderates; the grand mufti had silenced them.

Another event occurred in 1929—one that went unnoticed on the world scene, but one that would have great repercussions for the future nation of Israel. In the midst of all the rioting that summer, a child was born to the Husseini clan. A distant relative, and future protégé, of the grand mufti, the child was named Mohammed Abder Rauf Arafat al-Kudwa al-Husseini. Nicknamed Yasser ("easy-going"), the child would be raised in a hotbed of Arab nationalism and virulent anti-Jewish sentiment. And he would one day inherit the mantle of terrorism from his kinsman and mentor, Haj Amin.

A CHANGE OF DIRECTION

Although Churchill had been responsible for removing 78 percent of the mandated territory to create the nation of Transjordan, and thereby cutting it off from Jewish settlement, he was still very much pro-Zionist. But a new Labour government had come to power in Britain, and no one among the new leaders felt so warmly about the idea of a Jewish homeland. During the last half of the 1930s, the Labour administration effectively overturned the Balfour Declaration and its provisions.

By 1936, Britain was increasingly preoccupied with Hitler. And Nazi propaganda in the Middle East was playing heavily on the anti-Zionist fears of the Arabs. The British had been able to enlist the Arabs on their side in the First World War; now Germany was trying to marshal the Arabs of Palestine to their side.

England's response was to become increasingly friendly

toward the Arabs in an attempt to win their favor. One of the chief ways they did this was to impose restrictions on Jewish immigration. As usual, though, the British appeasement only served to spur the Arabs to more aggression. As chairman of the newly-formed Arab Higher Committee, Haj Amin called a general strike that lasted for six months. The strike was accompanied by an armed uprising among the Arabs that was aided and abetted by Iraqis, Syrians, and other Arab groups. But in the mufti's distorted arrangement of priorities this Arab Revolt, as it became known, turned upon itself.

While the Jews and the British suffered losses, the real bloodletting was among the Arabs themselves. Haj Amin used the Arab Revolt as his opportunity to destroy his enemies, particularly the rival Nashashibi clan. But it didn't stop with that. Haj Amin's fears of landowners, schoolteachers, clerks and virtually anyone who was literate, especially in English, rose hysterically to the surface. Men were gunned down in the marketplace and in their beds. The mufti's henchmen became so adept at these executions that they began to be hired out for the use of others.

More than two thousand Arabs died in the melee. Haj Amin's grip on the Arab community was firmer than steel. But it was a grip that choked the life out of that community. Those who might have led the Arabs into vital and dynamic growth were either killed or cowed into silence. This was not the case in the Jewish community, where a generation of leaders and thinkers was being carefully nurtured and groomed.

In the midst of the slaughter Haj Amin's own decorous and refined behavior was a strange anomaly. But he lived in no dreamland. Never did he venture out in the streets without a bulletproof vest and the company of his six Sudanese bodyguards. His automobile was armor-plated, and he never arrived at an appointment on time—he would be careful to arrive either late or early.

During 1937, Nazi broadcasts into the Middle East increased greatly. Zionism was portrayed as the handmaiden of French and British imperialism. Arab unrest kept increasing. In July the Peel Commission issued its report after five months of preparation. It bespoke, more than anything, British despair of finding a solution to the Arab-Jewish conflict. Britain had made commitments to both groups that, it was now beginning to realize, were irreconcilable.

Therefore, since the British were unwilling to turn over four hundred thousand Jews to Arab domination, or conversely to put nearly a million Arabs under Jewish rule, the only solution was partition—to divide the territory into two separate states: one Arab (which would be joined to Transjordan), and one Jewish. Jerusalem, the Royal Commission said, should be set aside with Bethlehem in a British enclave with access to the coast; they intended to hang on to that foothold in the Middle East, as they had held on to Hong Kong in Asia.

The League of Nations rejected the idea of partition. King Abdullah of Transjordan and his friends the Nashashibis of Palestine probably favored it, but dared not say so. The Jews were willing to accept partition as the least undesirable alternative, but the point was moot. Officially, the status quo would continue: the mufti and his followers contemptuously rejected the partition plan. And that assured the rejection of the plan by the Arab Higher Committee. It also assured continued violence.

Following the Peel Commission report, Haj Amin dropped in to see the German consul-general in Jerusalem. He wanted to tell this Nazi official how much he admired the Third Reich, and how much he would appreciate a little help from them in his struggle against the British and the Jews. From there the negotiations progressed until the head of German intelligence delivered quantities of weapons from German manufacturers to the mufti by way of Iraq and Saudi Arabia.

AGGRESSION AND GENOCIDE

In the wake of the political assassination of some British officials in Galilee by Arab gunmen, the British deposed the mufti and abolished the Supreme Muslim Council and the Arab Higher Committee. Orders were given to arrest Haj Amin, but once again he had escaped, slipping past British police disguised as a beggar.

Exiled from Palestine, Haj Amin sought refuge in the neighboring Arab countries. But as the war in Europe heated up, he moved to Italy, where he made friends with Benito Mussolini. Eventually, in 1941, he was the honored guest of Adolph Hitler in Berlin. Haj Amin was convinced that the Nazis held the key to the two great goals of his life: to destroy the Jews, and to drive the British out of the Middle East.

In 1942 Haj Amin succeeded in getting both Hitler and Mussolini to agree in a secret document to "the abolition of the Jewish National Homeland in Palestine." He then moved to Germany, where he helped the Axis war effort in every way he could. In radio programs broadcast into the Middle East, Haj Amin called for a holy war against the British. He recruited Arabs to perform sabotage behind British lines. He helped raise two divisions of Balkan Muslims for the S.S. And the mufti's agents provided useful intelligence for the Axis powers.

But his greatest zeal was spent in destroying Jews. When the "Final Solution" was invoked, the mufti was one of its most enthusiastic supporters. He worked assiduously to ensure that none of the Jews intended for the gas chambers and ovens were mistakenly diverted to Palestine or other places of refuge. He personally lodged a complaint with Ribbentrop, the Nazi foreign minister, when he got word that almost seven thousand Jewish children and eight hundred Jewish adults were going to be exchanged for German, Romanian, and Hungarian citizens living in Palestine. Thanks to Haj Amin, none of these Jews ever left Europe.

After the war, the mufti narrowly escaped arraignment for war crimes before the Nuremberg tribunals. With help from the French, who were feeling vindictive toward the British because of their eviction from Syria and Lebanon, he fled to Egypt. From Cairo he resumed leadership of the Arab cause in Palestine. And it was Haj Amin who would once again determine the Arab response to the momentous events of 1947 and 1948.

Back in Palestine, it had taken substantially reinforced British troops until the summer of 1938 to break the hold of Arab rebels on Jerusalem. But the Arab revolt was not completely quelled until 1939, when the British finally ditched the Peel Commission's partition plan in an effort to stop the fighting. While the Jewish community was trying to persuade the British to allow increased Jewish immigration, the Arabs were threatening to cut off access to Middle Eastern oil supplies if immigration were increased. The British responded with another White Paper, which effectively overturned the Balfour Declaration.

The 1939 White Paper specified three guidelines for Palestine: (1) Jewish immigration would be slowed, then halted; (2) Jews would only be allowed to buy land in areas where they were already the majority population; (3) Britain would support an independent Palestinian state, controlled by the Arabs, after the war. Winston Churchill called it "a gross breach of faith."

A turning point was reached on November 9, 1938, a night which lives in the bitter memory of millions of Jews as *Kristallnacht*, so named because of the sound of shattered glass as Jewish shops in Germany were destroyed by Hitler's storm troopers. More than 260 synagogues were burned that night and 20,000 Jews were arrested. The Jewish community was then fined $400 million for damages inflicted by the soldiers to their property. From that moment on Adolf Hitler began to speak openly of annihilating the Jews. It was unconscionable for Britain to halt immigration to Palestine just at the moment Hitler began his campaign of destruction against the Jewish people. But the White Paper of 1939 condemned millions of European Jews to the concentration camps.

Britain was not alone in her guilt, however. As reports of Hitler's "Final Solution" were confirmed, other countries, including America, followed suit. Fear won out over compassion as first one country and then another halted Jewish immigration. From that time on we read agonizing tales of shiploads of Jewish refugees from Europe perishing in the waters of the Mediterranean because their unseaworthy ships could find no harbor to receive them.

Of Europe's eight million Jews, only one and a half million survived the war. Some six million of them became Hitler's burnt offering on the altar of Aryan supremacy. The genocidal slaughter became known as the Holocaust, a term derived from the Greek *holokaustos*, literally "burnt whole," referring to a sacrifice consumed by fire.

ARCHITECTS OF A NEW ISRAEL

In October 1943, three men in London sat down over lunch to discuss the latest proposal for partitioning Palestine between the Arabs and the Jews. Called the Morrison Plan, it established Jerusalem as a separate territory under a British high commissioner. The three men were Winston Churchill, who had been elected prime minister in 1940; Chaim Weizmann, head of the

World Zionist Executive; and Clement Attlee, the leader of the Labour opposition in Britain's parliament.

The Morrison Plan would have to be kept secret until after the war, Churchill explained, but he wanted both of these men to know that Israel had a friend in him. "When we have crushed Hitler," he said," we shall have to establish the Jews in the position where they belong. I have an inheritance left to me by Balfour and I am not going to change. But there are dark forces working against us."

The prime minister probably did not know just how dark or how powerful those forces truly were. No matter how firm his own commitment to Zionism, he was steadfastly resisted by the British Foreign Office and the authorities in Jerusalem who had charge of the mandate. And in 1945 Churchill was forced out of office by a new Labourite government led by Clement Attlee. At war's end, Palestine remained closed to the hapless survivors of the concentration camps, most of whom were now homeless. More than a million Jews were homeless, but their national homeland was closed to all but a few thousand immigrants per year.

Ernest Bevin, foreign minister in the Attlee administration, continued to limit immigration to Palestine, in spite of postwar appeals. U.S. President Harry Truman was moved by the plight of Jewish refugees and urged Britain to open Palestine and increase immigration. Bevin's reply was that "the Jews have waited two thousand years; they can wait a little longer."

Yet thousands of them refused to wait a minute longer. They stuffed themselves in the holds of patched-together ships, only to be turned back at the harbor. They marched hundreds of miles on foot, over snow-covered mountains and through parched deserts, only to be arrested at the border and sent to detention camps.

Most of them were returned to the very concentration camps in Europe from which they had been freed. The gas chambers were no longer in use, of course, but the camps had become refugee centers for the former prisoners.

The Haganah, authorized by Churchill as an independent Jewish brigade within the British Army, became the leading Jewish defense force after the war. Before long, however, the Haganah had moved from self-defense to open hostility. In 1946 the Haganah attacked British military installations and attempted to destroy their communications systems.

Then on July 22, 1946, the Irgun, a radical resistance group, blew up the King David Hotel in Jerusalem, the city's leading hotel, where the British government kept an office. Ninety-one people were killed, including forty-one Arabs and twenty-eight British. In retaliation the British not only arrested the Irgun leaders, they made possessing a weapon a capital offense.

By the beginning of 1947 the British had decided they wanted nothing more than to wash their hands of the whole mandate affair. In February, Bevin tossed the hot potato of Palestine into the lap of the United Nations and announced the British would be leaving soon, so the UN needed to come up with a plan.

It was Andrei Gromyko, the Soviet ambassador, who called for partition along the lines of what Lord Peel and his commission had recommended ten years before. Chaim Weizmann appealed to the UN to support partition, saying: "We realize that we cannot have the whole of Palestine. God may have promised Palestine to the Jews; it is up to the Almighty to keep his promise in his own time. Our business is to do what we can in a very imperfect human way."

So in May 1947 the UN created a committee to study the Palestine question. The Arab countries refused to participate in the committee's deliberations, which was a tactical mistake.

Abba Eban, the Jewish liaison for the UN committee, persuaded the committee members to travel to Palestine.

While there they witnessed British soldiers arresting four thousand illegal Jewish immigrants whose ship had just arrived in harbor. These Holocaust survivors were hauled off their ship, placed in wire holding cages, and then bodily dragged to other ships destined for the refugee camps in Germany. The committee members were visibly shaken by the emotional scene of four thousand Jews—a few strong enough or desperate enough to attempt to resist, some so emaciated and weak they had to be literally carried by the soldiers, most of them simply distraught to the point of screaming and wailing—being manhandled and denied their only hope for a safe haven.

The committee released a report in favor of partition. Jerusalem, instead of becoming a British colony as the Peel Commission had proposed, would be withheld from both the Arabs and the Jews and established as an international zone administered by the UN. The Jews were blackmailed into accepting the idea of Jerusalem's internationalization by the Vatican. At its urging the Catholic nations of Latin America made it plain to the Jews that they would cast their votes at the UN in favor of partition only if the Jews let the city go.

It was an incredible price to pay—after all, the name of their movement, "Zionism," was linked to this city—but what could they do? They agreed and hoped that God would overrule. On November 29, 1947, the Latin Americans delivered their vote in the General Assembly and the necessary two-thirds majority in favor of partition was achieved. The Arab response was swift and violent. The next day Haj Amin's followers took to the streets of Jerusalem. The fight was on.

Part III:
Prophecy Unfolding

Nine

Reclaiming the Land

O N the eve of the United Nations partition vote, Israeli leader David Ben-Gurion sent Golda Meir to meet with King Abdullah of the Transjordan. They would rendezvous at night at an out-of-the-way little spot near where the Jordan flows out of the Sea of Galilee.

Golda was, in many ways, an American. She had been born in 1898 in Kiev, the ancient capital of the Ukraine. At the age of eight she had emigrated to America with her family and settled in Milwaukee, Wisconsin. She grew up there and worked for a time as a school teacher. But by the age of seventeen she had discovered her Zionist faith, the cause to which she would dedicate the rest of her life.

The electricity that served the king's palace and the rest of the city of Amman came from a hydroelectric station built and run by the Jews along a stretch of the east bank of the Jordan that lay just inside Galilee. It was here, at the home of the plant's director, that Golda Meir and King Abdullah held their secret meeting.

Though it was their first meeting, they greeted each other as friends with a common enemy: the mufti Haj Amin. In the event of partition, Abdullah confided, he would prefer simply to annex the Arab sector to his kingdom. Mrs. Meyerson (Golda's name at the time) thought that sounded much better than a separate state led by Haj Amin. She pledged that the Jews would leave the Arab sector to its own devices and devote themselves entirely to the establishment of their own sovereignty within the borders assigned to them by the UN.

Abdullah was not an anti-Semite. Instead he recognized the Zionists as fellow Semites returned to their homeland after long exile. Their presence in Palestine had already profited him and his people immensely. And he knew better than to think he could put a stop to the establishment of a Jewish state. The mufti was a fool who thought of the Jews in terms of the pale rabbinical students so easily cowed by his ruffians' clubs.

The Syrians and Iraqis were perhaps deceived by the relatively docile and subservient Jewish communities of Damascus and Baghdad. But Abdullah knew the Zionists for what they were: a vigorous and capable people who could put up a stiff fight.

Despite his desire for peace with his Jewish neighbors, however, Abdullah would be pressured intolerably by the other Arab states in the coming months. He met a final time with Golda Meir just before Israel declared its statehood. He offered the Jews autonomy within his kingdom and full representation in parliament, but was not surprised when the Zionists turned him down. Reluctantly, Abdullah entered the war against Israel when the nation eventually declared its independence.

In the months between November 29, 1947, when the UN General Assembly voted for partition, and May 14, 1948, when the last British troops left Palestine, Jerusalem was the scene of almost interminable conflict. It was Haj Amin's season of opportunity to seize final control and turn Palestine into an Arab state with himself at its helm.

To lead this crusade, he selected one of his kinsmen, Abdul Khader. Khader was a uniquely charismatic leader who aroused the admiration and zeal of his fellow Arabs as few others could. A member of the Husseini clan, his father had been mayor of Jerusalem—the same one who was deposed and exiled by the British in 1921 in the wake of the bloody Nebi Musa riots.

Abdul Khader had been a small child when that had happened, so he grew up fighting the British. He was wounded twice in the Arab revolts in 1936–39. Under Haj Amin's sponsorship, he had received considerably more education than most of the mufti's lieutenants, including training with explosives in Germany during World War II. Khader became the military leader of the Arab Higher Committee. Around his kitchen table in Cairo, young Arab nationalists were taught how to make bombs. A seventeen-year-old relative from the Husseini clan, Yasser Arafat, was assigned to buy up weapons that had been left behind in Egypt when the war ended.

In December 1947, Khader slipped back into Palestine and began to organize the holy war against the Jews that his cousin had called for. The centerpiece of his strategy was Jerusalem. His goal was to strangle the city. Before Abdul Khader's arrival the mufti had already launched his crusade by calling for a three-day strike in the immediate wake of the partition vote. The Arabs had opposed partition because it acknowledged the right of the Jews to exist unmolested in the Middle East. Haj Amin denied that right with all his being.

Thereafter, relations between the Jews and Arabs in the Holy City grew more strained and distant. Fellow workers—Jews and Arabs—who had co-existed peacefully for years in close quarters were now compelled to search each other for weapons at the start of each day.

JERUSALEM BETRAYED

A SEASON OF DEFEAT

During that cold December, neither Christmas nor Hanukkah was celebrated with their usual gusto. The UN had called for internationalization of the city, but its citizens were aware that no one—not Britain nor the U.S. nor France nor any of the smaller nations—was willing to give the UN policy a strong arm with its own troops. And that was probably the Arabs' greatest victory that winter—the admission from UN headquarters in New York that its Palestine resolution could not be implemented without armed force. Only the Jews and Arabs were willing to spill their blood for this city, and the world stood by and watched.

Abdul Khader's first thrust was a desultory raid against a house in which a detachment of Haganah men were stationed. The Haganah, with its roots in the early informal Jewish efforts at self-defense in the days prior to World War I, was the nucleus that would become the Israel Defense Force in the new state. Many Haganah members had gained some formal military training in the Jewish Legions that were part of the British army in both wars.

Abdul Khader brought in a truckload of 120 men from Hebron, an Arab center about thirty miles south of Jerusalem in the Judean hills. The brief skirmish was broken up by a British armored car; there were no casualties.

Meanwhile the Jews were doing everything they could to strengthen their hold on their most vulnerable and isolated population center: the Jewish quarter of the Old City—the part surrounded by walls. Living inside the Jewish quarter were people who were not representative of the rest of the Yishuv. Rabbis, sages, and students, most of them were pale and stooped from long years of studying the Torah—not the sturdy sort who would be potential recruits for the Haganah. So the task of the Haganah was to smuggle fighting men into the quarter past the watchful eyes of both the British and the Arabs.

Another thing the Haganah lacked almost as much as men to defend the Jewish quarter was arms. The Arabs had access to arms by way of shipping routes from all around the Middle East. But military hardware could only reach the Jews through the Mediterranean ports where British agents maintained a close watch. Smuggling was developed to a fine art. Rifles, mortars, machine guns—all sorts of materiel—arrived disassembled and disguised. Then the stuff had to be left disassembled and carefully hidden in secure storage areas pending the departure of the British. Meanwhile, Golda Meir made a memorable trip to the United States to raise money to pay for all the weapons and war materiel, entirely from private funds.

The man David Ben-Gurion appointed to defend Jerusalem was David Shaltiel. He was a bit of a maverick by Haganah standards. He'd gained his military training in the French Foreign Legion, fighting Arabs in Morocco. Later he settled in France and only became involved in Zionism in the late thirties with the rise of Nazi anti-Semitism. He was captured by the Gestapo, underwent torture, and ended up in Dachau. It was in the concentration camp, ironically, that his leadership abilities began to shine.

Released from the camp, he managed to return to Palestine before the outbreak of World War II. And there he continued as a Haganah counterintelligence operative. As he rose through the ranks of the Haganah, his background in the French military establishment came clearly to the surface. He was a spit-and-polish disciplinarian, a man who would put starch into the Jewish defense of Jerusalem.

And starch it would need. Shortly after he arrived, Shaltiel got a taste of the way things would be in Jerusalem. A British sergeant-major arrested four Haganah men who had been exchanging fire with the Arabs. He simply took the four men into the Arab sector and turned them over to the mob. One they shot to death. The other three were stripped, beaten, emasculated, and hacked to death.

But Abdul Khader was after bigger game. His chief demolition expert was Fawzi el Kutub, a graduate of an SS terrorism course in Nazi Germany. Kutub blew up the offices of *The Palestine Post*, a Jewish newspaper, on February 1, 1948. Before the end of that month, with the help of two British deserters, he managed to plant an enormous explosive device on Ben Yehuda Street in the heart of Jewish Jerusalem.

Fifty-seven people—almost all of them civilians—died; eighty-eight were injured. Kutub's greatest accomplishment, from his point of view, came on March 11, when a U.S. consulate car carried one of his bombs into the headquarters of the Jewish Agency—the most closely guarded Jewish building in the city—killing thirteen people.

STARVATION AND DEFIANCE

But the most severe threat to Jewish Jerusalem was that of starvation. Abdul Khader's militia held the strategic points along the main highway that leads from the coastal plain up into the Judean hills in which Jerusalem sits. And Khader's stranglehold was working. Virtually every convoy bringing supplies from the coast (and the British would not permit the transport of any sort of war materiel in these convoys) was ambushed and sustained losses before reaching the city—if they reached it at all. By the end of March nothing was getting through. The Jewish city had only a few days' supplies left.

On March 20, 1948, Ben-Gurion summoned his Haganah

commanders to a meeting to determine how to reopen the road to Jerusalem. Yigael Yadin, an archaeologist in civilian life, but now chief of operations for the entire Haganah, put it plainly: The Yishuv, both in Jerusalem and in Galilee, was being strangled. Convoys and mere defensive measures were no longer getting the job done. Bolder measures were required.

The Zionist leaders debated the question for three hours. They would have gone longer if Ben-Gurion had not pugnaciously said, "Enough!" It was time to take action in spite of the enormous risks involved.

The first requirement was for weapons in sufficient quantity to launch a sizable operation. Ben-Gurion had already cabled his agent in Prague, and a Dakota transport arrived at a deserted British airstrip less than twenty miles south of Tel Aviv during the night of April 1. Two days later the main shipment arrived via freighter off a coastal inlet unpatrolled by British guards. Hundreds of machine guns and thousands of rifles were ferried ashore.

From there, they went by truck directly to the untested troops that would use them. The men had to use their own underwear to get packing grease off their new weapons, but by April 5, three battalions of five hundred men each started clearing the way for a convoy of 250 trucks to relieve Jerusalem.

During the fighting, Abdul Khader was killed. Caught in the face of a more intense Jewish assault than he had ever experienced, he had called on Fawzi al-Kaukji, an Iraqi leader on his northern flank, to send help—weapons for the peasants who would join him if he could arm them. But Kaukji was Abdul Khader's rival. Haganah agents were monitoring the conversation and report that Kaukji's reply was: *"Ma'fish—*I have not any!" It was a lie. Abdul Khader was betrayed and died in the fighting soon after the conversation.

When his people found his body the next day, mourning and wailing broke out in their ranks. Khader's leadership of the Arab peasants had been decisive and, with his death, Haj Amin's cause was lost. Never again would the Palestinian Arabs offer so serious a threat to the Haganah.

But as the Arabs mourned Abdul Khader and buried him, the Jews of the New City shed tears of rejoicing for the arrival of truck after truck loaded with supplies. The siege had been broken—for the moment at least. Before long, even without Abdul Khader's leadership, the Arabs would manage to resume their ambushes of the convoys. Supplies in the city would begin to dwindle again.

Added to that, the city would be shelled increasingly. As the British withdrawal progressed, they often turned over their arms and other materiel to the Arabs. In this way the Palestinian Arabs came into possession of more and more artillery with which, naturally, they began to fire on the Jewish sectors of Jerusalem.

The British Mandate was set to end at 6:00 P.M. New York time on May 14, 1948. The British were more than happy to be leaving. Sir Alan Cunningham, the last British high commissioner for Palestine, left his official residence in Jerusalem and was driven to Haifa, where he boarded a British cruiser.

By midday Egyptian forces had massed in the Negev, Jordanian and Iraqi troops were stationed all along the river, and Syrian forces were marching toward Palestine from the north. In Tel Aviv the founding fathers of the nation of Israel, led by David Ben-Gurion, were meeting to debate whether to declare their independence; the vote was six to four in favor of declaration.

At the United Nations, the mood was especially tense. The Arab states, who had rejected partition, were trying to force a vote on a last-minute resolution to prevent the creation of a Jewish state. Israel's only hope was for the United States to recognize the new nation. As the clock ticked past the six o'clock deadline, no action had been taken.

Finally, eleven minutes after the British Mandate officially expired, the U.S. ambassador went to the podium to address the UN. He announced that the U.S. had just learned that the State of Israel had been declared and its provisional government had requested recognition. Therefore, he said, the United States government officially recognized the new state. There was little time for celebration in Israel. At midnight Jordanian troops crossed the Allenby Bridge and headed for Jerusalem. At 5:00 the next morning, May 15, 1948, Tel Aviv was bombed by Egyptian aircraft. The War of Independence was on.

Few people gave the new nation of Israel much hope for survival. Forty-five million Arabs were intent on pushing four hundred thousand Jews, bunkered on a tiny strip of earth (one-sixth of 1 percent of the 7.5 million miles of Arab lands), into the sea. That Israel did survive, against such impossible odds, truly is a miracle.

THE DIVINE WITNESS

The Arab arrogance in rejecting partition was somewhat understandable. Vastly outnumbering the Jews, and far better equipped and armed, the Arabs thought it would hardly be a fair contest. They expected to drive the Jews into the sea and occupy all of Palestine in a matter of days.

Actually, the Arabs did not have the right perspective on the battle at all. It was never really a contest between the Arab world of forty-five million people and four hundred thousand Jews struggling to become a nation. Those forty-five million Arabs were going up against four hundred thousand Jews defended by the innumerable hosts of heaven. So the Arabs were right that it was hardly a fair contest. They were just grossly mistaken as to who the winner would be.

When you look at the history of the founding of the State of Israel, you have to marvel at the hand of God in human events. Modern historians find it remarkable that Israel was created in a tiny window of opportunity. It happened at precisely the right moment—a moment so precise that it had to be more than coincidence.

For example, had Israel declared independence when Franklin D. Roosevelt was president, it is unlikely the United States would have recognized Israel. And without that recognition, there would have been no world support for the Jewish state and it would have been doomed. Roosevelt was anti-Zionist and would probably have opposed the creation of an independent Israel.

Also, Roosevelt's successor, Harry Truman, would have been unlikely to go out on a limb to recognize Israel had it not been for the intercession of his old business partner—the two had endured bankruptcy together in Kansas City years before—a Jew named Eddie Jacobson, who tearfully urged him to meet with Zionist leader Chaim Weizmann.

Truman agreed to meet Weizmann at the White House, making sure he entered by a side door, unnoticed by the press. He later referred to Weizmann as "a wonderful man, one of the wisest people I've ever met." The meeting was cordial and Truman promised his support for the Jewish state.

But just as Churchill had battled the pro-Arab bent of his foreign office, Truman contended with what he called the "striped-pants boys," the pro-Arab officials in his own State Department. Truman's recognition of Israel was bitterly opposed by the State Department and the influential American oil interests such as the Arabian American Oil Company

(ARAMCO). The Arab nations were threatening all the western governments that if they wanted Arab oil, they had better not try to help the Jews.

Or, as another example, had Israel's move for independence come just a year or so later, the Cold War would have been underway and Truman, although a Zionist, might not have had the courage to buck the powerful forces allied against Israel. Consider the Soviet Union, which followed America's lead in recognizing the State of Israel. The Soviets, who had been the first to recommend partition the year before, had been pro-Zionist only as a way to get Britain out of the Middle East and extend their own influence.

By the early 1950s the Soviets were courting Arab interests in the Middle East and had withdrawn their support for Israel. So Israel's declaration of independence on May 14, 1948, came at precisely the right moment—not a moment too soon or too late. As historian Paul Johnson notes, "Israel slipped into existence through a crack in the time continuum."

Had more people been reading the writings of a prophet named Ezekiel, they would not have been so surprised by the birthpangs of the nation of Israel or the regathering of Jews from all over the world to Palestine. The creation of modern Israel made possible the fulfillment of a prophecy made some twenty-five centuries before the fact: Ezekiel's foretelling of the scattering and regathering of the exiles of Israel. His vision of the valley of dry bones is one of the most vivid and moving passages in all of the Bible. (See Ezekiel 37:1–10).

Ezekiel relates how he was taken to a vast open cemetery, a great valley full of bones. After long exposure to the sun and wind, the skeletons had become dry, bleached, and disconnected. As he viewed this grisly sight, the Lord asked him if the bones could live. He simply replied, "O Sovereign Lord, you alone know."

He was then given the responsibility of prophesying over the bones, promising them that they would receive flesh, breath, and life. As he obeyed the Lord, there was a great shaking and a loud noise as the bones came together, were covered with flesh, and received the breath of life, then stood to their feet and became a great army.

The prophet said the Lord showed him that the bones represented the whole house of Israel. Their dry and disconnected condition represented the dispersion of the Jews around the globe, and their hopeless despair at ever becoming a nation united again. The Lord instructed Ezekiel to say to them, "I will bring you back to the land of Israel . . . and I will settle you in your own land" (37:12, 14).

So Ezekiel proclaimed the message God had given him, and his words helped keep a glimmer of hope alive in the hearts of the Jewish people across the centuries from their "boneyards" in every nation of the world. In the midst of incredible persecution and suffering, the promise of God offered something to hold on to: "For I will take you out of the nations; I will gather you from all the countries and bring you back into your own land" (Ezek. 36:24). Those words of the Lord from Ezekiel's prophecy were like a bright light cutting through the gloom and darkness of the Jewish ghettos and death camps.

The establishment of the new nation of Israel in 1948, and the subsequent emigration of Jews from more than one hundred nations to populate the Jewish state, brought obvious and undeniable fulfillment of this part of Ezekiel's prophecy.

THE VOICE OF PROPHECY

I once talked about the importance of the prophecies with Benjamin Netanyahu, years before he became the prime minister of Israel. "The truth of the matter is, Mike, that if it had not been for the prophetic promises about returning to our homeland, the Jewish people would not have survived," he said.

"There is something about reading the statements of the prophets in the original Hebrew language—the powerful impact of those words bores deep into your heart and is implanted into your mind. There is absolutely no question but that those ancient prophetic promises kept hope alive in the hearts of Jewish people and sustained us over the generations when we had nothing else to cling to."

From the beginning of their independence—while they were still at war—Israel threw open her doors to Jewish refugees. Within the first four months after independence, some fifty thousand Jews fled to Israel; most of them were Holocaust survivors. Within the first three years the total number of immigrants climbed to almost seven hundred thousand, doubling Israel's population.

In 1950 the Knesset unanimously passed the Law of Return, stating that all Jews everywhere had the right to make Israel their home. Over two and one-half million, coming from the four corners of the earth, have done just that, settling in a land they have never seen but have always longed for. "Next year in Jerusalem" has become a reality for them.

The nation of Israel has gone to great expense to help them get there, putting together mass airlifts of thousands of Jews at a time, sometimes taking them out of hostile countries during war situations. The logistics of the airlifts are staggering, but the Israelis quickly became masters of the process.

The first major airlift, in 1950, was dubbed Operation Magic Carpet. The entire Jewish population of the Arab country of Yemen was airlifted to Israel. Then over fifty thousand Jews were airlifted out of Baghdad, under a tight deadline given by the Iraqi government before making immigration to Israel a capital offense.

Two mass airlifts have brought the Jews of Ethiopia, believed to have existed there since the time of Solomon, to a new home. In 1984 Operation Moses brought fifteen thousand Ethiopian Jews to Israel. When the country broke into civil war, thousands of more Jews were stranded. Months of difficult negotiations were concluded in 1991, with the assistance of the U.S., resulting in permission to rescue the remaining Jewish population. And in less than thirty-six hours the Israeli Air Force completed Operation Solomon, airlifting some fourteen thousand Jews from Addis Ababa to Tel Aviv—all of them shuttled to Israel before word leaked out to the press.

The largest group of immigrants—and one that is prophetically significant—comes from the former Soviet Union. Some one hundred thousand Jews were allowed to emigrate in the 1970s. Many of them had waited years for exit visas. With the collapse of Communism, however, the floodgate was opened. From 1989 to 1994, over five hundred thousand Soviet Jews arrived in Israel—for a while they were coming at the rate of ten thousand every month.

Even though Israel has a Ministry of Absorption to help the new arrivals integrate into Israeli society, it has been a tremendous economic burden on the nation. But the *raison d'être* of modern Israel is to be the home of the Jewish people—a safe haven from a future holocaust—so the doors will never be closed, in spite of the hostility of the surrounding Arab nations or the political pressure of the Western nations. The prophetic ingathering of exiles continues.

JERUSALEM AND PROPHECY

In light of all the blood that has been shed over this ancient soil, it is important to understand the biblical prophecies that either have been or will be fulfilled regarding Jerusalem. This city is the centerpiece of Bible prophecy, and it is to this place that Messiah will return. Jesus will not return to a Muslim city. Not because he is prejudiced against them, but because he promised two thousand years ago that Jerusalem would be trodden down by the Gentiles until the time of the Gentiles was over (Luke 21:24). Through the centuries this prophecy has stood as an immovable landmark by which we may gauge the often confusing events of Jewish history.

Today Jerusalem remains the capital of Israel, the very heart of the nation. Jesus' words, spoken so long ago, make the city's recapture by the Jews the single most prophetic event in history since John concluded his writing of the Revelation on the Isle of Patmos. The time of the Gentiles is now past and there has been a changing of the guard. Men may argue and pontificate, but something irrevocable has happened: Jerusalem is no longer trodden down by non-Jews. History has turned a corner—even if few have noticed it.

During the nineteenth century, Jews began to make up the majority of the population of Jerusalem. But until June 7, 1967, the walled city—the Old City with the Temple Mount—remained trodden underfoot by the Gentiles. On the last day of three days of fighting between the Jordanians and the Israelis in and around Jerusalem, a pattern of history that had held steady for 1,832 years (since the Bar Kochba Rebellion) was dramatically reversed. Jerusalem was restored and reunited, and once again under the control of an independent Jewish nation.

No one can deny that Jerusalem looms large in history. As every chapter of this book has shown, the City of David has always had a special destiny and a unique calling before God. The prophet Daniel called it God's "holy mountain." As the site of the Temple of Israel, and as the city to which Messiah will return to usher in his earthly Kingdom, Jerusalem is known throughout the earth as the City of God.

Several New Testament writers speak of Jerusalem. John provides more information about the city than any other gospel writer, detailing the visits of Jesus during his brief but dramatic ministry. But it is Luke, the Gentile, who gives the prophetic nature of the city greatest attention. Luke's opening announcement of the birth of John took place in Jerusalem. He tells how Jesus visited the city at age twelve. We learn that on the mount of transfiguration Jesus was transfigured with Moses and Elijah as they spoke of his coming death, resurrection, and ascension.

All of the resurrection appearances in the Book of Luke take place at Jerusalem, and the disciples are told by Jesus to wait there until Pentecost. At that time, he had said, the Holy Spirit would come upon them. This event would introduce a new spiritual age, a New Covenant, in which the truth of God's relationship with mankind would no longer be experienced through ritual and sacrifice but through the Word of God dwelling in the hearts of believers. After the experience of Pentecost, Jerusalem suddenly became the heart of the church, and the center of evangelism that would extend to the ends of the earth.

But Jerusalem also figures prominently in John's vision of the End Times recorded in the book of Revelation. It is here that the earthly Jerusalem appears for the last time after the thousand-year reign of Christ. It is here that the forces of the Man of Sin will be marshaled and the great last battle will take place. It is here that Satan will be finally defeated and the forces of evil will be destroyed by fire from heaven.

John describes the luminous vision of the new Jerusalem descending from heaven. A beautiful new city of gold and silver and precious stones is the home of the faithful who have sought the kingdom of God and his righteousness, who have fought the good fight, who have resisted unto death, and who have loved the Lord their God with all their heart, mind, soul, and strength. Clearly, in this sense, Jerusalem is the ultimate home and the goal of believers. It is, after all, our eternal home.

Today the nations wage a war of words against the City of God. Washington demands that the peace process continue, and a chorus of world powerbrokers sounds the Amen. From every side we hear, "Peace, peace!" But as an American Jew bitingly observed, "If this is *peace*, then what is *war*?" God's Word shows there will come a time when national leaders will seek to calm the people with claims of peace. But peace will not come. "They dress the wound of my people as though it were not serious. 'Peace, peace,' they say when there is no peace" (Jeremiah 6:14).

Ezekiel prophesied, "Because they lead my people astray, saying, 'Peace,' when there is no peace, and because, when a flimsy wall is built, they cover it with whitewash, therefore tell those who cover it with whitewash that it is going to fall. Rain will come in torrents, and I will send hailstones hurtling down, and violent winds will burst forth. When the wall collapses, will people not ask you, 'Where is the whitewash you covered it with?' Therefore this is what the Sovereign LORD says: In my wrath I will unleash a violent wind, and in my anger hailstones and torrents of rain will fall with destructive fury. I will tear down the wall you have covered with whitewash and will level it to the ground . . . So I will spend my wrath against the wall and against those who covered it with whitewash. I will say to you, 'The wall is gone and so are those who whitewashed it, those prophets of Israel who prophesied to Jerusalem and saw visions of peace for her when there was no peace, declares the Sovereign LORD.'" (Ezekiel 13:10–16).

JERUSALEM BETRAYED

THE PARABLE OF THE FIG TREE

Jesus gave an indication of how we would be able to identify the time immediately preceding his return: He told us to learn a lesson from the fig tree. "As soon as its twigs get tender and its leaves come out, you know that summer is near. Even so, when you see all these things, you know that it is near, right at the door" (Matthew 24:32–33). Then he added a startling comment: "I tell you the truth, this generation will certainly not pass away until all these things have happened" (v. 34).

How are we supposed to understand that? To answer that question, we first have to decide what he meant by the phrase "this generation." There has been a lot of disagreement on how to interpret this. Did that mean the generation of people of which Jesus himself was a part? I don't think so. We need to let the context of the verse help us interpret it, and the context talks about a fig tree. "This generation" is the generation of people who see the fig tree putting forth leaves from tender twigs.

But what is the significance of the fig tree? We must resort to symbolism at this point to help unlock the mystery, but the symbolism Christ intended here is not difficult or obscure. The fig tree stands for restored Israel. If you've ever been to Israel, you've noticed that the leaves of the fig tree are common ornaments on government buildings. I challenge you to order breakfast anywhere in Israel without its being served with some figs. In the Bible, references to the fig tree are generally symbolic of the nation of Israel. Jesus uses the fig tree to talk about the end of the age because he meant that Israel itself would be the key sign to his return.

The generation of people who see the blossoming of the fig tree (Israel's rebirth and establishment in the family of nations) is the generation that will see the completion of "all these things" (the signs of the end recorded in Matthew 24). The generation of people that saw this "blossoming" of modern Israel were born between 1925 and 1935. Their lifespan will be roughly seventy years according to the Bible and the actuarial tables. Some of them will live much longer, but I believe the Lord will have returned before their entire generation passes away.

The Bible tells us no one will know the day or the hour of Christ's return, but we are exhorted to recognize the season. The rebirth of Israel, then, is a sign that his return will occur within the lifetimes of some of us now living.

But nothing stands in the way of its happening tonight or tomorrow. If ever a generation of people had reason to believe they were living in the days immediately prior to the Lord's return, it is our generation. So where are we now in the countdown to the beginning of the last chapter in the history of mankind? What events must yet take place to trigger the ticking of God's prophetic clock?

Bible scholars say there is nothing to delay the return of Messiah for those who serve him. It could take place at any moment, and no one can say for sure when it will be. Jesus said, "No one knows about that day or hour, not even the angels in heaven, nor the Son, but only the Father" (Matthew 24:36). He also warned: "You also must be ready, because the Son of Man will come at an hour when you do not expect him" (Luke 12:40).

Ten

The Struggle for Autonomy

A FTER the UN recognized Israel's independence in 1948, Haj Amin al-Husseini, the grand mufti, declared: "The entire Jewish population in Palestine must be destroyed or driven into the sea. Allah has bestowed upon us the rare privilege of finishing what Hitler only began. Let the *jihad* begin. Murder the Jews. Murder them all!"

The Arab countries launched an all-out attempt to do just that. Within hours of the declaration of statehood, some thirty-five thousand soldiers from six Arab nations, armed with state-of-the-art British and French weapons, were arrayed against the men, women and high-school students who made up the Israeli Army—the majority of whom had never seen a day of real training, let alone battle.

Caught in the middle was King Abdullah of Transjordan. As all this was happening, he was sitting alone with a newspaperman in Amman. "The Arab countries are going to war," he explained, "and naturally we must be at their sides; but we are making a mistake for which we will pay dearly later. One day we will live to regret that we did not give the Jews a state to satisfy their demands. We have been following the wrong course, and we still are." Abdullah paused. Then, he added, "If you quote me on that, I will deny it publicly and call you a liar." In the early days of the War of Independence, the Israel Defense Force (IDF) had to put Jerusalem on hold while they gave all their attention and limited manpower to holding off the Egyptian onslaught coming up through the Negev. Soon, however, their attention would have to be divided—because the thing Abdullah wanted most was Jerusalem. It was the third holiest shrine in Islam, and since his father's loss of Mecca and Medina to the Saudis in 1925, its capture by Abdullah's legionnaires would serve as a compensation for his family as well—a vindication of the Hashemite dynasty.

Abdullah's army, the Arab Legion, led by the British officer John Bagot Glubb, was the only thoroughly professional army in the Arab Middle East at the time. Glubb, nevertheless, was reluctant to commit his Bedouin soldiers to street-fighting in Jerusalem. If he had known how poorly defended the city was at that point, he would have felt differently.

The first units of the Legion—a small detachment—arrived in the Old City on May 19. At the same time over two thousand of them invaded the heights north of the city and began to advance against the New City, the center of Jewish population, where roughly one hundred thousand people lived. And their approach struck terror. This was a real army, not an undisciplined bunch of irregulars.

In Jerusalem, David Shaltiel had roughly the same number of men under his command, but they were virtually weaponless. In fact, it was a group of teenagers armed with Molotov cocktails, a bazooka, and an armored car, who encountered the first column of the Legion. The Jordanians had made a wrong turn near the Mandelbaum Gate and were taken completely by surprise in the ambush. Before the Arabs withdrew, the teenagers managed to knock out three of their armored cars. It was a victory that gave fresh heart to the Israelis.

They would need it. What followed was ten days of savage fighting in which the Jews turned back the Arab assault on the New City. On May 28 Glubb called off the attack. His men had been seriously mauled in the fighting. Besides, the strategy of this assault was wrong. He was convinced the battle for Jerusalem would be decided on the heights of Latrun, which overlooked the supply road from Tel Aviv.

While the New City was momentarily safe from capture by the Arabs, the Jewish quarter of the Old City was not. On May 18 a second company of Haganah men had managed to fight its way into the quarter to join the lone company that had previously been defending the place. The quarter, of course, was behind the ancient Turkish walls. Here Glubb's Legion held a real advantage. Its artillery prevented any further reinforcement by the Jews and the death grip tightened.

The Old City defenders surrendered on May 28. The Arab armies looted and burned the Jewish quarter, destroying dozens of synagogues, as the residents of the Old City fled outside the walls. It was an enormous symbolic loss not only to the other inhabitants of Israel but also to the entire Jewish community throughout the world.

SUPPLY LINES TO JERUSALEM

But David Shaltiel only knew he had done what he could, and that the population of the New City was his primary responsibility. By early June the Jewish sector there had taken more than ten thousand rounds of Jordanian artillery. Two thousand homes had been destroyed, and there had been twelve hundred civilian casualties.

Dov Joseph, a Canadian Jew who was the civilian governor of the city during this crisis, could take much of the credit for the orderly and disciplined life of the city. The people were remarkably steadfast, courageous, and patient. Once the Egyptian threat from the south had been reduced at the end of May, the Israeli high command could focus its attention on the relief of Jerusalem. The city was again entirely cut off from supplies and on the verge of starvation. Ben-Gurion summoned Yigal Allon from the fighting in Galilee to lead the assault on Latrun and break the Arab stranglehold on Jerusalem's supply route.

Haganah troops, augmented with large numbers of raw recruits—many of them just off the immigrant ships that were at last arriving in Israel's ports unimpeded by British authorities—were rushed up to the front by bus and taxi. In blistering heat, these troops were hurled into a direct frontal assault on the entrenched Jordanians, without artillery support or adequate reconnaissance. The Arabs raked them with artillery and mortars and the Jews withdrew with heavy losses.

In the midst of the campaign to take Latrun, Ben-Gurion assigned a new and special volunteer to oversee the assaults. He was David Marcus, an American, a West Point graduate, a Normandy veteran, a Jew, and a colonel in the U.S. Army who had left a prestigious post at the Pentagon to help his brothers in Israel. Marcus joined with Shlomo Shamir, the commander of the first assault against Latrun, and together they tried harder to make the succeeding assaults work. But in spite of beefing up their operations considerably, the Fourth Regiment of the Arab Legion stood firm in the face of the next attack, and more Jewish bodies littered the slopes in front of their positions. It seemed that the hope of relieving Jerusalem was being bled dry at Latrun.

Another matter made their task more urgent. A UN ceasefire was due to go into effect on June 11. When that happened, all troop positions would be frozen and everything would come to a standstill. If the road to Jerusalem had not been opened by then, it would be too late.

Marcus began to look for a different way. There was a path by which troops had been getting to Jerusalem on foot. Marcus got Vivian Herzog and Amos Chorev to take a Jeep trip with him. Together they discovered that it was possible to traverse this path from Tel Aviv to Jerusalem on wheels. Now, if it could somehow be made passable for trucks, the seige of Jerusalem could be lifted and a new supply road opened.

Dirty and unshaven, the three men headed directly for Ben-Gurion's office as soon as they got back into Tel Aviv. The prime minister listened carefully to their report—a jeep could get through. It would be a race against time, but perhaps the path could be turned into a new supply road before the UN truce went into effect, they told Ben-Gurion. They decided to take the gamble.

The heat wave continued as hundreds of workers set out from Tel Aviv to undertake the strenuous work of building a road in the wilderness. Given the shortage of machinery for such a job, it was a gigantic undertaking. They called it the Burma Road, after the route Chinese coolies had hacked out of jungle-covered mountains to resupply Chiang Kai-shek's troops in their struggle against the Japanese during World War II.

Meanwhile, in Jerusalem, the situation was growing desperate. Only a few days' supplies were left. The ordnance officer estimated that enough ammunition remained for a sustained battle of no longer than twenty-four hours.

On Saturday, June 5, Dov Joseph was still reeling under the grief of his daughter's death. She had been killed in the fighting in the south a few days before. But he kept at his job in Jerusalem. That day he had to cut the citizens' rations once more. From now on he and his fellow Jerusalemites would subsist on four thin slices of bread a day, supplemented by half a pound of dried beans, peas, and groats each week. Each resident had to make do with one pail of water a day—for all purposes.

Marcus started the Burma Road with just one bulldozer at his disposal. The work inched forward at an agonizing pace. Each hundred yards of progress toward Jerusalem required three hundred yards of winding roadway. Alternate crews kept the work going day and night. Then a second bulldozer became available.

But conditions in Jerusalem remained desperate. On Monday, Joseph cabled Ben-Gurion: The city couldn't hold out beyond Friday. Ben-Gurion weighed his alternatives. Marcus still had three miles to go. Could he make it in four more days?

Ben-Gurion couldn't risk the wait to find out. He called out the Home Guard and sent them on foot with forty-five-pound packs on their backs full of food for Jerusalem. Three hundred middle-aged men were bused to the end of the Burma Road and from there set out to hike the three miles over ridges and through ravines until they reached the point where they could turn over their burdens to be trucked the rest of the distance to the Holy City. In this way, Ben-Gurion's answer to Dov Joseph's cable arrived on June 8. A final assault on Latrun almost succeeded on June 9. But the Arab Legion was destined to hold that plot of land for the next nineteen years.

Something else happened that day, though, to compensate for the failure to take Latrun. David Marcus and his two bulldozers emerged from the wilderness through which they had been digging since the end of May. The first trucks, filled with food and water, to make their way over that anguished and primitive roadway were greeted in Jerusalem with tears and cheers of joy.

Two days later, at ten o'clock in the morning, the UN ceasefire went into effect. It was just the breathing space Israel needed to rearm and replenish itself for the completion of her struggle for independence. But in Jerusalem the war was over. The Jordanians held the eastern half of the city—including the Old City with the holy sites, the Western Wall, and the Jewish Quarter, now abandoned—and all the surrounding country north and south and east.

The Israelis held the New City and a secure western corridor leading to the coast. Jerusalem, throughout history, had been besieged and destroyed many times before, but now the knife was thrust in her heart. For the first time in her history, Jerusalem was divided.

PLANS FOR JERUSALEM

Israel's War of Independence continued off and on for the rest of 1948. But, as already noted, Jerusalem ceased to be a focus of any serious fighting after June. Instead it became the focus of the efforts of Count Folke Bernadotte, the UN mediator for Palestine, to find a basis for a binding peace treaty.

His proposal, issued on June 27, was that two independent states—Israel and Transjordan—should become members of a union. Abdullah would get the Negev and Jerusalem, Western Galilee would go to Israel. Israel would be permitted unlimited immigration for two years; thereafter, the UN would govern immigration. With the exception of Abdullah, everybody hated the plan, all of the other Arab groups and the Israelis alike. And Abdullah was constrained by his loyalty to his fellow Arabs not to express his glee at the proposal.

Sobered by the hostile reception everyone gave him and his idea, Bernadotte went home to Sweden to rest and reflect on the matter. He returned to the Middle East later in the summer and issued a second proposal on Septebmer 16. This time he opted for the internationalization of Jerusalem under United Nations control.

The next day Bernadotte and some of his staff were driving through Jerusalem on their way home to their headquarters at the YMCA building in the New City. Their three cars had just entered a neutral zone between the Jordanian and the Israeli sector when a jeep pulled out of an alley and blocked their passage. The Jeep's occupants, four men, were wearing Israeli Army uniforms. Three of them got out and walked up to Bernadotte's car. One of them then thrust the muzzle of his Sten gun through the driver's window and fired a burst. Bernadotte and the man beside him were both killed.

The Israeli government launched a massive manhunt to find the culprits. They suspected the Stern gang, but later evidence indicated that the culprits were even more fanatical zealots who regarded Bernadotte as a secret agent. They were never apprehended. Bernadotte's assassination elevated him to the status of a martyr. And his September 16 proposal began to take on greater weight than it might have otherwise.

During November 1948, the Israelis and Jordanians conducted a series of meetings in which they hammered out a workable cease-fire. Glubb did not attend these meetings. Abdullah had been disappointed by his performance in the war, and on July 12, Glubb was sent to Europe for a rest.

So it was Abdullah Tell, the on-site Jordanian commander, and Moshe Dayan who fixed the dividing line and hammered out the details. Early in 1949 at a series of meetings on the island of Rhodes chaired by Bernadotte's successor, American diplomat Ralph Bunche, armistice agreements between the various Arab nations and Israel were signed.

With the armistice between Israel and Jordan, the division of Jerusalem was established as a permanent fixture. It also provided for Israeli access to two important areas of Jerusalem that were controlled by the Jordanians: Mount Scopus where the campus of the Hebrew University and the Hadassah Hospital were located, and the Western Wall and synagogues of the Old City. The most that ever came of these provisions was that the Jews were allowed to keep police stationed on Mount Scopus. No access of any sort to the holy sites of East Jerusalem was ever allowed during the Jordanian administration. The citizens of Israeli Jerusalem participated in the general elections for the Knesset, Israel's parliament, in January 1949. The first Knesset convened in Jerusalem on February 14 and stayed in session through February 17, long enough for its members to take the oath of office, and for Chaim Weizmann to be elected first president of the state. When Jerusalem came up again on the UN agenda in New York, it was November 1949. Israel argued against internationalizing the city and offered instead to sign an agreement which guaranteed free access to all holy sites in their part of the city.

However, on December 10 the General Assembly passed a resolution calling for the internationalization of the city under UN trusteeship. Israel's government reacted promptly. On December 13 it announced that it would speed up the transfer of its offices from Tel Aviv to Jerusalem, proposed that the Knesset locate there permanently, and proclaimed that Jerusalem was the eternal capital of Israel. The Knesset resumed sitting in the city on December 26, using a bank building until more permanent quarters were ready.

In the face of these actions and Jordan's equally vehement opposition to the UN resolution, the UN's Trusteeship Council recognized that implementing the resolution could only be accomplished by armed force. Consequently, the resolution was set aside.

JERUSALEM BETRAYED

THE HOLY CITY DIVIDED

So, by January 1950, a new arrangement had been established which would endure for the next seventeen and one-half years. The City of Jerusalem remained divided—one side belonging to Jordan, the other to Israel.

In East Jerusalem the Jewish quarter stood in almost total ruin as a result of the sacking it endured after its surrender in May 1948. Nearly all the synagogues, schools, and other notable buildings were destroyed. The ancient Jewish cemetery on the slope of the Mount of Olives was desecrated. Many of its headstones were used to build latrines and other facilities for the garrison of the Arab Legion permanently stationed in the city.

Any government services that had been housed in East Jerusalem during the British Mandate were transferred to Amman. King Abdullah annexed the city and the "West Bank" (more accurately described as the hill country of Samaria and Judea that lie north and south of Jerusalem) to his kingdom and renamed it the Hashemite Kingdom of Jordan (rather than Transjordan). Although East Jerusalem was proclaimed the "second capital" of Jordan, it meant little in actual practice. The city was cut off from its usual access to the Mediterranean Sea by the new arrangement and tended, as a result, to be somewhat isolated up in the hills.

For several years after the armistice East Jerusalem was without electricity. Water was in short supply. The economy was based on tourism and institutions devoted to religious research. The only significant factory in town made cigarettes. Construction of new housing in the city was limited to its northern reaches. Only a small number of large building projects—hotels, churches, hospitals, etc.—were undertaken during the Jordanian administration. The existence of a hostile frontier so near at hand and the pervasive presence of a Jordanian garrison created an uneasy atmosphere throughout the eastern city.

The Israelis took a much more aggressive attitude toward their western half of the city, in spite of the fact that it was situated at the end of a long corridor and virtually surrounded by Arab population and territory. Larger water pipelines replaced the emergency pipeline that had been laid in conjunction with the building of David Marcus's Burma Road in 1948. In addition, an immense reservoir for water was constructed southwest of the city. The city's already functioning electrical network was connected to the national grid, and train service in and out of the city was resumed by May 1949.

Israeli Jerusalem was a thriving city, the proud capital of a new nation—but it belonged to a people who could never forget that it was a divided capital, with its soul lying dormant in a desolated quarter sealed off from their sight, but not their hearts.

One of the most serious consequences of the War of Independence was the creation of two parallel refugee problems: Arab refugees who fled their homes in Palestine when their leaders attacked Israel, and Jewish refugees who were forced to leave Arab countries where they had been living.

So many Jewish refugees streamed to Israel that the population doubled within three years. Israel welcomed the refugees and integrated them into society, helping them find jobs and housing, and making them citizens. Arab refugees who remained in Israel were also offered citizenship in the new nation. But the Arab refugees who fled Israel were regarded by the surrounding Arab nations as political pawns. The feeling was that if world attention could be focused on the miserable plight of these refugees, then world opinion would be turned against Israel—and that has been the primary Arab strategy to this very day.

Only Jordan welcomed the Arab refugees from Palestine and offered them citizenship. The Palestinians repaid Abdullah's kindness with nothing but grief. While availing themselves of the king's hospitality, many of them remained loyal to Haj Amin al-Husseini, who had fled to Cairo; they still spent their days scheming to get Palestine back in Arab hands and to somehow vaporize the Jewish nation that had been planted there. The other Arab nations repaid Abdullah with isolation, cutting him off for having opened Jordan to their Palestinian-refugee bargaining chip.

In July 1951 the former Lebanese prime minister was assassinated while visiting in Amman. Death threats were also made on Abdullah's life, and he was warned not to go near Jerusalem. But Abdullah insisted on going to Friday prayers on July 21 at the Al-Aksa mosque, where the king intended to deliver a eulogy for the slain Lebanese leader.

Abdullah and his sixteen-year-old grandson, Hussein, joined two thousand Muslims who had gathered for noon prayers in the mosque. As they entered, a man fired a pistol at Abdullah, killing him with a single bullet to the head. A second bullet, aimed at Hussein's chest, was deflected by a medal on his military uniform, which his grandfather had insisted he wear. The assassin turned out to be a young Palestinian associated with a terrorist group sponsored by Haj Amin. Even in exile, the former grand mufti had subjected Jerusalem to yet more bloodshed.

KEEPING A PROMISE

I was sitting in a barber's chair one sunny June morning in Philadephia when I learned that the Six-Day War had started. Of course, no one knew at the time that it would be over in a matter of days. The radio in the barber shop was playing popular music when an announcer suddenly interrupted with a news bulletin: "Early this morning war broke out between Israel and three of its Arab neighbors—Egypt, Syria, and Jordan." The sketchy news report quickly concluded and the music resumed.

"Looks like Israel has had it," the barber said. "It's all over for her this time."

"Sorry, my friend," I responded. "But you're wrong. Israel is going to win this war, and win it quickly."

The barber just shrugged and smiled at my enthusiasm. He was probably thinking that I was young and cocky, which I was. But I was also a student of God's Word and I was convinced he would defend Israel. And I had also been keeping up with events in the Middle East. As the major military powers became entrenched in the Cold War, the Soviet Union began courting the Arab countries and increasing tensions in the Middle East. In 1955 the Soviets signed an arms deal with the Egyptians.

At Egypt's urging, British troops guarding the Suez Canal were pulled out of the area from 1954 to 1956. With the reduced British military presence, and emboldened by Soviet assistance, Egyptian President Gamal Abdel Nasser decided to seize control of the canal. In 1956 Nasser closed the canal to all ships sailing to or from Israel and blockaded the Straits of Tiran, effectively cutting off Israel from most of the world. He openly called for the destruction of Israel.

Israel joined Britain and France, whose economies depended on shipments moving freely through the canal, in mobilizing against Egypt in the brief Sinai Campaign. In the ground war, Israel took possession of the Gaza Strip, which had been the launching point of numerous guerrilla attacks into Israel. The military action against Egypt was halted when the United States put financial pressure on the European powers and forced them to withdraw, a strong-arm tactic President Eisenhower later said he regretted.

The United Nations quickly censured Israel and the Europeans for aggression without, as usual, condemning Egypt for the extreme provocation, and without imposing sanctions on the Soviet Union, who happened to be invading Hungary at the same time. The decade between the Sinai Campaign and the mid-sixties was the most peaceful in Israel's troubled history. Relations with Jordan, while not cordial, were largely quiet—disturbed now and again by purely isolated events.

It was Egypt and Syria who were giving the Israelis their worst headaches. In 1965 and 1966 Egypt received an enormous amount of military and economic aid from Russia; so did Syria. During those same years, guerrilla attacks by Arabs crossing into Israel's borders increased dramatically. The terrorist raids were calculated to provoke Israeli retaliation, which, it was hoped, would provoke the Arab countries to declare war on Israel.

By the spring of 1967 the situation had markedly deteriorated. Israeli kibbutzim were attacked dozens of times. In early April, Syrian troops opened fire on one of Israel's northern settlements. Israel retaliated by engaging the Syrian Air Force, destroying six of Syria's Soviet-supplied MIGs in the brief airfight.

At that point Soviet diplomatic rhetoric began accusing the Israelis of ominous arms buildups, particularly along the Syrian border below the Golan Heights. Completely untrue, it was a prime example of Soviet disinformation. In fact, it was Syrian artillery aimed at the Israeli settlements that had been moved into position on the Heights.

In mid-April the Soviet ambassador to Israel complained to Prime Minister Levi Eshkol about heavy concentrations of Israeli troops along the Syrian border. Eshkol offered, on the spot, to drive the ambassador—Leonid Chuvakhin—to the Syrian border so that he might inspect it personally and discover the truth that no such troop concentrations existed.

But the truth was beside the point. To the Soviets just the rumor of Israeli mobilization was a useful diplomatic tool, because if, after the rumor was spread by means of accusations, the Israeli aggression failed to materialize, then the Soviets could say that it was their support of the Syrian Ba'ath regime that kept the Israelis from acting. Colonel Hafez al Assad and his henchmen in Damascus would be grateful. However, the Soviets kept the pot over the flame a little too long. It suddenly boiled over and scalded them.

ESCALATING HOSTILITIES

In May the Soviets told Egypt that Israel was planning to attack Syria. Nasser immediately amassed an army on the Sinai Peninsula—eighty thousand of his troops—opposite Israel's southern border. He also demanded that UN peacekeeping forces leave the Sinai, and Secretary-General U Thant quickly acquiesced. By May 19 the Egyptians stood threateningly at the border with nothing in their way.

On May 22, Nasser again blockaded the Straits of Tiran and closed off the Israeli port of Eilat. This was Israel's only access from the Gulf of Aqaba to the Red Sea, and from there to the Gulf of Aden and the Arabian Sea, and it meant Israel's access to oil from the Persian Gulf was cut off. The blockade, considered an act of war by Israel, was provocation of the first order. Israel had already notified the UN Security Council that it would soon have to act in its own self-defense. But the UN failed to enforce the conditions of the truce that had existed since 1956, instead complying with Nasser's request to withdraw.

On May 30, Jordan's King Hussein flew to Cairo to bury the hatchet with Nasser and to sign a mutual defense pact. Israel was once again surrounded by hostile neighbors: Syria to the north, Jordan to the east, and Egypt to the south. Iraq and Saudi Arabia also pledged to send troops to the Arab federation. And, unseen but threatening behind the scenes, was the vast military power of the Soviet Union.

Prime Minister Eshkol and the defense minister, Moshe Dayan, had remained remarkably cool, not moving to strike until all other alternatives proved fruitless. The Israeli intelligence establishment, headed by Isser Harel, had spent a considerable amount of time studying the Arab character. They knew, therefore, that collective efforts among Arabs seldom held together for long.

Hussein knew that too. But by befriending his old enemy Nasser, he was evidently seeking to avoid what happened to his grandfather, Abdullah. Abdullah's assassination had been attributed to the fact that he did not share fully his fellow Arabs' goal of expunging the Jews from the face of the earth. The best the Israelis could hope for was that the signing of the pact would be as far as Hussein felt he had to go to demonstrate his Arab solidarity—that he would refrain from real aggression and leave the Israelis alone to fight it out with the Egyptians and the Syrians.

But the tension in Israel was overwhelming. If war started, where would it end? Would there be another Holocaust? Arabic rhetoric was inflammatory—radio broadcasts called for a *jihad* to avenge 1948, and Nasser vowed to completely destroy the nation of Israel and push the Jews into the sea once and for all. It was obvious that war was inevitable. The only question was when.

The Israeli cabinet met on June 4 to decide their response to the Arab aggression and illegal blockade. Despite the potential for catastrophe, the vote was unanimous: Israel would go to war to defend herself. At ten minutes after seven in the morning on June 5, the commander of Israel's air force, Major General Mordechai Hod, ordered his forces to undertake a carefully planned preemptive attack on Egypt's air force. With 340 combat aircraft, Nasser's air force was the largest in the Middle East; it was also poised within easy striking distance of Israeli civilian targets.

Well before noon that day three hundred of those aircraft were flaming wrecks, and the Egyptian Air Force was effectively wiped out. Simultaneously, the Israeli ground forces struck the Egyptian army amassed in the Sinai and virtually demolished Egypt's capacity to fight. By the end of the second day of battle, Israel was in command of the Sinai Peninsula.

As an important part of the Israeli strategy for victory, Dayan had ordered a complete blackout of news. None of the stunning victories of June 5 were acknowledged by the government of Israel for over twenty-four hours. That permitted loudly-proclaimed Egyptian announcements that they had destroyed Israel's armed forces to go unchallenged. It would be three days before the Egyptian people learned they had actually been defeated by the Israelis.

The result Israel anticipated from the news blackout was that the Soviets would stall any moves toward ceasefire at the UN as long as they thought their Arab clients were winning. But the ploy had an unanticipated result: King Hussein's entry into the war.

PREPARATIONS FOR VICTORY

Through diplomatic channels, Israel had sent messages to Hussein urging him to stay out of the fight and promising not to infringe on his territory if he kept his forces in Jordan. But

Nasser called Hussein, knowing his air force was destroyed, and bragged that Egypt had dealt Israel a severe blow and was winning the war. Unaware the Egyptian air force had actually been wiped out, Hussein ordered a Jordanian airstrike and the Legion began shelling Jerusalem.

Dayan ordered Uzi Narkiss, the front commander in Jerusalem, to grit his teeth and take no retaliatory action. They hoped this would be as far as Hussein would go in terms of a gesture of Arab solidarity. And, just to be on the safe side, Israeli jets destroyed Amman's air force of twenty Hunter jets that same day. But Jordan did not back down from the ground assault.

At one o'clock the Jordanians made their move. It was not where the Israelis expected it, namely on Mount Scopus where the tiny garrison was bracing itself for a savage attack, but it came at a site on the south side of the city.

There stood Government House, a large stone mansion the British had built as a residence and headquarters for their high commissioner. Now it was the headquarters of the chief of the United Nations Truce Supervision Organization. The building was surrounded by seven hundred acres of fenced land and stood atop the Hill of Evil, *Jabal Mukaber* in Arabic. The Jordanians wanted it because it gave them easy access to Israeli Jerusalem—access for their Patton tanks.

At about two o'clock Dayan gave the go-ahead for the achievement of some limited objectives in Jerusalem: first, take Government House from the Jordanians; second, link up with the detachment on Mount Scopus; third, protect the high ground north of Jerusalem by whatever means necessary.

Narkiss assigned the job of taking Government House to the Jerusalem Brigade. It was a haphazard affair. The Israeli Army had no elaborate plans for the capture of Jerusalem. They were flying by the seat of their pants. Still, the Jerusalem Brigade attacked and drove the Jordanians away from Government House and proceeded to drive the Legionnaires out of a series of entrenchments further south. Before midnight their mission was accomplished with the loss of only eight men.

By the first light of dawn one of the Harel Mechanized Brigade units had managed to reach the outskirts of Tel el-Ful, where the roads from Ramallah and Jericho met to form one road into Jerusalem. Israeli air support arrived and all the Jordanian tanks that had ventured out in the open came under rocket attack. That broke the thrust of their attack and the Jordanians turned around and headed for Jericho. As the rest of the tank and infantry units started arriving, the road to Jerusalem was firmly blocked.

It was the decisive moment of the battle for Jerusalem. Once the route by which the Jerusalem garrison of the Jordanian Arab Legion could be reinforced was effectively blocked, the outcome of the battle in and around Jerusalem was not in doubt.

THE BATTLE FOR JERUSALEM

However, the Israelis still had a battle with time, and the outcome was far from certain. The time factor was injected by the ability of the United Nations to impose a cease-fire. The Israelis had entered the war with no intention of storming East Jerusalem. But since Jordan had launched the attack, and since an Israeli victory seemed imminent, they wanted to be in full physical possession of the city before a cease-fire was called. If not, the haggling would go on forever.

So it was that on the very first day of the war, Uzi Narkiss, commander of the defense of Jerusalem, got a call from military headquarters in Tel Aviv. The 55th Paratroop Brigade under Colonel Mordechai Gur had been scheduled for use in the Sinai, but things were going so well there that the high command had decided to offer them to Narkiss to bolster his position.

Colonel Gur and his staff arrived in Jerusalem late in the afternoon, a few hours ahead of their paratroopers. Gur had to draw up a plan on the spot; it called for penetrating the Green Line—as the border with Jordan was called—at three points north of the Old City. The Jerusalem Brigade was already engaging the Jordanian troops south of the Old City. And it was from the northern approaches that the garrison on Mount Scopus could be most directly relieved.

The most difficult question facing Gur's planners was whether to attack at night or to wait for the dawn. Since air support had been ruled out by Dayan, who wished to protect the holy sites, there was little point in waiting for daylight, and a night attack might give the Israelis an advantage. By 8 P.M. they started installing powerful searchlights atop the Histadrut Building. At 2 A.M., the troops were finally in position. The searchlights went on to illuminate the area in front of the paratroop positions.

A volley of wire-guided rockets—until that moment a secret weapon—was let go against the Jordanian line. Simultaneously the paratroopers pounded machine gun and artillery emplacements with their Jeep-mounted recoilless rifles. They were joined by two tanks from the Jerusalem Brigade's tank unit.

By 2:30 A.M. the paratroopers had cut their way through the fences and started moving across no-man's land. On the northern flank they encountered light resistance at the Police Training School. The Jordanians withdrew to entrenched positions behind the school at a site called Ammunition Hill, where they put up a terrific fight. For the Israelis, Ammunition Hill was probably the costliest assault of the entire war.

On the southern flank the other two prongs of the paratrooper attack went across the Green Line at the same spot, just north of the Mandelbaum Gate. The first group turned right and headed south toward the Old City walls. The second unit set a more westerly course which led to the Augusta Victoria Hospice, a suspected Arab strongpoint. Both of these routes involved fierce street-to-street combat. But before the morning was over, Jordanian resistance was broken.

On Tuesday morning Uzi Narkiss ordered the Jerusalem Brigade, which had been fighting around Government House the previous day, to storm and capture Abu Tor, a steep and heavily populated hill that forms the other side of the Hinnom Valley immediately south of Mount Zion and the Old City. Here, as at Ammunition Hill, the Jordanians held fortified positions. The Israeli infantrymen would have support from tanks and mortars, but once again, air strikes were too risky.

The ensuing battle was bloody and involved savage hand-to-hand combat. One Israeli company accidentally came under friendly mortar fire and suffered severe casualties. But by the late afternoon, Abu Tor was in Israeli hands and only the Old City remained in Jordanian hands.

THE FINAL ASSAULT

Perhaps the most critical struggle for Jerusalem was fought on Monday night in the cabinet of Prime Minister Levi Eshkol. At seventy-two, Eshkol had been prime minister since 1963. Shortly before the breaking of the crisis his nation was now facing, he had brought a number of opposition people into the cabinet to form a wartime unity government.

Among those brought in were Moshe Dayan—who took up the defense portfolio—and Menachem Begin. On Monday morning in answer to Narkiss's query as to how he should respond to the Jordanian shelling, Dayan had told him to surround the Old City if necessary, but not to enter it. But when the cabinet gathered on Monday evening, with the news of a tremendous victory in the Sinai still ringing in their ears, they pressed for liberation of the Old City. Dayan resisted their pressure. Such an assault would likely be costly. He would rather surround and choke the city into surrender.

Throughout Tuesday, Dayan's plan remained in effect. Tuesday at noon he and Narkiss drove out to Mount Scopus when they got word that the way was clear. As it turned out, they reached the outpost before the relief column of paratroopers got there. As Dayan looked down from this height on the Old City—Jerusalem the Golden—he knew it would have to be taken the next day or it would be too late.

So that night he gave in to the cabinet's demands and issued the orders through Chief of Staff Yitzhak Rabin: the 55th Paratroop Brigade would take the city Wednesday morning. Gur arranged for detachments of his paratroopers to enter the city by every gate, but the main thrust would enter through the Lion's Gate—also known at St. Stephen's Gate—on the Eastern Wall opposite the Mount of Olives.

At no point did they encounter any really stubborn resistance. At 10 A.M. Gur radioed Narkiss, "Temple Mount is in our hands." Simultaneously the first men were reaching the Western Wall. The rest of the day was devoted to rejoicing and the costly work of cleaning out the last pockets of Jordanian resistance.

That same day columns of Israeli tanks and infantry continued pressing the Jordanians throughout the regions of Samaria and Judea which Jordan had occupied since 1948. Called the West Bank by the Jordanians, it was, after nineteen years of unfriendly occupation, inhabited almost exclusively by Arabs. The former

Jewish inhabitants had left for Israel. But now the Jews were back with the overpowering might of their air force. And by sundown of June 7, the Israeli columns had reached the Jordan. The West Bank—and, most importantly, the Old City of Jerusalem—was in their hands.

By June 8, Israel had captured the Suez Canal and the Eilat blockade was ended. The next day the Israelis turned their attention back to their northern border and engaged Syria, who had initially provoked the war. After another day, the Israelis owned the entire Golan Heights. On June 10 the Arabs called for a ceasefire.

At the end of six days it was all over. And tiny Israel, who had once again been surrounded and outnumbered by Arab armies, was now in possession of territories which had increased her size four-fold. For the Arabs it was a crushing and humiliating defeat.

King Hussein, grandson of Abdullah, paid dearly for his gamble. He suffered over fifteen thousand casualties—dead, wounded, or missing—in his army. His air force was gone, as were half his tanks. Proportionately, it would have been as if the United States suffered a million and a half casualties in three days. But Hussein lost more than his military strength. The West Bank had been his richest agricultural land. And the income from tourism in Jerusalem and Bethlehem had accounted for forty percent of Jordan's income.

Further, he lost the Hashemite dynasty's last claim on Islamic holy places. As his great-grandfather had lost Mecca and Medina to the Saudis, so now he had lost Jerusalem to the Israelis. He had only one meager source of solace. The Jews had suffered more casualties taking his territory from him than they had in the much larger Sinai campaign. A quarter of Israel's heavy losses against Jordan had been taken in the battle for Jerusalem.

But few Israelis found room in their hearts for mourning. For nineteen years they had been shut out of their holiest places. There would be time for mourning later; now was the time for rejoicing. On the day they took the Old City, the chief rabbi of Israel's armed forces, Shlomo Goren, managed to reach the Western Wall—even before the firing had died down—to sound the victory with his ram's horn, the shofar.

Dayan, Eshkol, and Rabin were close behind him; it was still hard to believe it was really theirs. Hardened veterans ran to touch the ancient wall and to weep with gratitude.

In the aftermath of the Six-Day War, the Arab countries held a summit conference in Khartoum. On September 1 they signed a declaration that specified "the main principles by which the Arab States abide." Those principles were "no peace with Israel, no recognition of Israel," and "no negotiations with it." In addition to the three noes to Israel, the fourth principle was their "insistence on the rights of the Palestinian people in their own country."

The Arabs, who had never been willing to help solve the refugee problem they created in 1948, were still using the Palestinian Arabs as their bargaining chip almost twenty years later, still pretending that Israel would just go away and they could reestablish Arab hegemony on all the land "from the river to the sea."

In November 1967 the UN Security Council adopted a resolution written by the British and American delegates calling for Israeli withdrawal "from territories occupied in the recent conflict." Because the wording was somewhat ambiguous—it didn't call for "immediate" withdrawal from "all" the territories, as the Soviet Union and Arab nations were demanding—and because it called for "acknowledgment of the sovereignty . . . of every State in the area," which would, of course, include the state of Israel, Israeli leaders viewed it favorably.

BROKERING THE PEACE

Resolution 242 was intended to provide a foundation for peace agreements between Israel and the Arab countries which had gone to war against her. But because it called for recognizing Israel's right to exist, none of the Arab nations would acknowledge it, and they remained technically at war with Israel. And Israel, understandably, would not release any territories gained in the war unless her security was guaranteed—which at the very least would include recognition of her sovereignty. The situation in the Middle East was stalemated.

It would be a full ten years, and another war later, before one Arab leader, Anwar Sadat of Egypt, courageously decided to make peace with Israel. The rest of the Arab nations refused to accept Resolution 242 and make peace with Israel unless Israel first recognized the principle stated at Khartoum, the right of the Palestinians to have their own country—and that meant, they later specified, turning over the occupied territories to the Palestine Liberation Organization.

It would be twenty-six years after the Six-Day War before Israel would finally buckle under the pressure, by then international pressure led by the U.S., and sign another peace treaty—not with an Arab nation, but with a terrorist organization. Even then, only one other Arab nation, Jordan, followed by signing a peace treaty with Israel.

And Israel might as well have signed a peace treaty with the devil himself as with the PLO.

Eleven

The Navel of the Earth

O N Tuesday afternoon, September 24, 1996, Jewish worshipers were evacuated from the Western Wall as angry
Palestinians cried out, *"Allahu akhbar!"* From their vantage point
outside the Al-Aksa Mosque, located directly above the Wall,
young men and old shouted their rage with the words, "Allah
is great!" As the disturbance grew, Israeli police fired rubber
bullets to disperse the rioters who were pelting Jewish worshipers with stones.

But this time the incident didn't end with a few stones being thrown. Instead, the violence escalated stage by stage until
the entire nation teetered on the brink of civil war. By the next
day, the Palestinian Authority had called an official strike by
Arab workers and urged massive demonstrations throughout
the West Bank, Gaza, and East Jerusalem. And this time, as
Israeli soldiers tried to break up the renewed rioting, they were
fired on by the Palestinian police—using the guns the Israelis
had given them under the Oslo Accords.

From Jerusalem the fighting spread to other towns and villages.
The worst fighting broke out in Nablus (biblical Shechem), where
Israeli soldiers and settlers had been mobbed at Joseph's Tomb, a

Jewish holy site. The Palestinians ransacked a nearby yeshiva and burned thousands of holy books. To prevent a massacre, the Israel Defense Forces (IDF) moved tanks and attack helicopters into position. Six soldiers were killed in the ensuing skirmish, but the majority of Israelis trapped at the site were rescued.

After four days of fighting, more than seventy people were dead and hundreds were wounded. A state of emergency was declared by the nation of Israel. President Bill Clinton summoned the Israeli and Palestinian leaders to Washington for a hastily-arranged summit conference. Once again, the world's attention was focused on Israel, and particularly on Jerusalem, where the violence had started. Reporters, photographers, and non-stop TV cameras trumpeted the story to an international audience.

Governments around the world rushed to weigh in with pronouncements on the situation in Jerusalem. And, following their long-standing pattern, the United Nations Security Council passed a resolution condemning Israel for provoking the violence.

A FORTY-FIVE ACRE TINDERBOX

The pretext for the initial rioting was the opening of a new exit to the Hasmonean Tunnel, an archaeological site that runs along the Western Wall and under a portion of the Old City, a few hundred meters away from the Temple Mount area. The tunnel had been open to tourists for about ten years. But with only one opening, visitors have to double back and exit the same way they entered. The new opening allows one-way traffic in the tunnel, and at the same time allows many more tourists to visit this important historical site in the heart of Old Jerusalem.

What Washington and most of the world failed to understand is that this most recent outbreak of violence in Israel was not simply another example of the smoldering tensions between Israelis and Palestinians. This battle was not about the Arab-Jewish nationalist conflict. This war was about sovereignty over Jerusalem, and, specifically, about who owns the title deed to the forty-five-acre plot in Jerusalem that is home to the holy sites of Jews and Muslims.

This forty-five-acre tract of land is called the Temple Mount by Jews and the Haram esh-Sharif, or Noble Sanctuary, by Muslims. Today it is a landscaped park, home to the Islamic shrine known as the Dome of the Rock, and the Al-Aksa Mosque.

All traces of Jewish ownership of the site, including Solomon's and Herod's temples, lie buried beneath the bedrock platform—and that is the way the Muslims intend to keep it. They will allow no archaeological work to be carried out on the site. In fact, over the years they have purposefully destroyed archaeological finds on the Temple Mount.

To most students of Bible prophecy it appeared that the "age of the Gentiles" came to an end in 1967, when Israel regained control of the entire city of Jerusalem, including the Temple Mount. Indeed, the re-establishing of Jewish sovereignty over the Holy City during the Six-Day War was one of the most significant prophetic events in modern history.

But within days of the war's end, the Temple Mount area had been restored to Arab supervision. Israel's Defense Minister, Moshe Dayan, met with the leaders of the Jordanian *wakf,* the Muslim religious body with oversight of mosques and holy sites, and essentially turned control of the Temple Mount back to them.

Many of Israel's secular Jews viewed Dayan's action as a political necessity, believing it would bring an end to the Arab nations' historic conflict with Israel. But religious Jews viewed it as a sin against God, who had miraculously won a victory for his people in the short war, resulting in the return of many Bible lands to Jewish control.

And returning the Temple Mount area to Muslim control has not brought peace with Israel's neighbors as Dayan naively hoped. Instead, in Arab eyes it was seen as weakness on Israel's part, as appeasement inevitably is. So the *jihad* over Jerusalem, and particularly over this forty-five acre tinderbox at the heart of the Old City, continues today.

When Israel opened the new exit to the Hasmonean Tunnel Yasser Arafat complained that it was just one more attempt to "Judaize Jerusalem," which, in his view, is the capital of a *de facto* Palestinian state. It is hard for those familiar with the Bible to understand how the Arabs can grumble about making Jerusalem more Jewish, since the Jewish association with the city— and particularly with the Temple Mount area—extends back at least four thousand years.

However, Palestinian youth are educated using textbooks which contain no mention of Israel. Maps of the Middle East used in Arab schools label the area of the nation of Israel as Palestine. Against all historical (not to mention biblical) evidence, Arab youth are taught that Jerusalem has always been an Arab city and that the Jews are illegal occupiers in the region.

To bolster their claims on the land, Palestinians now boast that they are descended from the Canaanites who occupied the land before the ancient nation of Israel—and, therefore, they have a prior legal right to the land. Again, the claim defies all historical evidence.

But that's not the point, as a report from the *Wall Street Journal,* written just after the riots over the tunnel opening, shows. Reporter Amy Dockser Marcus writes, "Archaeologists and biblical scholars say they are often amazed at the historical liberties taken by political leaders, who disregard or sometimes rewrite ancient stories to suit current needs."

Marcus described an August 1996 ceremony held by the Palestinian Authority in the ancient amphitheater in the village of Sabatsia, near Nablus. "Young people recreated the pagan legend of Ba'al, the Canaanite god, as a narrator read aloud an ancient text designed to resonate with the modern political troubles of its audience: warnings about the Hebrew tribes led by Joshua that were then starting to conquer Canaan."

After pointing out some of the "scholarly holes" in the ceremony, Marcus indicates that the purpose of the celebration was entirely political, not historical—a fact that doesn't bother the Palestinians one bit. "Mr. Abu Khalaf of the Islamic archaeology institute says those insisting on rigorous academic standards are missing the point. Though scholars say it isn't likely that the Canaanites originated in Arabia, he argues that life in traditional Palestinian villages today isn't much different than it was when the Canaanites lived there. It also doesn't bother him when Palestinians call Jesus Christ the first Palestinian. Jesus lived in Bethlehem, Mr. Abu Khalaf says, and Bethlehem's current inhabitants are Palestinians."

So when Yasser Arafat accuses the Israeli government of "Judaizing Jerusalem," he is simply rewriting history to suit his political purposes. He would like very much for the world to ignore the Jewish history of Jerusalem, and especially the Jewish connection to the Temple Mount.

THE NAVEL OF THE EARTH

What makes the Temple Mount sacred to both Jews and Muslims? It is home to the Foundation Stone, the exposed bedrock of Mount Moriah which lies under the Dome of the Rock.

Both Jews and Muslims regard the Foundation Stone as the place where God created the world—the navel of the earth. They believe it was on this spot that God created Adam, who was later placed in the Garden of Eden, which was "to the east" according to the Book of Genesis. In fact, there is an Arabic inscription on the Dome of the Rock which reads, "The Rock of the Temple from the Garden of Eden."

Jews also call the Foundation Stone the "rock of Abraham," because it was here on this particular outcropping of Mount Moriah that Abraham offered his son Isaac in obedience to God. "By this act," Gershon Salomon says, "Mount Moriah became the most holy place on earth and the place for the worship of G–d." Salomon is the founder of the Temple Mount Faithful movement, dedicated to the reintroduction of Jewish worship on the Temple Mount site.

Muslims also believe the Foundation Stone to be the site of Abraham's great sacrifice. However, they believe—totally without warrant—that it was Ishmael, not Isaac, who was offered as a sacrifice to God here on Mount Moriah.

The Tabernacle of Moses is also associated with Mount Moriah. The tabernacle functioned as a portable temple, used for the Israelites' worship as they traveled out of Egypt and into the Promised Land. After Joshua led the conquest of Canaan, the tabernacle came to rest in Shiloh, where it stayed for approximately four hundred years.

Shiloh was destroyed around 1050 B.C. and the Ark of the Covenant was carted off by the Philistines. Some time later the tabernacle was moved to Jerusalem, King David's new capital, where he eventually set it up on Mount Moriah. He also recovered the Ark of the Covenant and brought it to Jerusalem. David had bought the "rock of Abraham," which was being used as a threshing floor by Araunah the Jebusite, as a location for a permanent house of God.

When Solomon built the First Temple, on this sacred site on Mount Moriah, the old tabernacle was dismantled. Many Jews believe the tabernacle was put into storage underneath the Foundation Stone—where it may remain to this day.

GOD GAVE US THIS LAND

The First Temple, Solomon's temple, was completely destroyed by the Babylonians in 586 B.C., and rebuilt on the same spot seventy years later by the returning Jewish exiles. This so-called Second Temple was enlarged and lavishly restored by Herod the Great beginning in 20 B.C.

It was this Second Temple that was in existence during the lifetime of Jesus Christ. Here he was named and circumcised, and here he was found in dialogue with the religious teachers when he was twelve years old. Here Jesus preached and taught, and here he overturned the tables of the money changers who had turned God's "house of prayer" into a "den of thieves." And here the church was born on the Day of Pentecost, as the disciples continued in prayer. Peter's great sermon was probably preached in the outer courts of the Temple grounds.

Since the Second Temple was destroyed by the armies of Rome and leveled to the ground, it has never been rebuilt. For two thousand years the Jewish people have been without a temple for worship or sacrifices. For centuries, in fact, the Temple Mount lay in ruins. Pagan temples built on the site by the Romans were destroyed by the Byzantine Christians. And Christian churches were built in Jerusalem beginning in the early fourth century, but not on the sacred rock of Mount Moriah. This was not out of consideration for the Jews, but was more likely a commentary on the failure of the Jewish state.

When the Muslim invaders captured Jerusalem, however, they turned Mount Moriah back into a place of worship. But it was not Yahweh, the God of Abraham, Isaac and Jacob, who was worshiped at the holy place. Allah, the Muslim god, is not the same as the God of the Bible worshiped by both Jews and Christians, the "people of the Book."

Prior to Muhammad, the Arabs worshipped many gods—the Ka'aba shrine in the city of Mecca was home to some 360 idols. But the Arabs' chief god was the moon god, who was known by the title al-Ilah, "the deity." Even before Muhammad's time the moon god's title had been shortened from al-Ilah to Allah. Muhammad "promoted" Allah, making the moon god the only god of Islam. Allah's symbol, adopted by Islam, was the crescent moon. This was one of the reasons Islam, although monotheistic, was rejected by both Jews and Christians as an unscriptural religion: The people of the Book recognized that Allah was not the God of the Book.

In the late seventh century, the Muslims built a shrine over the Foundation Stone, the sacred bedrock of Mount Moriah. Called the Dome of the Rock, it remains the most prominent landmark in Jerusalem today. Outside of one brief period, approximately one hundred years under Crusader rule, when the mosque was turned into a church, the Dome of the Rock has stood its ground for thirteen centuries.

Muslim hostility toward both Judaism and Christianity can be found in the Arabic inscriptions on the walls of the Dome of the Rock. There are over seven hundred feet of inscriptions, many of them quotes from the Koran. Here are but a few examples:

O People of the Book, do not go beyond the bounds in your religion and do not say about Allah anything but the truth.

There is no God but Allah alone; he has no co-partner.

The Messiah, Jesus, son of Mary, is but a messenger of Allah and His word which he cast upon Mary, and a spirit from Him. So believe only in Allah and of his messenger, but do not say "Three" [Trinity] and it will be better for you.

Allah is only one God. Far be it from His glory that he should have a son.

Verily, the religion in Allah's sight is Islam.

From this brief history of Mount Moriah, we can see that tensions between Muslims and Jews over the Temple Mount is a centuries-old conflict. Jewish ownership of the site, however, pre-dates Muslim control by at least fifteen centuries. If title deed to this forty-five-acre tinderbox could be proved by any party, it would definitely be the Jewish people. God promised them the land, Jerusalem included. And God's Word records that King David bought this particular spot on Mount Moriah, paying fifty shekels of silver for it.

Why would David pay for a place God had promised to give his people? Gershon Salomon offers this answer: "Three places in the land of Israel were bought by the people of Israel even though the land had been promised by G–d, because when the nations come and say, 'This land does not belong to you,' the answer to them will be: 'This land was given to us by G–d Who is the owner of all the universe, and we also paid for those three places which symbolize this land.' These three places are the Temple Mount, the Machpelah cave of the Patriarchs in Hebron, and the tomb of Joseph in Shechem."

All three of those places have either been turned over to Muslim control already, or soon will be if the peace process continues unhindered. The Palestinians have told the Israelis, "This land does not belong to you." And they backed up their words with bullets: They recently killed six Israeli soldiers at Joseph's Tomb, and Palestinian police returned fire on the Israeli soldiers who tried to break up the Arab riots on the Temple Mount. It is time for a voice to be raised in Israel: "God gave us this land, and we also paid for it."

PLANNING TO REBUILD

While Christian worship was never established on the Temple Mount, we consider it a very important site historically and spiritually. And many of us believe that Jewish custodianship of the holy site is mandated in Scripture. For in order for prophecy to be fulfilled, there must be a Third Temple built by the Jews on the same spot as the previous two temples.

In the Old Testament, Daniel spoke of the prince who will make a covenant with the Jewish people and guarantee them religious freedom to make sacrifices and oblations. These can only be done in the Temple. The prophet also predicted that after three and one-half years, the Temple would be desecrated by this prince, the Antichrist, who would invade the inner sanctum and proclaim himself God. So it is certain that the Temple will ultimately be rebuilt.

The New Testament also describes Jewish worship in a future Temple. Jesus quoted the prophecies of Daniel regarding the Antichrist and the Temple (see Matthew 24:15). The apostle Paul also referred to Daniel's prophecy: "Don't let anyone deceive you in any way, for that day [the return of Christ] will not come until the rebellion occurs and the man of lawlessness is revealed, the man doomed to destruction. He opposes and exalts himself over everything that is called God or is worshipped, and even sets himself up in God's temple, proclaiming himself to be God" (2 Thessalonians 2:3–4).

So again and again we're confronted with the presence of the Temple in descriptions of the last days. But are the Jewish people today planning on building the Third Temple?

Without a doubt. Walk the narrow alleyways of the Jewish quarter of the Old City. Talk to the people in the shops and yeshivas. You'll find ample evidence of the spiritual longing of the Jews for their ancient Temple and the worship associated with it.

If you visit Jerusalem electronically, via the Internet, you'll find the same enthusiasm for rebuilding the Temple. For example, the home page of the Jerusalem Temple Store features this sign:

> PRE 3RD TEMPLE SALE—
> Buy now before the temple is rebuilt and prices go up

The light-hearted sign follows this description of the Temple Store, a shop in the Old City featuring collectibles related to the First and Second Temples: "With the return of the Jewish people to her own land, the dream of the Holy Temple is once again becoming a reality."

Gershon Salomon, founder of the Temple Mount Faithful movement, is convinced that the temple will be rebuilt in his lifetime. He writes, "There are three biblical conditions for the complete redemption of the people of Israel and for the coming of Mashiach ben David [Messiah]: the regathering of the Israeli nation from all over the world to the Promised Land; the foundation of the Israeli state in the land which G–d promised to Abraham, Isaac, and Jacob in the eternal covenant . . . and the rebuilding of the Temple, the Third Temple.

"The first two conditions have already been met in our time through mighty godly miracles. The third condition, the rebuilding of the Temple, is soon going to be fulfilled. This is the right time to do it immediately. So many houses were built during the last fifty years in the land of Israel and only one house, the biggest house and most holy house in the world, the House of G–d, is still in ruins."

To devout Jews, rebuilding the temple is seen as a *mitzvah*, or commandment. And of the 613 commandments codified in the Mosaic Law, 202 of them are contingent upon the Temple for their fulfillment. Therefore, many in the religious community in Israel have been earnestly preparing to fulfill these *mitzvot* (commandments).

All that remains now is the temple itself; the Levitical priesthood is being re-established, yeshivas (seminaries) are training the priests, and craftsmen are recreating the garments, vessels, and musical instruments used in temple worship.

According to Rabbi Chaim Richman of the Temple Institute in Jerusalem, "the Torah enumerates ninety-three categories of *klei sharet*, sacred vessels, to be used in the Beit HaMikdash [Holy Temple]. Of this number, the Temple Institute has already constructed more than half." The Temple Institute maintains a museum displaying the temple vessels, including such items as the copper washbasin, the golden crown of the High Priest, the silver trumpets, and the priestly garments.

"These vessels are not models, copies, or replicas," Richman says, "but are actually kosher, functional pieces, made from gold, copper, silver, and the other original source materials. The restoration is so accurate that should the Temple be rebuilt immediately, the Divine service could be resumed without delay, utilizing these vessels."

The Temple Institute is only one of several organizations in

Jerusalem actively researching and preparing items for use in the future Temple.

Beged Ivri was established in 1983 for the purpose of reviving the Levitical ministry. Their promotional literature states: "Behind the tumultuous scenes and out of view of the news media, a dedicated group of people are quietly restoring ancient customs, rebuilding the original vessels and instruments, and a number of special schools are training those who will use them."

SOUNDS OF THE TEMPLE

Every person who has seen a Christmas pageant has heard of frankincense and myrrh—two of the gifts brought by the Wise Men to the Christchild. But what exactly were frankincense and myrrh? They were two of the eleven "holy spices" that made up the *Ketoret*, or incense offering, burned every morning and evening on the altar of incense in the ancient Jewish temple.

Researchers at Beged Ivri have authenticated all eleven of the original ingredients of the *Ketoret*: balsam, clove, galbanum, frankincense, myrrh, cassia, spikenard, saffron, costus, aromatic bark, and cinnamon. Because the *Ketoret* was used in every ceremony conducted in the Temple, the identification and production of these aromatic oils is an important step in the preparations for the Third Temple. Perhaps it will not be long before the fragrance of the *Ketoret* fills the air from Jerusalem all the way to Jericho, as the Talmud describes.

The Talmud also says that there were so many harps played during the Passover and Tabernacles festivals, when thousands of pilgrims converged on Jerusalem, that the sound of the harps could be heard in Jericho, as well. And one Jewish couple in Jerusalem today has a vision of recreating the joyful sounds of thousands of temple harps.

Micah and Shoshanna Harrari have devoted the last decade of their lives to researching and recreating the musical instruments invented by King David for use in temple worship. At their Jerusalem workshop, the House of Harrari, beautifully hand-crafted replicas of the *kinnor*, David's ten-stringed harp, can be purchased. These hand-held harps are true objets d'art, pleasing to the eye as well as the ear.

In honor of the official celebration of the 3,000th anniversary of Jerusalem as David's capital, the Harraris began a new direction in their biblical work: building three thousand Levitical harps to be used in the Third Temple. They have asked Jewish congregations around the world to sponsor a harp for the Temple. According to their promotional literature, the sponsoring congregation will receive one of these three thousand Levitical harps, "which will be built and delivered as a centerpiece cared for and prayed for and finally returned to Jerusalem when the temple is rebuilt."

A scroll with the sponsors' names will be maintained and presented to the chief Levite of the Temple orchestra, and when the time of fulfillment has arrived, a call will go out for the three thousand harps to be returned to Jerusalem. The Harraris say, "For us personally this represents the beginning of a new era as we draw closer to the time of redemption and the rededication of the Holy Temple, A House of Prayer for All Nations." Can the day be far away when the fragrance of the *ketoret* and the harmony of Levitical harps fill the air from Jerusalem to Jericho once again?

WHERE WILL IT BE?

As we have seen, preparations for a revived Levitical service in the Temple are far advanced. All that remains is for the

Temple itself to be rebuilt. But that's the problem: how to rebuild the Temple without starting World War III. If just opening a new exit to the Hasmonean Tunnel could spark a civil war in Israel, what would happen if the Jews attempted to build a Temple anywhere close to the Temple Mount, let alone right on top of it?

And that's where it would have to be built, for according to rabbinical law the only place the Jewish temple can be built is on the exact spot where the first two temples were erected. There is one major obstacle to building the Temple there—the third holiest place of the Muslim faith, the Dome of the Rock, is squarely in the middle of the old Temple site.

Shortly after the recapture of Old Jerusalem in 1967, a reporter interviewed a famous Israeli historian, Israel Eldad. He asked, "Do your people intend to rebuild the Temple?"

Eldad said, "From the time that King David first conquered Jerusalem until Solomon built the Temple, just one generation passed. So will it be with us."

"What about the Dome of the Rock which now stands on the Temple site?" asked the reporter.

"It is, of course, an open question," said Eldad. "Who knows, maybe there will be an earthquake."

It is conceivable that God might use an earthquake to settle the question—the Bible records many earthquakes, some of them said to result from God's judgment. The Bible also predicts that the great tribulation period will be preceded by severe earthquakes.

And it happens that Jerusalem lies very close to the African Rift Zone, the deepest break in the earth's crust, which runs from Africa through the Red Sea, the Dead Sea, and the Jordan River Valley. Many seismologists say that, like California, Israel is overdue for "the big one."

Tradition has long held that the ancient Temple stood on

precisely the same spot occupied today by the Muslim shrine, the Dome of the Rock—the most prominent and eye-catching structure in all of Jerusalem—although it was uncertain whether the sacred rock was the original site of the Altar of Sacrifice or the Holy of Holies.

Consequently, it seemed that reconstruction of the temple would require demolition of the Dome of the Rock—something unthinkable to all but the most zealous advocates of reconstruction, because it would surely provoke war with neighboring Islamic states.

Although the traditional view still holds sway with the majority of archaeologists and rabbis, two other views have gained a growing number of adherents in recent years. Both of these theories conclude that the Temple site is adjacent to, but not directly over, the Dome of the Rock. The advantage of these views is that, at least theoretically, the Third Temple could be built on the Temple Mount area without destroying the Muslim holy sites.

About twenty years ago, Dr. Asher Kaufman, a professor of physics at the Hebrew University, proposed a northern location on the Temple Mount as the original Temple site. Kaufman has investigated the Temple Mount intensively for years, and he concludes that the ancient Temple did not stand on exactly the same ground occupied by the Dome of the Rock. Rather, he thinks it stood about one hundred yards north of the Dome of the Rock's location.

His first reason for believing this is the location of the Eastern or Golden Gate. This gate, which has long been sealed shut, led directly to the front entrance of the temple, which lay on an east-west line with the Holy Place and the Holy of Holies at the western end.

But the Dome of the Rock sits roughly one hundred yards south of the east-west line that would run through the Eastern

Gate. And archaeologists have discovered remnants of the ancient Eastern Gate directly beneath the location of the present one. So the location is not in doubt.

Kaufman also believes that a small cupola, standing largely unnoticed in the northeast corner of the Temple Mount about one hundred yards from the Dome of the Rock, preserves the original site of the Holy of Holies, possibly the very spot on which the Ark of the Covenant rested. Called in Arabic the Dome of the Tablets or Dome of the Spirits, it covers the only other spot on the platform where the bedrock of Mount Moriah is not covered by paving stones.

Perhaps the Arabic names convey a sense of the original purpose of the spot: "Tablets" could refer to the tablets of stone on which the Ten Commandments were written. These tablets were stored in the Ark of the Covenant, which was housed in the Holy of Holies. And "Spirits" could refer to the presence of God, which was said to dwell in the Holy of Holies.

There is some documentary evidence for Kaufman's theory. *The Mishnah*, a collection of Jewish laws and traditions dating from the time of Herod's temple, and other ancient extrabiblical records provide evidence that the ancient Temple stood with its northern wall outside and north of the platform on which the Dome of the Rock now stands; likewise its shorter eastern wall probably stood slightly east of the platform wall that exists today.

Recently a southern location on the Temple Mount has been proposed as the original Temple site. Israeli architect Tuvia Sagiv developed this theory about five years ago. Sagiv places the original Temple on a spot that is today occupied by the El Kas fountain, about halfway between the Dome of the Rock and the Al-Aksa Mosque.

Sagiv offers a tremendous amount of documentation to back up his theory of a southern location. First, he has reconstructed the Temple Mount area using topographical maps of Mount Moriah, comparing them to ancient records recording the relative height of the various buildings known to have been on the Temple Mount.

The Antonia Fortress, Sagiv believes, was actually on the spot now occupied by the Dome of the Rock. That would put the original Temple site south of the Dome of the Rock, since ancient records agree that the fortress was adjacent to and just north of the Temple.

Another critical consideration in Sagiv's theory is the location of the Temple in relation to the aqueduct bringing water to the Temple site. Rabbinical law required that "living" or flowing water, not water stored in cisterns, be used for the *mikvah*, the ritual bath for the temple priests, as well as for cleaning the area where animal sacrifices were offered.

That means the water would have to flow from a higher source down to the Temple area. But surveys of the ancient aqueduct put the location of the water source about sixty yards below the bedrock on the site of the Dome of the Rock. Therefore, the Temple could not have been located on that site or the flowing water would have to defy the laws of gravity to reach the Temple site above. In Sagiv's proposed southern location, the Temple would be positioned well below the water source, as required.

Additional methods Sagiv has used to back up his theory include ground-penetrating radar and thermal infrared imagery. According to Sagiv, the results of this high-tech testing support his conclusion that the original Temple site was lower than, and therefore, to the south of, the Dome of the Rock.

Which of these theories about the precise location of the First and Second temples might be correct is impossible to prove at the moment, because excavation of the Temple Mount is prohibited. But a review of these newer studies gives the impression that careful analysis may have uncovered a long-overlooked truth. And, if that is true, then the rebuilding of the Temple may be closer than we think.

Twelve

Rumors of War

Just two days after Washington strong-armed the signatures of Benjamin Netanyahu and Yasser Arafat onto the Hebron Agreement, the Clinton administration began pressuring Israel to reopen negotiations with Syria. Sandy Berger, Clinton's new national security advisor, told reporters on January 17, 1997, that "there can be no comprehensive peace in the Middle East that does not include Syria."

When I first read newspaper accounts of America's latest attempt to coerce a "paper peace" in the Middle East, I was dumbfounded. The ink had barely dried on the Hebron protocol. Israeli troops were redeploying rapidly from the oldest city in Israel's history, the biblical City of the Patriarchs, leaving eighty percent of Hebron in the hands of the Palestinians. Under the new arrangement, joint mobile units of Israeli soldiers and Palestinian police will be required to escort Jewish worshipers to the holy sites where Abraham, Isaac, and Jacob are buried.

Now, even before the heartache of Hebron has time to heal, administration officials have implied that Israel's next sacrifice for peace will be the Golan Heights, perhaps her most strategic asset. Washington knows that Syria has made its position absolutely clear: Israel must cede the entire Golan Heights *before* there will be any peace talks. Washington also knows that Syria has backed up that hard-line negotiating precondition with military maneuvers. Syrian troop movements in the fall of 1996 positioned the 14th Commando Division almost at the front line on the Golan. By December, intelligence reports on both sides calculated the risk of war as being greater than at any time during the past decade.

If Washington's demand for peace talks seems unrealistic in light of Syrian threats, it is doubly absurd when you consider that Syria is officially listed by our State Department as a terrorist state. What on earth does Berger mean by "there can be no comprehensive peace in the Middle East without Syria"? What about other terrorist states in the region, such as Libya? Will Israel be forced to negotiate with Libya in the pursuit of this comprehensive but elusive peace? Syria and Libya have much in common: They both are ruled by dictators. They both harbor terrorists at home and even send them abroad to wreak havoc on governments and terrorize civilian populations. And if there is to be a "comprehensive peace" in the Middle East, then what about Iraq and Iran?

Why is Israel, the only democracy in the Middle East, perceived as the chief obstacle to true peace?

FEEDING THE ALLIGATOR

For decades the United States government has been controlled by the liberal mindset, and the majority of career bureaucrats in the State Department have fallen into the pro-Arabist camp. In spite of press reports about a powerful Jewish lobby in this country, Israel has not had many true friends at the highest levels of our government. And when it comes to the Middle

East, many politicians still hold to the alligator-feeding school of thought: *If we just feed Israel to the alligator, then the alligator will leave us alone.*

But the alligator—the antagonism of the Islamic world toward the West—raged for a millennium before Israel was ever added to the mix of Middle East powers. Islamic extremists, terrorist-sponsoring dictators, and oil-rich sheiks do not hate the West because of Israel; they hate Israel because of the West. In their eyes, America was the Great Satan long before the modern nation of Israel came into existence. The principles of democracy, firmly rooted in the Judeo-Christian tradition, are an enigma to the Islamic world.

What many in our government fail to realize is that there can be no true peace in the Middle East unless the Arab world embraces democracy. As Bernard Shapiro, director of the Freeman Center for Strategic Studies, points out, democracies rarely go to war with each other. "All our major wars of the last two hundred years have been between dictators or between democracies defending themselves from dictators." That's why, in Shapiro's view, "it seems a bit odd that our State Department is pushing democracy and human rights from one end of the globe to the other—with the remarkable exception of the Middle East. Why are the Arabs insulated from pressure to democratize their societies?"

But how effective would attempts to democratize Arab countries be? The Islamic resurgence sweeping most of the Arab world makes a true democracy in the region virtually impossible. My experience during the Persian Gulf War made this fact clear. I was part of a group of journalists allowed to accompany General Khalid, Saudi commander-in-chief of the multi-national forces, on an inspection of troops positioned at the Kuwaiti border. When we returned to Dhahran the next day, it appeared that a major development in the war was looming on the horizon. The king called a meeting and virtually everyone of significance was summoned, including General Schwarzkopf and the American top brass.

Word spread like wildfire that an invasion of ground troops into Iraqi-held territory was imminent. There were indeed a lot of sweaty palms in the room that day as a momentous decision was made. But this top-level meeting had nothing to do with an imminent ground war; this meeting had to do with the breakfast menu. A decision was being made whether American troops would be allowed to have bacon with their eggs. The Saudis had refused to allow supplies of bacon to be unloaded from American ships. Officials feared that if our troops ate pork on Saudi soil it could cause the overthrow of their government by Islamic fundamentalists.

That may sound silly to most Americans, but the Saudis had a genuine concern. With a groundswell of fundamentalism advocating a government based on strict Islamic law, there was indeed a threat to the stability of the Saudi kingdom. So the momentous breakfast decision was made: ship-based troops could have bacon with their eggs, but not U.S. ground troops.

Now imagine for a moment that this scene had taken place in Israel. Orthodox Jews keep to a strict kosher diet. Like Muslims, they do not eat pork, and they can be very adamant about adhering to the injunction against it. But the idea of Jewish extremists keeping American troops from eating bacon for breakfast is absurd. It would never happen. Israel was birthed from the womb of democratic ideals. There is a healthy debate over the boundaries between religious faith and government in Israel. Even among Jewish extremists it would be hard to find a single person who believed that the sanctity of the nation would be defiled by foreigners eating pork on Israeli soil.

Yet a violation of the Islamic prohibition against pork would be a political problem of enormous consequence in many Arab countries today. Islamic fundamentalists have risen to power in these countries, causing a backlash against Western culture and values. Fundamentalists have plunged the nation of Sudan into civil war. Algeria's president was assassinated by fundamentalists in 1992, shortly after he attempted to prevent an Islamic takeover of his country. Egypt, whose former president, Anwar Sadat, was assassinated by Muslim extremists, is again struggling with a growing fundamentalist movement.

LIBERATING AL-QUDS (JERUSALEM)

But one key element ties these different movements in different countries together: the desire to return to the glory days of Islam by forcefully liberating former Muslim lands. And at the top of every Islamic movement's list is the liberation of one particular city: al-Quds, the Arabic name for Jerusalem.

The impetus for this rising tide of fundamentalism is the Iranian Revolution, which ousted the shah in 1979 and swept the Ayatollah Khomeini to power. The mullahs of Iran visualize a vast Islamic republic under their control. And the presence of Israel, a pro-Western democracy occupying a tiny speck of sand in the middle of the vast desert lands of the Arab world—just under 11,000 square miles compared to more than six million square miles—is a perpetual threat to the Islamic ideal.

Because the crown jewel of Israel, Jerusalem, is also the third holiest city of Islam, the ayatollahs are not much interested in peace agreements between the Israelis and Palestinians. Since the Madrid Peace Conference in 1991, Teheran has made every effort to undermine a Washington-brokered "comprehensive peace in the Middle East." Intelligence sources say that Teheran spends up to $200 million annually to fund extremist groups dedicated to destroying prospects for peace, primarily through attacking Israeli and American targets in the area.

The Iranians' determination to destroy peace and export their revolution can be seen in the creation of a special force within the Islamic Revolutionary Guard Corps. The Special Qods (Jerusalem) Force, is charged with planning and executing all revolutionary activities outside of Iran. The Qods Force's 2nd Corps, with command headquarters in Damascus, is stationed in the Bekaa Valley, adjacent to the security zone in southern Lebanon where Israeli troops are positioned to defend against Hezbollah incursions into the Upper Galilee.

Today Syria, without which "there can be no comprehensive peace in the Middle East," has more than thirty thousand troops stationed in Lebanon, complemented by these special Iranian forces. Why have Syria and Iran taken over 75 percent of the territory of war-torn Lebanon? For one reason only: as a launching pad for an invasion of Israel and the subsequent capture of Jerusalem for a revived Islamic Empire.

Which brings me back to the question of America's misguided foreign policy regarding Syria and a "comprehensive peace" in the Middle East. Why, in spite of intelligence reports showing a likely outbreak of aggression against Israel, does the Clinton administration continue to put pressure on our democratic ally to give up yet more land in the hope of securing a fragile paper agreement for peace? Shouldn't we also be putting pressure on the Arab nations to give up land, or give up *something*, for the sake of peace?

There are two important reasons for the Clinton administration's tendency toward appeasement. The first reason is that peace agreement signings play well to the home audience. Much of the American public has lost patience with protracted negotiations and endless rounds of shuttle diplomacy. But most Americans do not understand the convoluted politics of the Middle East, and they do not realize that it will take far more than signatures on a series of agreements, like the Hebron Agreement and its predecessors, to bring true, lasting peace to the Middle East.

The second reason for Clinton's foreign policy direction has to do with what advice he chooses to heed and what he chooses to ignore. For example, Clinton has totally disregarded a Congressional report from the Task Force on Terrorism and Unconventional Warfare, which states that another Arab-Israeli war is imminent. Instead we read that Clinton's new national security advisor, Sandy Berger, is making pronouncements that Israel must get back to the bargaining table with a terrorist state.

Interestingly, an Egyptian assessment of the new Clinton cabinet, published in the Arabic weekly *Al-Ahram*, had this to say about the national security advisor: "Berger happens to be Jewish, but his religious orientation doesn't color his views or alter his commitment to the peace process. He was an active member of the Peace Now movement, which supports the Palestinian right to self-determination." Peace Now is a left-wing activist group, one of the strongest political voices in Israel urging the government to make territorial concessions. If Berger is indeed a former peacenik, what does that tell us about the kind of advice he will give President Clinton? Can there be any doubt that Israel will be asked by Washington to make still more territorial concessions?

It is also possible that President Clinton has been receiving advice about the Middle East from terrorist front groups. When the campaign fund-raising scandal broke just before the 1996 presidential election, it was widely reported that Indonesian business interests had donated millions of dollars to the Democratic party in an effort to influence Clinton's foreign policy in the Far East. What was not as widely reported was that radical Islamic forces were also trying to influence the Clinton White House. Investigative journalist and terrorism expert Steven Emerson reported in the Pittsburgh *Tribune-Review* of November 3, 1996, that "known Middle East terrorist supporters" had also tried to cultivate a relationship with the Clinton administration. Emerson, who has tracked radical Muslim groups in the United States for several years, said: "Two major groups fronting for radical Islam in the U.S. are the Council on American Islamic Relations (CAIR) and the American Muslim Council (AMC), both headquartered in Washington, D.C. Records and documents obtained from both the White House and internal publications of the groups themselves show that CAIR and AMC have been invited repeatedly into the White House."

How radical are these groups with access to the Clinton White House? Emerson says that CAIR has been an open advocate of Sheik Omar Abdel Rahman, the blind Egyptian cleric now serving a life sentence for masterminding the World Trade Center bombing in New York. And CAIR was created by a front group for Hamas—the leading sponsor of suicide bombings and terrorist attacks against Israel.

ARM-TWISTING FOR PEACE

Few newspapers picked up the story of these Clinton meetings with Islamic terrorist front groups. At the same time a secret report predicting imminent war in the Middle East was being issued by the Congressional Task Force, Americans were treated to extensive press coverage of a letter to the Israeli prime minister signed by three former secretaries of state, three former national security advisors, and two former peace negotiators.

This letter, written on December 14, 1996, put tremendous pressure on Israel to make concessions on the Hebron issue. It is not coincidental, in my view, that a Hebron Agreement was signed just thirty days later.

Initiated by former secretary of state James A. Baker, the letter contains a thinly-veiled threat against Israeli settlements in the West Bank. It says, "We write because we are concerned that unilateral actions, such as the expansion of settlements, would be strongly counterproductive to the goal of a negotiated solution and, if carried forward, could halt progress made by the peace process over the last two decades. Such a tragic result would threaten the security of Israel, the Palestinians, friendly Arab states, and undermine U.S. interests in the Middle East."

Former secretaries of state Lawrence Eagleburger and Cyrus Vance also signed the letter. But perhaps more telling of the letter's true intent was the fact that three other former secretaries of state *refused* to sign the letter: Henry Kissinger, George Shultz, and Alexander Haig. Is it possible they did not sign the letter because they knew this approach would undercut Israel's negotiating position and encourage those who prefer terror as a bargaining tactic to unleash a new round of violence?

Even as American negotiators were pushing through an agreement on Hebron, intelligence reports were monitoring Syrian troop movements in the Golan and illegal arms shipments flowing to the Palestinians. These reports were conveniently ignored, while tremendous pressure was put on Israel to make concessions. I do not know exactly what classified intelligence was available to the Clinton administration. But they surely had access to the type of information detailed in the Task Force report. And that report, leaked to the public via the Internet in mid-January, is shocking in its assessment of the likelihood of a war in the Middle East.

Congressman Jim Saxton, chairman of the House Task Force on Terrorism and Unconventional Warfare, criticized the Clinton administration for ignoring the Task Force report while pushing through a Hebron Agreement. "The Administration continues to apply pressure on Jerusalem to make additional concessions to Mr. Arafat while ignoring the concurrent developments in the Middle East," he said. "Instead of pressuring the democratically-elected government of Israel to deviate from the policies it was elected for, the U.S. should concentrate on helping Israel meet the growing threat of war."

Titled *Approaching the New Cycle of Arab-Israeli Fighting*, the Task Force report documents Syrian troop movements on the Israeli border, the existence of nuclear weapons in Iran and Pakistan, the rise of militant Islam, and the inevitability of another war designed to destroy Israel. The report states, "Numerous sources in the region report that the supreme leaders—both civilian and military—in most Arab states, as well as in Iran and Pakistan, are convinced that the present vulnerability of Israel is so great that there is a unique opportunity to, at the very least, begin the process leading to the destruction of Israel. These circumstances are considered to be a historic window of opportunity the Muslim world should not miss."

Documenting the evidence showing that the Arab states intend to take advantage of this window of opportunity, the report states that "this crisis is escalating even as all key players continue to reassert their commitment to the U.S.-inspired 'Peace Process.'" This "slide to war," the report says, is the "dominant dynamic" in the region.

Potentially explosive situations could erupt in Iraq and Syria as Saddam Hussein and Hafez al Assad determine who will succeed them. In Saudi Arabia, Prince Abdallah has consolidated power over other contenders in the royal family. Abdallah, who plans to oust the United States from the region, has developed a close relationship with Assad of Syria. According to the Task Force report, "Prince Abdallah has already promised Damascus to deliver a comprehensive oil embargo against the West in case of a major crisis with Israel."

In painstaking detail the report analyzes strategic military moves that indicate active preparations for war:

- In the spring of 1996, Hafez al-Assad and Saddam Hussein met secretly for a summit. They were later joined by Iran, and plans were made to dispatch Iranian forces and weapons to the Syrian front.

- In May 1996 Iran conducted its largest military exercise ever, simulating a long range advance equal to the distance between Iran and Israel.

- In June, Iran and Syria signed an agreement for military cooperation against Israel. In August, Iraq joined the agreement and a tripartite "joint command" was established for the conduct of "a major war against Israel."

- In September, the Palestinian Authority (PA) signed a military agreement with Syria, providing for Palestinian forces and terrorist groups to flare-up the Israeli interior in the event of an escalation in the north. Meanwhile, the PA's security services are stockpiling anti-tank and anti-aircraft weapons, including missiles, even though they are forbidden by the Oslo Accords.

- Also in September, the Egyptian Armed Forces conducted their largest military exercise since the late 1970s, simulating a strategic offensive against Israel. In October, Egyptian Army officers conducted a tour of the Sinai, near the Israeli border, in violation of the Camp David Accords.

- Beginning in October, several coordination sessions between Egypt, Iran, Iraq, Syria, and Jordan were held to discuss imposing "a military blockade on Israel from the north, east, and south."

- In early November, second-tier states, such as Pakistan, were brought into "the circle of confrontation."

- In late November, Damascus shared a comprehensive intelligence assessment with its Arab allies to warn of an impending major war.

These strategic moves were followed by tactical preparations: Syria moved troops to the edge of the Israeli-held security zone in southern Lebanon, a position that puts them within striking distance of Israel's early warning station on Mt. Hermon. In addition to Syria's march on the Golan, Iran stepped up shipments of arms to Hezbollah and terrorist forces stationed at the Israeli border. The Hezbollah weapons airlift reached its peak in the first week of December, just before the Task Force report was released.

Instead of this information making its way to the American public, however, it was ignored by the Clinton administration and shelved by the news media. Instead of reading this hard military intelligence about an imminent outbreak of war in the Middle East, we were reading about former secretaries of state criticizing the prime minister of Israel and slapping him on the hand over Jewish settlements in the West Bank. Our government *knows* that Israel is being surrounded by hostile Arab armies intent on her destruction. Yet, driven by the rubric of "a comprehensive peace in the Middle East," we keep pushing Israel to make concessions.

Much of the world has been lulled into a false sense of security because of peace agreements signed in the last few years.

But just how solid is this "paper peace"? In early January 1997, Egypt threatened that her peace agreement with Israel might not be worth the paper it was written on if Israel does not sign an agreement with Syria. Five days before the Clinton administration announced there could be "no comprehensive peace in the Middle East without Syria," Egypt gave what amounts to a formal warning to Israel. In an interview for Israeli media, Egyptian ambassador to Israel Mohammed Bassiouny said, "The agreement between Israel and Egypt will break if Israel doesn't sign [an agreement] with Syria and the rest of the Arab states. I want to make it clear that when Egypt signed the peace agreement with Israel [in 1979], it made the agreement subject to a general agreement with the Arab states. Both Egypt and Jordan are part of the Arab nation, and will never agree to remain the only partners of Israel."

Taken in light of the Task Force report on the Syrian and other Arab military buildup surrounding Israel, that is a chilling statement. Egypt and Jordan are the only two Arab countries to have signed peace treaties with Israel. Now Israel is told that if she doesn't sign an agreement with Syria—which would, of course, mean giving up the strategic Golan Heights—then she stands to lose her only peace partners in the Arab world. And, as we have already seen, we can expect the Clinton administration to fall right in line with this latest threat against Israel.

THE SAMSON OPTION

Perhaps the most frightening aspect of the current situation in the Middle East, reflected in the Task Force report, is the threat of nuclear war. Both Iran and Pakistan now possess nuclear weapons. And the Arab nations have a simple philosophy of nuclear warfare: the Muslim World, with its six million square miles of land and millions of soldiers, can absorb a massive nuclear attack and still survive; Israel cannot.

"The nuclear factor is essentially irrelevant," the report says, "for as long as Arab leaders can hold their position in a strategic nuclear brinkmanship. While Teheran and Damascus are willing to gamble on such a brinkmanship, Jerusalem cannot afford to be wrong—Israel will not survive as a viable country in the aftermath of a strike with the few tactical nuclear warheads Iran has." Nor can Israel necessarily rely on the United States to come to her aid in the face of a credible nuclear threat by Iran or Pakistan. Washington will be very hesitant to commit troops to the region if there is a serious risk of exposure to nuclear, biological or chemical weapons.

The extent of Israel's nuclear capability was completely unknown until 1986, when a disgruntled employee of Israel's top secret chemical reprocessing plant gave inside information and photographs to the London *Sunday Times*. Fired for his outspoken pro-Palestinian views, Mordecai Vanunu provided extensive details about Israel's nuclear capability, and estimated that Israel had stockpiled more than two hundred nuclear warheads—almost ten times the number of warheads estimated by our intelligence agencies at the time.

In 1991 Seymour Hersh, a Pulitzer Prize-winning journalist, published a political history of Israel's nuclear program, titled *The Samson Option*. According to Hersh, Vanunu's information was carefully analyzed by American weapons designers. "They concluded," he wrote, "that Israel was capable of manufacturing one of the most sophisticated weapons in the nuclear arsenal—a low-yield neutron bomb."

Israel's nuclear reactor at Dimona, in the Negev Desert, was built in 1958. For years its existence was one of the best kept secrets in military intelligence. Proponents of nuclear technology in Israel believed the only way to insure the nation's survival against its Arab enemies, who were backed by the Soviet Union, would be the deterrence of a bomb. They were right in that assessment. After the Six-Day War, the Soviet Union routinely targeted major Israeli cities with nuclear weapons. Israel returned the favor by repositioning some of its mobile missile launchers at Soviet targets.

In 1991, when Saddam Hussein began launching Scud missiles at Israel, the U.S. pledged support, including batteries of Patriot missiles, in return for an Israeli pledge not to retaliate. But what most people didn't know, according to Hersh, is that in those first few hours after the Scud attacks American satellite intelligence showed that Israel "had responded . . . by ordering mobile missile launchers armed with nuclear weapons moved into the open and deployed facing Iraq, ready to launch on command."

That Israel may once again face a barrage of Scud missiles from a hostile Arab nation requires no stretch of the imagination. Whether Israel would show such restraint again is uncertain, depending perhaps on the extent of damage inflicted on Israel and the amount and reliability of U.S. support offered. Some analysts foresee an escalating situation in which it might be conceivable that Israel, isolated by enemies and abandoned by allies, would be forced to use a doomsday weapon of massive destruction.

It is fascinating to me that three decades ago Israel coined the sobriquet "Samson Option" to describe its nuclear warfare option. Anyone familiar with the Old Testament will see the connection immediately: Samson was the biblical strongman who destroyed himself in the process of destroying Israel's enemies. But note the name and location of Israel's enemies as described in the Old Testament account of Samson (Judges 16).

Samson was in *Gaza* when he prayed to die with the enemies of Israel, the *Philistines*. Israel's so-called Samson Option was in place decades before Yasser Arafat, who claims his Palestinian people are descendants of the Philistines, was handed the Gaza Strip on a peace process platter. Now Arafat is building a concrete command bunker in Gaza, four stories underground, and his Palestinian "police" force is being armed by Iran and trained by Syria.

What is Arafat preparing for, if not war? And why does our government not acknowledge what he is doing? After the Hebron agreement, President Clinton invited Prime Minister Netanyahu to Washington. I was there, in the White House, for the press conference following their private meeting in mid-February 1997. Reporters threw only softballs to the president. No questions were asked about the military buildup of Israel's neighbors. No questions were asked about the illegal weapons being stockpiled by the Palestinian Authority.

I left Washington more convinced than ever of the conclusions drawn in this book. Without doubt the Arab world is preparing for war. They will be patient, but they will not let that "window of opportunity" close. Yet such a positive twist is put on the situation by Washington spinmeisters that the public is left with the impression of peace, not imminent war.

An illusion of peace when the reality is war—that calls to mind a verse of Scripture: "While people are saying, 'Peace and safety,' destruction will come on them suddenly . . ." (1 Thessalonians 5:3). The possibility of sudden destruction is very real in Israel. A few days after the Clinton-Netanyahu meeting, Maj. Gen. Meir Dagan, head of the prime minister's Anti-Terrorism Task Force, told the Israeli newspaper *Yediot Ahronot* that Israel is preparing for the prospect of nuclear or chemical terrorism. Dagan also stated his concern that Iran may be funneling unconventional weapons to terrorists.

Arms control reports show that Iran ranks third, behind China and North Korea, in nuclear weapons and ballistic missile development. Iran has stockpiled some two thousand tons of mustard gas. And China recently sold four hundred tons of chemicals to Iran, including the components for nerve gas.

Long-range ballistic missiles armed with nuclear or chemical warheads—does this sound like peace and safety . . . or a potential for sudden destruction?

Thirteen

The Voice of Prophecy

I CLIMBED to the top of the hill and looked out over the valley below. A few miles to the north I could see the city of Nazareth, its white-walled buildings glistening in the bright sunlight. Farther beyond, and to the east, was Tiberias, on the shore of the Sea of Galilee. Some eighteen miles to the northwest were the Mediterranean and the beautiful, modern port city of Haifa.

I was overlooking Megiddo, and the great plain that stretched out before me is the site where the Battle of Armageddon will take place. Countless bloody battles have been fought there. And for centuries various prophets have warned that the final conflict between the forces of good and evil would take place at Megiddo.

Napoleon is reported to have stood upon this hill to survey the great battlefield. Gazing in awe at the huge expanse of the Plain of Jezreel, which extends from the Mediterranean to the Jordan, he exclaimed, "All the armies of the world could maneuver for battle here."

As I looked down into what the Old Testament prophet Joel called the "valley of Jehoshaphat," I found myself wondering how long it would be until this scenic, tranquil spot would once again be filled with the men and machines of death and war.

It seems inevitable. When the Jews reestablished their nation in Palestine in 1948, they were immediately embroiled in a controversy—one that has never ended—over the ownership of the land. The Middle East conflict has become a sore that never heals, a pit of white-hot coals that can burst into roaring flames at any second. And it is a fire which could well draw in and involve all the nations of the world.

WHAT DANIEL SAW

For hundreds of years, Jewish and Christian Bible scholars have studied the scriptural prophecies. Many agree that there is one inescapable conclusion: the Middle East crisis will continue to escalate until it threatens the peace of the whole world. The problem will eventually involve all the nations of the earth, and will bring them to the precipice—to Armageddon—to what many now predict will be a thermonuclear holocaust.

One of the most accurate outlines of the future is found in the writings of the Prophet Daniel. His first recorded prophecy was actually the interpretation of a dream which came to Nebuchadnezzar, the powerful king of the Babylonian Empire. According to the late Dr. H. A. Ironside, this interpretation, which has come to be known as the ABC of Prophecy, "contains the most complete, and yet the most simple, prophetic picture that we have in all the Word of God."

History has already proved the accuracy of much that Daniel foretold, as world events have fulfilled what he said would come to pass. Now it appears that the stage is set for the remainder of the prophecy to develop.

Nebuchadnezzar's dream revealed the image of a man. His

head was of gold, his breast and arms were of silver, his midsection and thighs were brass, his legs were iron, and his feet were part iron and part clay. As the king watched, a great stone crashed down upon the statue, smashing it so completely that the wind blew away the pieces. Then the stone became a great mountain that filled the whole earth (see Daniel 2:31–35).

Daniel's interpretation of the dream was simple, yet profound. He said the head of gold represented Nebuchadnezzar, whose power in the Babylonian Empire was absolute. The other parts of the statue, Daniel said, represented future kingdoms that would follow Nebuchadnezzar, and a final kingdom that would crush all the other kingdoms and itself endure forever.

Many scholars now see relationships between Daniel's interpretation and later events in world history. The silver breast and arms of the image represented the Medo-Persian Empire which came to prominence after the fall of Babylon. The Grecian Empire, headed by Alexander the Great, was symbolized by the belly and thighs of brass. The legs of iron represented the might of the Roman Empire—and its division, both politically and spiritually, into east and west—while the feet, part iron and part clay, foretold the revival of the Roman Empire in the last days. The ten toes represent the ten leaders of this future European federation.

The stone that crushed the statue represents an all-powerful divine force that will ultimately destroy all earthly kingdoms and be recognized as supreme. This refers to the coming kingdom of the Messiah which will be established upon his return to earth. Remember that Jesus is called in Scripture the Cornerstone, "the stone the builders rejected."

Some forty years after Nebuchadnezzar's dream, Daniel had a vision which was a confirmation and extension of his first interpretation of the future. The vision consisted of the appearance of four beasts, which he saw as representing major world empires. Daniel saw a lion with eagle's wings, a bear with three ribs in its mouth, a leopard with four wings and four heads, and a strange ten-horned beast, "terrifying and frightening and very powerful" (Daniel 7:2–7).

Like the statue in Nebuchadnezzar's dream, the beasts in Daniel's vision represent succeeding kingdoms. The lion represents the Babylonian Empire headed by Nebuchadnezzar. The bear was the Medo-Persian Empire that followed, and the ribs in the bear's mouth indicated the three major conquests of that empire. Alexander the Great's Grecian Empire was represented by the leopard, the four heads indicating the division of the empire between four generals upon Alexander's death.

According to this system of interpretation, the beast with ten horns was the symbol of a revived Roman Empire to appear in the last days. Daniel noted that after a time another little horn grew up on the beast and plucked up three of the other horns by the roots. With eyes like a man and a mouth speaking great things, the little horn portrayed a powerful leader who would come in the end time.

THE LAST GREAT NATION

It could very well be that recent events in Europe fulfill the prediction of a revived Roman Empire described by Daniel. For several decades prophecy teachers have been saying, based on this prophecy, that the European Common Market (later called the European Economic Community) would develop into a political entity that would constitute a revived Roman empire.

That became a reality in 1993 with the advent of the European Community (EC). It united all of Western Europe—almost 350 million people—into a single market for goods and services.

The EC has also made provisions to establish a central bank, and a single currency will be issued for all EC countries by the end of the decade. At a special meeting with the president of the EU, he told me that by the twenty-first century United Europe would be the strongest economic democracy in the world, with an annual income of one trillion dollars.

The 1991 Club of Rome report, *The First Global Revolution*, applauds the move toward globalization by the EC. The authors state, "This new surge of integration among the ancient nations of Europe is not simply an economic or technocratic matter. It is essentially a process of historic political significance." Notice the recognition that it is the "ancient" nations of Europe who have formed this federation. And to the statement that the reunification is "of historic political significance," I would add that it is of great prophetic significance.

What many people don't realize is that the EC is more than just an economic alliance. It has also united Europe politically, under the leadership of a body called the European Union (EU). The national sovereignty of the member nations is being eroded by the increasing political power of this supranational entity.

And now that Western Europe is united into a common political body, there is even talk of establishing a common defense force—something else that would be of great significance prophetically. A defense alliance, called the Western European Union, has already been in place for several years and the EU is now working toward their stated goal of a Common Foreign and Security Policy. The next logical step would be a combined military force.

In 1960 Charles de Gaulle of France spoke of a unified Europe that would extend "from the Atlantic to the Ural Mountains." That, too, is coming to pass as alliances are being formed between the EU and the CEEC (Central and Eastern European

Countries). Already Bulgaria, the Czech Republic, Hungary, Poland, Romania, and Slovakia have been granted associate status, meaning they are eligible for potential membership in the EU.

The economic and political influence of the EU has reached into the Middle East. Israel signed a free-trade agreement with the EU in November 1995, and has also been accepted as an associate state in the EU's research and development scientific program.

However, the relationship is not without friction. Israel's foreign minister, David Levy, recently asked EU officials not to visit Palestinian Authority offices while in East Jerusalem. (The PA is not allowed to maintain government offices in Jerusalem under the Oslo agreements and the Netanyahu government is trying to force the closure of such offices.) EU officials, however, flatly refused the Israeli request.

Look for the political influence of the EU to expand dramatically in the coming years. Also look for the EU to put financial pressure on Israel over the Palestinian issue. Israel's economy is dependent on exporting products to the EU countries; the EU leaders could use that dependence as leverage to further the new world order's land-for-peace policy by demanding that Israel make territorial concessions in order to remain a trading partner with the EU.

And look for a leader to arise out of the EU—a "little horn" that will pluck three of the other horns up by the roots.

IDENTITY OF THE BEAST

Who is this "little horn," the powerful leader Daniel says will arise? He is also called the Antichrist in Scripture. While the Antichrist has yet to be revealed, the antichrist spirit is abroad in the world at this hour, as the gospels clearly indicate. Jesus said, "False Christs and false prophets will appear and perform great signs and miracles to deceive even the elect—if that were possible" (Matthew 24:24).

Over the centuries many have tried to usurp the authority and power of Christ, to seduce true believers by altering or misusing Scripture. Some of these have been as crafty and cunning as the snake in the Garden. But those who are fed on the Word should not be misled. Those who know the true Messiah will not be tricked by a mere imitation.

This general spirit of antichrist, and the many apostates who have trampled on the name and reputation of Jesus Christ, have been among us from the beginning. Paul and John make that very clear in their writings. But in the end times, one will come who is more attractive, more insidious, more deceptive, and more powerful because he will have on loan, as it were, the power of Satan himself. This "man of sin" or "man of lawlessness," as he is also called, is *the* Antichrist, the ultimate expression of hatred toward God and his Messiah.

Who is this Antichrist? Is he present now? Is he already visible in the world? Although he has not yet been revealed, I am convinced that Antichrist is a man among us; he is alive and well. Even at this hour he is perfecting his pitch and leading many astray, to be his followers and apologists when the hour comes that the wicked one will be revealed.

The true nature of this "man of sin" is indicated by the very theme of this book: the use of a phony peace process to betray Jerusalem. The Antichrist is not only the enemy of Christ, he is a destroyer of the Jews. He will make a treaty with Israel, drawing the nation into an evil alliance under the guise of a "comprehensive" peace. But this treaty will be a trick designed to deceive and destroy God's chosen people. The Antichrist will set up his kingdom; then, by shrewd judgments and apparently miraculous powers, he will convince millions that he is the most brilliant and gifted leader of the day. The originator of his powers, though, will be the False Prophet, who will operate behind the scenes to orchestrate his great and miraculous feats.

I do not believe we have enough information at this moment to name the Antichrist, even though there are a number of candidates who might be named. But there are clues in Scripture about this man and the false prophet who will go ahead of him. Even if we cannot discern who he is at this hour, I am certain these signs will help to confirm the identity of the Antichrist once he appears.

We know that Antichrist will make a miraculous recovery from an apparently fatal head wound. He will rule with such wisdom and insight that millions will idolize him. At first, they will be adoring fans; they will idolize him as a popular hero. But in time they will worship him as a god. And eventually, Revelation tells us, he will stand in the Temple at Jerusalem. He will declare himself to be God and command the nations to bow down before him.

The Antichrist will control currency and approve or disapprove of all commercial activities. He will command that everyone have a mark or ID number of some type on their hands or their foreheads to identify them as his followers. Anyone who does not have what John calls the "mark of the Beast" will not be allowed to buy or sell. They will be cut off, pariahs, unable to feed themselves or their children. John's vision gives this ominous warning:

> If anyone worships the beast and his image and receives his mark on his forehead or on his hand, he, too, will drink of the wine of God's fury, which has been poured full strength into the cup of his wrath. He shall be tormented with burning sulfur in the presence of the holy angels and of the Lamb. And the smoke of their torment rises forever and ever.

There is no rest day or night for those who worship the beast and his image, or for anyone who receives the mark of his name. (Revelation 14:9–11).

DANIEL'S SEVENTY WEEKS

Near the end of his life, Daniel began praying about returning to Jerusalem. He may well have remembered the prophecy of Jeremiah that had specified that the captivity of the Jews in Babylon would last seventy years. As that period of time came to an end, he began confessing his own sins and the sins of his people, crying out to God for forgiveness.

During his prayer, the angel Gabriel appeared to Daniel and revealed a timetable of coming events that would especially affect Israel. The angelic message, referred to as the vision of seventy weeks, is considered to be the backbone of end-time prophecy. This mathematical revelation gave the Jews the exact time at which to expect the coming of their Messiah. It also foretold his death, the destruction of Jerusalem, the rise of the Antichrist, and the establishment of the Messiah's coming kingdom on earth.

The prophecy said that seventy weeks (literally "seventy sevens") of trouble were coming upon the Jewish people. These "weeks" were not units of days, but of years. These 490 years would cover a series of events that would determine the eternal destiny of the Jews. From a definite starting point—when the order was given to rebuild Jerusalem—a period of sixty-nine weeks, or 483 years, would elapse before Messiah would come—and be rejected (see Daniel 9:24–26).

Interestingly enough, the Bible gives the precise date for that starting point, when Artaxerxes, king of Persia, granted the request of Nehemiah and decreed that Jerusalem should be rebuilt. The Bible says it happened "in the month of Nisan, in the twentieth year of Artaxerxes the king" (Nehemiah 2:1). When a particular day of the month was not stated, it was the Jewish custom to date an event on the first of the month. Since Artaxerxes had taken the throne in 465 B.C., his twentieth year would have been 445 B.C. So 483 years after the first day of Nisan in 445 B.C. would be the time the Anointed One, or Messiah, would appear in Jerusalem.

In calculating ancient dates, several things should be kept in mind. First of all, the Jewish year consisted of 360 days, so it is not exactly equivalent to our calendar year. For example, the 483 year period of Daniel's sixty-nine weeks would be roughly 476 years by our calendar. This would put the date of the Messiah's arrival in Jerusalem at approximately A.D. 31.

You may remember from your schooldays that miscalculations were made in switching from a lunar to a solar calendar and in reckoning the birth of Jesus Christ as the dividing line of history between B.C. and A.D. calendar years. Most historians now say that the birth of Christ must have happened between the years we designate as 7 B.C. and 4 B.C. We know that he was born before Herod the Great died, an event which can be definitely dated in 4 B.C.

That puts the beginning date of Jesus' public ministry somewhere around 26 A.D. and his death and resurrection around 30 A.D. Again, these dates are approximate, because the Bible does not give the exact date of either Jesus' birth or his death. Some scholars, using Daniel's sixty-nine weeks, have calculated the fulfillment of his messianic prophecy at the precise date of 6 Nisan 32 A.D. While I don't think we can prove that date with absolute certainty, it is obvious that the time of the appearance of Jesus Christ in Jerusalem falls squarely within the parameters of Daniel's extraordinary prophecy.

Also, Daniel's prophecy went on to say that the Messiah would be "cut off," which is a euphemism for being killed. After that, an army would march in and destroy Jerusalem and the Temple, which had been rebuilt by the returned Babylonian exiles. Since the destruction of Jerusalem and the Temple were carried out by Titus of Rome in 70 A.D., the Messiah had to have appeared before then. There again, the most logical choice to have fulfilled Daniel's prophecy is Jesus of Nazareth. But what happened to the last "week," the last seven years covered by Daniel's vision of seventy weeks? These events are yet to come.

Many Bible scholars see a break between Daniel's sixty-ninth week, when the Messiah is cut off, and the beginning of the seventieth week, which marks the end of the age. This gap before the final week of Daniel's prophecy represents the entire church age. As the time arrives for that seventieth week, the church will be "raptured," or caught up in the air to meet Messiah (see 1 Thessalonians 4:16–18, 1 Corinthians 15:51–52).

Then the seventieth week begins—the last seven years of time on earth before the Millennium, the establishment of the kingdom of God on earth for a thousand-year reign of peace. But these seven years are to be the most awful time in the history of the world, a period characterized by great tribulation, the Bible says.

It is also called the "time of Jacob's trouble." The Prophet Jeremiah said, "How awful that day will be! None will be like it. It will be a time of trouble for Jacob, but he will be saved out of it" (Jeremiah 30:7). Messiah said, "For then there will be great distress, unequaled from the beginning of the world until now—and never to be equaled again" (Matthew 24:21). The Prophet Daniel declared, "There will be a time of distress such as has not happened from the beginning of nations until then" (Daniel 12:1).

As this fearsome era nears, the "terrifying and frightening and very powerful" ten-horned beast that Daniel had prophesied about earlier appears on the scene in the form of a revived Roman Empire. Out of this ten-nation European federation will emerge a powerful political leader whose magnetic charm and personal appeal will win the confidence and loyalty of the world.

The specific marker Daniel gives that will begin the final seven-year period is the making of a covenant of peace with Israel by this immensely powerful leader, whom the Bible identifies as the Antichrist (Daniel 9:27). He will offer solutions to the perplexing problems and international crises that threaten the very existence of the world.

At first everything will appear to be going well. The centuries of armed tension will be relieved by the peace imposed by the power of Antichrist. Israel will be able to turn its full attention to the development of the country and its resources, and will prosper as never before. Some arrangement will even have permitted the rebuilding of the Temple in Jerusalem and the resumption of sacrifices and oblations.

Just when peace seems to have come for Israel, however, it will be taken from her. After three and one-half years, the Antichrist will break his treaty with Israel. He will go to the Temple and cause the sacrifice and offering to cease and bring about the "abomination of desolation" by proclaiming himself to be God.

THE BRINK OF ARMAGEDDON

Let's look now to Ezekiel and Revelation to see how the world situation could erupt in a crisis that would bring about the fulfillment of Daniel's prophecy. With the regathering of the Jews to their land and the rebirth of Israel, Ezekiel's track record as a prophet is totally convincing. He speaks in specific detail about coming events which will bring the world to the awesome edge of Armageddon.

We often speak incorrectly of the "Battle of Armageddon" as if it were a single event. The Bible actually describes a series of battles that culminates on the plain of Megiddo in a cataclysmic event referred to as Armageddon.

In Ezekiel 38 and 39, the prophet gives a detailed account of a great military offensive which will be launched against Israel by Russia and a confederation of Arab and European countries. Ezekiel identifies the participants in the invading force with names such as Magog, Meshech, Tubal, Gomer, Togarmah, and such familiar appellations as Persia, Ethiopia, and Libya.

A great many prophecy scholars are convinced that the evidence identifies Magog as Russia, and Meshech and Tubal as the cities of Moscow and Tobolsk. Gomer refers to Germany and Slovakia, Togarmah is Southern Russia and Turkey, Persia is modern Iran (and may include Iraq), and Ethiopia and Libya include the black descendants of Cush and the North African Arabs.

This is the combined force that will arm itself and march against Israel. Russia will lead the invasion at a time when war is not expected. Having made a treaty with the Antichrist, the emerging world leader, Israel will have been lulled into a false sense of security as a result of the three and one-half years of peace and prosperity she has enjoyed. Ezekiel says Russia "will invade a land that has recovered from war, whose people were gathered from many nations to the mountains of Israel. . . . They had been brought out from the nations, and now all of them live in safety" (38:8).

Some people have thought that the collapse of the Soviet Union makes a coming invasion of Israel by that region unlikely. Just the opposite is true. Russia still controls most of the massive arsenal of the former Soviet Union, and because of economic hardship and unstable leadership, the country is more likely than ever to forge a strategic alliance that would give the Russians access to the vast oil reserves of the Arab nations.

There is already evidence that, following the collapse of the Soviet Union, some of the terrorist-sponsoring states are trying to buy nuclear weapons directly from disaffected military personnel in the former Soviet republics. In fact, they may already have done so. Russian president Boris Yeltsin told former president George Bush at a February 1992 meeting that he was concerned that "certain Islamic states" were trying to buy tactical nuclear weapons from the new republic of Kazakhstan, which has a Muslim majority.

Of even more concern is a report from Ukraine. At a 1992 Moscow conference conducted by the International Security Council, it was disclosed that a strategic base in Ukraine had been penetrated, with disastrous results: three nuclear weapons were missing. According to Russian military sources, the empty containers for the nuclear devices were found outside the security perimeter fence of the base. Russian officials are worried that, under economic pressure, some enterprising officer may smuggle out a few weapons and sell them to the highest bidder.

Iran, a terrorist state exporting Islamic fundamentalism throughout the world, has just purchased its third Soviet submarine. And Moscow, ignoring severe opposition from the United States, agreed to build two additional nuclear reactors in Iran. So a strategic alliance of the type foreseen by Ezekiel is highly plausible as well as possible.

Not only is such an alliance possible, but weapons capable of producing the incredible destruction described in Scripture are readily available. Equally as devastating as the threat of nuclear warfare is the specter of germ warfare, the uncontrollable spread of deadly disease as a weapon of war. Terrorist states are experimenting with deadly bacteria, and some are believed to have stockpiles of BW agent. There is no longer any doubt that biological as well as chemical weapons, and the means to deliver them, are in the hands of rogue regimes in the Middle East.

The lethal effects of germ warfare are startling. Dr. Kathleen Bailey, former associate director of the Arms Control and Disarmament Agency, testified before Congress that a container the size of a tennis ball could hold enough BW agent to kill or injure 100,000 people if released in an enclosed space. Invisible, odorless, and virtually undetectable, BW agent is a concentrated dose of lethal disease germs that can spread rapidly in the air.

Ezekiel's account of this great military offensive called Armageddon harmonizes with Daniel's prophecy. Daniel said, "At the time of the end the king of the South (probably Egypt, at the head of an Arab and African confederacy) will engage him (the Antichrist) in battle" (Daniel 11:40). The thought of Israel's Arab neighbors launching an attack on Israel stretches no one's imagination. There is an almost constant patter of anti-Israeli propaganda flowing from the Middle East. And with the exception of Egypt and Jordan, the other Arab nations have remained technically at war with Israel since 1948.

In the same verse, Daniel says that "the king of the North (Russia and confederates) will storm out against him with chariots and cavalry and a great fleet of ships. He will invade many countries and sweep through them like a flood" (11:40). Russia will choose this moment of instability and chaos to make its move into the Middle East and Africa. The Russians will keep moving right through Israel and down into Egypt (11:42–43). The mention of the northern king's large fleet points to amphibious assaults against Israel and Egypt from ships deployed in the Mediterranean.

Russia's attack on Israel, though seemingly unstoppable, will be her greatest military blunder. The brief battle will undoubtedly be one of the most destructive in history. Ezekiel says that when Russia's hordes have invaded Israel as "a cloud that covers the land," there will come a great shaking, with earth-splitting explosions, mountains toppling, and a deadly rain of hail and fire (Ezekiel 38:19–23).

The vision is strongly suggestive of nuclear warfare. Whatever it is, the prophet says that the defeat of the northern invaders will make it clear to the Jews that God has protected them. Ezekiel says that the destruction of Russia's great army will be so devastating that it will take Israel seven months to bury all the bodies left behind, and the burning of the weapons will go on for seven years.

THE CLASH OF TITANS

With the destruction of the Arab and Russian forces, only two great spheres of power will remain to fight the final battle in the Armageddon offensive. The combined forces of Western civilization under the leadership of the Roman dictator, Antichrist, will face the vast hordes of the Orient, probably united behind the Red Chinese war machine.

The attack by Russia will give the Antichrist the excuse for full occupation of Israel under the pretense of protection. With forty-two months remaining in the last prophetic "week," the Antichrist will suddenly begin asserting his power and trying to gain control of the entire world.

At this point he will break his treaty with Israel, and refuse to allow further sacrifices or rituals at the Temple. Instead, Antichrist will commit the "abomination of desolation" and desecrate the Holy of Holies by using it as a platform to declare himself to be God and demanding the worship of all mankind. He will also assume total economic control, requiring his mark on the hand or forehead in order for any person to transact any business. The penalty for opposing him will be death (Revelation 13:15–17).

Now a new challenge will face the Antichrist: a massive Oriental army marching toward the Middle East. "But reports from the east (China) and the north (perhaps the NATO allies) will alarm him, and he will set out in a great rage to destroy and annihilate many" (Daniel 11:44).

In Revelation 16:12 we read that an angel will empty his bowl over the great river Euphrates so that its water will dry up to allow passage for the kings of the East. And so the hordes of Chinese can move even more quickly toward the final battle (Revelation 16:16). The troop concentrations and the weight of armor committed to this battle will dwarf anything known in the history of warfare.

Cataclysmic is insufficient to describe the results of the final battle in the plain of Megiddo. The Bible says the casualties of this confrontation will total one-third of the remaining world population. John wrote in Revelation: "The number of the mounted troops was two hundred million. I heard their number.

"The horses and riders I saw in my vision looked like this: Their breastplates were fiery red, dark blue, and yellow as sulfur. The heads of the horses resembled the heads of lions, and out of their mouths came fire, smoke and sulfur. A third of mankind was killed by the three plagues of fire, smoke and sulfur that came out of their mouths" (Revelation 9:16–18). This might be describing an all-out nuclear attack, with the "horses" being motorized tanks or mobile-based missiles.

So here it is, the last great conflict. The battle lines are drawn throughout Israel, with the vortex centered in the Plain of Megiddo. The Apostle John predicts that so many people will be slaughtered in the conflict that blood will stand up to the horses' bridles for a total distance of two hundred miles northward and southward of Jerusalem (Revelation 14:20). It's almost unimaginable, but the bloodshed from the fighting in and around Jerusalem and along the Jordan valley will flow into the two-hundred-mile-long rift that runs from the Sea of Galilee in the north, down the Jordan River valley, down the length of the Dead Sea, and thence down the Wadi Arabah (a dry riverbed) the entire length of the Negev to Eilat on the Gulf of Aqaba.

In addition to the indescribable slaughter in the Middle East, there will be a worldwide shock wave that will race around the globe and destroy all the cities of the nations. The biblical record isn't clear as to whether the destruction will come from a natural force like an earthquake or from some super weapon. But in an instant, all the great cities of the world—Paris, London, Tokyo, New York—will be gone (see Revelation 16:19).

As the battle reaches its awful climax it appears that all life on earth will be destroyed—and at that moment Messiah returns to save man from self-extinction. Jesus prophesied, "If those days had not been cut short, no one would survive, but for the sake of the elect those days will be shortened. . . . They will see the Son of Man coming on the clouds of the sky, with power and great glory" (Matthew 24:22,30).

Only with the coming of the Messiah of Israel will lasting peace come to the Middle East, and to the world. Daniel declared, "the God of heaven will set up a kingdom that will never be destroyed" (2:44).

When the governments of men have finally fallen, God will set up his kingdom, and the long-awaited millennium will begin. The word *millennium* means "one thousand years," and in biblical interpretation, this refers to that period of time when there will be total peace among people and nations. Jerusalem will at last become the City of Peace and the capital of the world.

Isaiah described this glorious time which is coming by saying, "They will beat their swords into plowshares and their spears into pruning hooks. Nation will not take up sword against nation, nor will they train for war anymore" (Isaiah 2:4).

Prophecy is not given to us in Scripture just so we can know beforehand what will happen in the future. It is given so we will humble our hearts in repentance and seek God, to find out how God would have us participate in that prophecy, and to pray earnestly for its fulfillment. Prophecy is given not only so we can understand our times, but so we can be a part of God's plan.

That excites me. I want to be a part of what God is doing in these last days. And that's the reason so much of my ministry has centered on Israel—it's where God's attention is about to be focused for the final events of history. We need to reaffirm our commitment to the Bible as the true Word of God, and we need to hear it speak to us, urging us to stand with Jerusalem's defenders against those who are trying to bring about the final betrayal of the Holy City. We who have glimpsed God's mighty purpose for Jerusalem must pray and work to see God's prophetic program fulfilled.

THE MASTER CONSPIRATOR

Throughout these pages I have talked about a modern conspiracy against the nation of Israel in general, and against the city of Jerusalem in particular. The cast of collaborators in this conspiracy has been revealed: world powers, the United Nations, American presidents and their governments, European governments, Arab terrorists, Soviet agitators, and even the major news media. Many whose motives are essentially benign have been drawn into this ancient plot. But behind them all there is a single "master conspirator" who is calling the shots.

He is described in Scripture as the "prince of darkness."

Satan, the great deceiver, has deceived the governments of the world into carrying out his work of destruction against God's city in the name of "peace." Satan, the father of lies, has whispered slander and falsehood and the news media have unwittingly reported it as truth. Satan, who comes only to steal, kill and destroy, has sent his henchmen into the souls of murderers and hatemongers who kill and terrorize the Jewish people.

All these collaborators are convinced they are absolutely right about the situation in the Middle East. They do not know that they have been duped by the prince of darkness and are carrying out the work of darkness that the prophets had predicted many centuries earlier. In reality, this modern political conspiracy springs from an ancient spiritual conspiracy. And the real battle for Jerusalem is not taking place between Israelis and Palestinians, but between supernatural forces in the heavenly realms.

This spiritual conspiracy has been going on since the opening moments of time—since the day Lucifer said, "*I will* ascend to heaven; *I will* raise my throne above the stars of God; *I will* sit enthroned on the mount of assembly, on the utmost heights of the sacred mountain. *I will* ascend above the tops of the clouds; *I will* make myself like the Most High" (Isaiah 14:13–14, italics mine). His arrogance and pride, and his lust for God's own power cost this being of light everything: he was cast from heaven. Jesus the Messiah said, "I saw Satan fall like lightning from heaven" (Luke 10:18).

Having failed in the role for which he was created in heaven, Satan has since tried to stake claim to the City of God on this earth, to Mount Zion, the "sacred mountain" of God. The earthly throne of God and the site of the Jewish temple is also called in Scripture Mount Moriah, the place where Abraham prepared to sacrifice Isaac, the son of God's promise. If he could not have heaven, Satan would have Zion itself and draw people to himself from every nation. And if he could not defeat Jesus Christ in the heavenlies, then he has imagined vainly that he will defeat him at Jerusalem.

The Mount of Zion represents God's authority and rulership over all creation, and Satan covets it for his very own. Knowing that Jerusalem is not only the city of God, but the place to which Messiah will come, Satan would like nothing more than to destroy it and to thwart God's eternal plan.

No wonder Jerusalem has been the scene of so much conflict. As you have witnessed through the pages of this book, this ancient city has witnessed violence and rage and persecution since the time of King David, three thousand years ago. And we know that it will continue to be embroiled in controversy until Christ returns.

The fuse has already been lit that will ignite the final conflagration around Jerusalem before Armageddon. The nations of the world are aligned for spiritual and physical warfare against the City of God. Unless the world's course against Jerusalem is reversed, God's fury will ultimately be unleashed upon the nations of the world. God spoke through the prophet Zechariah, "On that day I will set out to destroy all the nations that attack Jerusalem" (Zechariah 12:9).

God has promised that he will one day even the score. There will come a time when he will no longer allow the nations of the world to wage war against Jerusalem. And those who have come against the city will pay an awful price. The prophet says: "This is the plague with which the Lord will strike all nations that fought against Jerusalem: Their flesh will rot while they are still standing on their feet, their eyes will rot in their sockets, and their tongues will rot in their mouths. On that day men will be stricken by the Lord with great panic" (Zechariah 14:12–13). What a frightening punishment for those who afflict God's city!

When I walk the streets of Jerusalem today, my heart is often broken by the evidence of hatred and destruction, all signs of the soon-coming approach of Apocalypse. Israel is now in great turmoil, isolated in the world, and deeply divided over the great land giveaway that has been extorted from her by diplomatic thugs.

The prophetic purpose of my calling and the motivation behind my ministry has been to warn the nations that those who oppose Jerusalem are opposing God's will. The purpose in writing this book has been to encourage Christians to become defenders of the Holy City. These historical accounts of Jerusalem and the stories of international conferences will no doubt fade from our memories. But may we never lose the sense of urgency to pray for the peace of Jerusalem.

> *Pray for the peace of Jerusalem:*
> *"May those who love you be secure.*
> *May there be peace within your walls*
> *and security within your citadels."*
> *For the sake of my brothers and friends,*
> *I will say, "Peace be within you."*
> Psalm 122:6–8

Afterword

The Light in the Tunnel

"When Israelis add an opening to a tunnel in Jerusalem, Arab regimes protest. When Jews excavate their archaeological sites, the PLO wages a guerrilla war, the Arab League stages diplomatic campaigns, and the world media are outraged. If Mr. Yasser Arafat is angry, the United States hurries to invite Israel's prime minister and Arab leaders to discuss the matter."

Such words might be expected from Jewish leaders in Israel or from someone on the right of the political spectrum, but in fact they are from the opening paragraph of an advertisement appearing in the Washington *Times*, October 9, 1996, headlined: "Who is the oppressor in the Middle East? Who is killing peace?"

The half-page ad is signed by representatives of seven different Arab, Islamic and Christian organizations, all based in the U.S., along with the Stockholm-based Middle East Christian Committee. The ad goes on to list the "criminals against humanity in that region" and to detail the oppression and persecution of Christians and ethnic minorities living there.

Well-timed and appropriately placed to draw attention to the plight of those who are truly suffering in the Middle East conflict, this announcement called on the U.S. government to invite the Arab leaders to meet with the South Sudanese, Lebanese Christian, and Kurdish leaders, "and the leadership of all endangered minorities in the Middle East." Several months have passed, and this urgent petition has faded into obscurity. Did anyone really expect the cries of suffering Christians and Jews to be heard in Washington, D.C.?

As a result of recent events in Jerusalem, perhaps tourists should now be included as "endangered minorities in the Middle East." As shown in these pages, the opening of a new exit to an archeological tunnel—to relieve congestion and allow more visitors to view what is surely one of the wonders of the ancient world—sparked deadly violence. What should have been an occasion for celebration turned into gun battles that left seventy people dead and hundreds more wounded. It was the worst fighting in the territories since Palestinian self-rule began.

Why should the harmless act of opening an exit to a popular tourist site create so much chaos? Even in the Middle East, where it is by no means rare for old passions to burst out from time to time, these Western Wall Tunnel incidents stand out as a symptom of the deep distress with the present political situation and a dire warning of worse things to come.

THE DARKNESS IN THE HEART

By now it should be obvious that disputes in the Holy Land are not about tunnels or territories. They are about Israeli sovereignty over Jerusalem, which the Palestinian Authority (PA) tries to undermine whenever and wherever the opportunity presents itself. The PA's attempts to establish "centers of power" inside Jerusalem cause a continual conflict. Attempts to freeze Jewish development in Jerusalem, whether in the building of new neighborhoods or in archeological excavations that reveal Jerusalem's Jewish past, are another source of conflict.

Yasser Arafat continues to make the baseless claim that the Oslo Accords prevent Israel from "Judaizing" Jerusalem. Nowhere do the agreements question Israel's absolute sovereignty over Jerusalem. Yet Arafat and the Palestinian leaders are looking to the outside world for authority to continue their offensive against the legitimate Jewish authority in Israel.

In the darkness of a Jerusalem tunnel, most observers failed to notice the only truly new historic event in the Middle East: that a Palestinian armed force, accepted reluctantly by Israel into its midst as an unavoidable part of the peace process, had turned its weapons on Israelis. Whatever one may think of the wisdom or even the timing of opening the tunnel exit, it is a simple fact of life in the Middle East that such violence and hatred will find new sources to feed on. The friction point may be an archaeological tunnel today, but it will be something else tomorrow. For the underlying cause is not the darkness in the tunnel, but the darkness in the human heart—and that will prove to be the flashpoint of an even greater terror sometime in the not very distant future.

The essence of a peace process should be overcoming issues that divide us in pursuit of a satisfactory common goal. A peace process that entails the possibility of war is a contradiction in terms. But that is where Israel stands at this hour. While her Arab neighbors continue to urge acceleration of the "peace process," they appear to be preparing for another major war.

But, as bad as the situation may seem, I remain optimistic about the future of Israel and the City of Peace. Israel is a miracle nation. It was born by a miracle and lives by a miracle. The

Jewish people have been preserved by the hand of God throughout history. Marked for extinction, they have survived and prospered against all odds. Scattered throughout the world, these "dry bones" of Ezekiel's vision have been miraculously restored in the land of the Bible.

As Christians, we believe in the blessed hope of Christ's return. The Jews also have a glorious hope that their Messiah, for which they have prayed for so many centuries, will indeed come. The great debate between Christians and Jews is not whether Messiah is coming. The debate is over this question: "What is Messiah's name?" But there is no doubt that Messiah will come. And when he does, the armies and navies of all the world powers combined will not be able to hinder his prophetic plan for the nation of Israel. The so-called new world order will pass into oblivion when God's new order is finally revealed. So when things look bleak, when the prospects for peace look dim—look up. Redemption is near.

Until that day of redemption arrives we must not succumb to complacency and we dare not compromise with the enemies of God. Rather, we must remain committed to obedience to the Word of God. If we desire God's blessing, then we must bless his people, the People of the Book, with unconditional love. We must stand not only with God's people, but with his city, Jerusalem. His word urges us to this commitment: "You who call on the Lord, give yourselves no rest, and give him no rest till he establishes Jerusalem and makes her the praise of the earth" (Isaiah 62:6–7).

God has promised to be an ever-vigilant sentry over the walls of Jerusalem. His word assures us that "he who watches over Israel will neither slumber nor sleep" (Psalm 121:4). Israelis and Palestinians may wrangle over a final settlement on the issue of Jerusalem, but the city's final status was decided millennia ago by her true Sovereign. Jerusalem may have been betrayed by the peace process, but that betrayal is not her final destiny.

Then I saw a new heaven and a new earth, for the first heaven and the first earth had passed away, and there was no longer any sea. I saw the Holy City, the new Jerusalem, coming down out of heaven from God, prepared as a bride beautifully dressed for her husband. And I heard a loud voice from the throne saying, "Now the dwelling of God is with men, and he will live with them. They will be his people, and God himself will be with them and be their God. There will be no more death or mourning or crying or pain, for the old order of things has passed away."

Revelation 21:1–4

Appendix A

In Their Own Words

The following list of direct quotations from media sources will provide a compelling portrait of what PLO Chairman Yasser Arafat and the Palestinians are saying about events and issues in Israel today. All but a few of these statements were made *after* the signing of the Declaration of Principles on September 13, 1993.

About Jerusalem and the Holy Places

"The Israelis are mistaken if they think we do not have an alternative to negotiations. By Allah I swear they are wrong. The Palestinian people are prepared to sacrifice the last boy and the last girl so that the Palestinian flag will be flown over the walls, the churches, and the mosques of Jerusalem."

> — *Yasser Arafat, a speech on August 6, 1995,*
> *at a party to celebrate the birth of his daughter;*
> *as reported in* Jerusalem Post, *September 7, 1995*

"There isn't a single stone here that has a connection with the Jews. We are willing to permit the Jews to pray outside the Wall. But that doesn't give them ownership rights."

> — *Ekrima Sa'aid Sabri, PLO-appointed mufti of Jerusalem;* Religion News Service, *November 8, 1994*

"Jerusalem is the capital of the Palestinian state, whether they like it or not. If they don't like it, let them drink out of the Sea of Gaza."

> — *Yasser Arafat, in a speech in Gaza;* Agence France Presse, *October 16, 1994*

"We are now preparing our national institutions for the establishment of the Palestinian state whose capital will be holy Jerusalem."

> — *Yasser Arafat, in a speech to the Organization of African Unity in Tunis on June 13, 1994. Reported in* Yediot Ahronot, *June 14, 1994*

"The jihad will continue . . . You have to understand our main battle is Jerusalem . . . You have to come and to fight a jihad to liberate Jerusalem, your precious shrine . . . No, it is not their capital. It is our capital."

> — *Yasser Arafat, in a speech delivered at a Johannesburg mosque on May 10, 1994;* Israel Radio, *May 17, 1994;* Jerusalem Post, *May 18, 1994*

"There will not be peace without Jerusalem. Our independence will not be complete without Jerusalem. Beloved Jerusalem will return to us, despite the obstinance and the Zionist hypocrisy."

— *General Haj Ismail,*
Palestinian Liberation Army commander in Jericho,
Yediot Ahronot, *May 15, 1994*

"We expect the Israelis to give us back these holy places . . . We believe in freedom of religion. But Jews won't have rights there because these are our places."

— *Hasan Tahboub, head of the PLO-backed*
Supreme Muslim Council,
Jerusalem Report, *December 16, 1993*

About Israel and the Jewish people

Israel is "a demon" that "swallows up everything, including the peace process."

— *Yasser Arafat,*
New York Times,
August 7, 1996

"We must remember that the main enemy of the Palestinian people, now and forever, is Israel. This is a truth that must never leave our minds."

— *Freih Abu Middein, PLO Minister of Justice, in a speech at*
Al Azhar University in Gaza;
Al-Nahar, *April 11, 1995;*
Jerusalem Post, *April 17, 1995*

"We as Palestinians must understand that the central enemy is Israel."

> — *Farouk Qaddumi*
> *head of the PLO Political Department*
> Ha'aretz, *December 16, 1994*

"I miss the shooting of the Israelis. I hope the Israelis come back again, so we can shoot them again. I always dreamed of the day the Palestinian troops would come to Palestine. Now, I hope we go to war against the Israelis and take all of the West Bank and all of Palestine."

> — *Arafat Abushabab, head of the Fatah Hawks*
> *in the Shabura camp in Rafah, Gaza*
> New York Times Magazine, *November 17, 1994*

"Our enemy is a lowly enemy. The Palestinian people know there is a state that was established through coercion and it must be destroyed. This is the Palestinian way."

> — *Farouk Qaddumi,*
> *head of the PLO Political Department,*
> *in a speech at a ceremony marking the closing*
> *of the PLO radio station in Algiers,* Reuters,
> *August 10, 1994;*
> Yediot Ahronot, *August 10, 1994*

"We warn our leaders to stop the negotiations with Israel."

> — *Fatah gunman*
> *at a rally in the Jabaliya refugee camp*
> *in Gaza,* Associated Press, *April 3, 1994*

Appendix A

"Rabin has to remove all the settlers from the West Bank and Gaza and transfer them to hell."
— *Jibril Rajoub, senior adviser to Yasser Arafat,*
Yediot Ahronot, *March 4, 1994*

"As a Palestinian police officer, I will not hesitate to give my gun to anyone who approaches me and tells me he is going to commit an attack against the army or the settlers. I will even kiss the gun before and after the operation."
— *PLO police recruit from Ramallah,*
Iton Yerushalayim, *December 10, 1993*

"Slaughter the Jews!"
— *Chant heard in mosques throughout Gaza,*
Yediot Ahronot, *November 26, 1993*

About the Phased Plan
"In order to obtain the goal of returning to Palestine, all of us sometimes have to grit our teeth. But it is forbidden that this harm the continued struggle against the Zionist enemy. Cooperation and understanding between the PLO and the rejectionist organizations is what will lead to the speedy retreat of Israel from the occupied territories in the first stage, until the establishment of a Palestinian state with its capital in Jerusalem. Only a state like that can then continue the struggle to remove the enemy from all Palestinian lands."
— *Yasser Arafat, in a letter to heads of the rejectionist front in neighboring*
Arab countries,
Jerusalem Post, *November 18, 1994*

"It is only a cease-fire until the next stage."
— *Abbas Zaki, member of PLO Executive Committee,*
Jerusalem Post, *March 16, 1994*

"We have to accept the deal and wait for a change in the circumstances that could lead to the elimination of Israel."
— *Abu el-Aynayn, PLO chief of a refugee camp in Lebanon,* US News and World Report, *September 27, 1993*

"Our slogan of the 'present phase' is not 'from the sea to the Jordan River.' We did not give up, and we will not give up, on any of the obligations to which we have been committed for more than seventy years. We have, in our Palestinian Arab society, the ability to struggle against the divided Israel society, which is characterized by conflicts that haunt it. Sooner or later, we will force Israeli society to join a larger society, that is, our Arab society, and we will thereby bring about the dissolving of the Zionist entity in stages."
— *Faisal Husseini, PLO Minister for Jerusalem Affairs, interview in the Jordanian newspaper* A-Ra'i, *November 12, 1992*

About Jihad (Holy War)
"The commitment still stands and the oath is still valid: that we will continue this long jihad, this difficult jihad . . . via deaths, via sacrifices."
— *Yasser Arafat, in a speech at Al-Azhar University in Gaza on June 19, 1995,* Jerusalem Post, *August 3, 1995*

"Holy war is our path. My death will be martyrdom. I will knock on the gates of Paradise with the skulls of the sons of Zion."

— *Ayman Radi, Traffic policeman in the PLO force, in a written note to his family before he carried out a suicide bombing in Jerusalem, New York Times, December 26, 1994*

About the Armed Resistance, or Intifada

"We have several options available, political, economic, and social, which we can exercise if Netanyahu's position does not change—among them is armed struggle, using the weapons which the Palestinian Authority has."

— *Col. Mohammed Dahlan, Commander, Palestinian Preventive Security in Gaza, Ha'aretz, September 3, 1996*

If Israel does not make concessions on Jerusalem, settlements, etc.

"We shall go back to the struggle and strife, as we did for forty years. It is not beyond our capabilities. . . . All the acts of violence will return. Except that this time we'll have thirty-thousand armed Palestinian soldiers who will operate in areas in which we have unprecedented elements of freedom."

— *Nabil Sha'ath, PLO minister, Jerusalem Post, March 15, 1996*

"There will be an intifada not just in Jerusalem, but in all the occupied territories and in all the Middle East."

— *Faisal Husseini, PLO Minister for Jerusalem Affairs, Voice of Israel radio, May 21, 1995; Ha'aretz, May 22, 1995*

"We must always remember that our enemy is the Israeli occupation, and it is incumbent upon us to continue to struggle against it through the blessed intifada. . . . Only the intifada can carry our nation to a more advanced stage."

— Farouk Qaddumi,
head of the PLO Political Department,
Ha'aretz, *December 16, 1994*

"If there are those who oppose the agreement with Israel, the gates are open to them to intensify the armed struggle."

— Jibril Rajoub, PLO security chief,
Yediot Ahronot, *May 27, 1994*

"The peace process will not prevent the continued struggle of our people against the illegal actions of the Israeli occupier."

— From a petition signed by Dr. Haidar Abdel-Shafi, former head of the
Palestinian delegation to the peace talks with Israel, and other PLO
leaders, New York Times, *April 26, 1994*

"There is no decision in Fatah to cease the armed struggle against the occupation."

— Abbas Zaki, member of the PLO Executive Committee and nominee to
head the police force,
Jerusalem Post, *March 16, 1994*

"In case the Israeli army tries to arrest any of us, we will not hesitate to shoot. I will never surrender."

— Hisham Jouda, Commander of the Fatah Hawks in Gaza, Jerusalem
Post, *September 27, 1993*

Appendix A

"Palestine is only a stone's throw away for a small Palestinian boy or girl."

— Yasser Arafat, Jordanian TV, September 13, 1993

About an Independent Palestinian State

"Soon we will declare the establishment of the Palestinian state on the lands of the homeland. I tell Israel, that if it doesn't carry out the agreement in practice, the Palestinians will not have an alternative."

—Yasser Arafat, visiting Nablus, Ha'aretz, September 1, 1996

The direction Arafat will take with the Netanyahu government

"In the end there'll be a collision. The Palestinians will never give up on their own state. It's the raison d'être for Palestinian existence. Netanyahu will find that out for himself. Nor is a state in Gaza the answer. The West Bank is the heart."

— Khalil Shikaki, political analyst and head of the Center for Palestine Research, Jerusalem Report, August 8, 1996

"We are going to continue the Palestinian revolution until the last martyr to create a Palestinian state."

— Yasser Arafat, in a speech in Gaza on the 30th anniversary of the founding of Fatah, Agence France Presse, January 1, 1995

"I am convinced that our people are now on the way to establishing a Palestinian state. The agreement signed in Cairo is the first step in establishing the state, and therefore it should be implemented."

> — *Yasser Arafat, in an interview immediately after the signing
> ceremony, Radio Monte Carlo, May 4, 1994*

"We are building a Palestinian national authority that we know will be a state in the future."

> — *Faisal Husseini, senior PLO leader,* Jerusalem Post,
> *February 4, 1994*

"Here is Palestine being reborn again as a national entity on its way to becoming an independent state."

> — *Yasser Arafat, from Algiers, Voice of Palestine radio,
> December 31, 1993*

"I am not Mr. Chairman. I am His Excellency, the President of Palestine."

> — *Yasser Arafat, in response to a greeting by Swedish Prime Minister
> Carl Bildt,* Jerusalem Post, *December 17, 1993*

After the wave of suicide bombings in early 1996
"Hamas is part of the national movement and it has its own style and approach to action. It is resisting the Israeli enemy."

> — *Farouk Kaddoumi, PLO Foreign Minister, in the Beirut newspaper
> Al Nahar, March 9, 1996*

"No one can complain about what Hamas and Jihad are doing. I say that it is the right of every Palestinian to struggle so long as there is a single Israeli soldier in the land of Palestine."

— Farouk Qaddumi, head of the PLO Political Department,
Al-Musawar, September 30, 1994

"For us, we have a political relationship with Hamas, a brotherly relationship."

— Nabil Shaath, PLO Minister of Planning,
Reuters, *October 28, 1994*

ﷺ

The above quotations were compiled from the following sources. For additional information, check out their web sites or contact them at the Internet addresses indicated. These addresses were current as of September 1996.

Freeman Center for Strategic Studies
http://freeman.io.com
e-mail: BSaphir@aol.com

IIS, Israel Information Service, Ministry of Foreign Affairs, Jerusalem Israel Line, Consulate of New York
http://www.israel-mfa.gov.il
e-mail: ask@israel-info.gov.il

IMRA, Independent Media Review and Analysis
e-mail: imra@netvision.net.il

IRIS, Information Regarding Israel's Security
http://www.netaxs.com/~iris/
e-mail: elbaum@dircon.co.uk

Jerusalem Insider, Guardians of Israel
http://www.netrail.net/~sidel/
e-mail: sidel@netrail.net
Jerusalem Post
http://www.jpost.co.il
e-mail: jpedt@jpost.co.il

Jerusalem Report
http://www.jreport.virtual.co.il/index.htm
e-mail: feedback@jreport@virtual.co.il

Zionist Organization of America
http://www.zoa.org/

Appendix B

Chronology

Timeline of Jerusalem and Jewish History from the time of King David

B.C.

ca. 1000   David captures Jerusalem, makes it his capital

ca. 970   King David, shortly before his death, anoints Solomon as his successor

953   Solomon dedicates First Temple in Jerusalem at Feast of Tabernacles

ca. 930   Kingdom divided into Israel and Judah

ca. 740   Isaiah begins prophetic ministry lasting 50 years

724–722   Israel defeated by Assyria; northern tribes exiled

625   Jeremiah begins prophetic ministry lasting until 586

605	Pharaoh Neco of Egypt defeated by King Nebuchadnezzar of Babylon at battle of Carchemish; Judah caught in the middle, Daniel and friends taken captive to Babylon
597	Babylonian army strikes Jerusalem; 10,000 deported, including prophet Ezekiel
588	siege of Jerusalem by Babylonian army begins
586	Jerusalem falls; Temple destroyed; most of the Jewish people exiled
538	Medo-Persian empire conquers Babylon; Cyrus issues decree allowing return to Jerusalem to rebuild the Temple
536	exiles begin to return to Jerusalem; Zerubbabel begins reconstruction of Temple
534	work on the Temple halted by opposition
520–516	reconstruction of Temple completed
458	Artaxerxes permits Ezra to return to Jerusalem with additional exiles
445	Nehemiah rebuilds walls of Jerusalem
332	Alexander the Great conquers area; beginning of Hellenistic rule in Jerusalem

168	Antiochus IV (Epiphanes) ransacks Jerusalem; prohibits practice of Judaism; sets up "abomination of desolation" in Temple
166–160	Maccabean Revolt; Temple recaptured 164; miraculous eight-day supply of oil (origin of Hanukkah festival)
142–129	Jewish autonomy under Hasmonean dynasty
129–63	Jewish independence under Hasmonean kingdom
63	Roman army under Pompey conquers Jerusalem
40–37	Parthians conquer Jerusalem
37	Herod the Great besieges Jerusalem
20	Herod begins reconstruction of the Temple
ca. 7–4	birth of Jesus Christ
4	death of Herod the Great; Jewish revolt put down by Rome

A.D.

ca. 26–30	ministry of Jesus; crucifixion under Herod Antipas

26-36	Pontius Pilate procurator of Judea; moves capital to Caesarea
37–41	Roman emperor Caligula attempts to have his image carved on the Temple
66	Jewish revolt; war against the Romans lasts five years
70	Jerusalem and Second Temple destroyed by army of Titus
73	Masada, last stand of the Jewish revolt, falls
132	Jerusalem destroyed by emperor Hadrian, who outlaws circumcision and observance of the Sabbath; plans to build a temple to Jupiter over Temple ruins
132–135	Bar-Kochba uprising against Rome wins back Jerusalem temporarily
135	Hadrian regains the city and bans Jews under penalty of death; rebuilds and renames the city *Aelia Capitolina* and the area *Syria et Palaestina*, and vows to wipe the former Jewish capital from the world's memory for all time; Jews not allowed in their capital city for the next 500 years
313	Emperor Constantine converts and Christianity legalized in the Roman empire;

Constantine, who rules from his Byzantine capital, sends his mother, Helena, to search out holy sites in Jerusalem

335	Church of the Holy Sepulcher completed in Jerusalem
614	Persians sack Jerusalem
628	Jerusalem recaptured by Byzantines under Heraclius
638	Jerusalem conquered by Caliph Omar; Moslem domination of Jerusalem begins; Jews allowed to return to city
691	Dome of the Rock, a Moslem mosque, built on the Temple Mount
750	Abbasid Dynasty of Baghdad seizes control of Jerusalem
ca. 950	Egyptian-based Fatimid Dynasty conquers Jerusalem; all synagogues and churches destroyed
1071	Seljuks conquer Palestine and vandalize Jerusalem, persecuting both Jews and Christians
1097	Godfrey de Bouillon leads First Crusade to Jerusalem

JERUSALEM BETRAYED

1099	Crusaders lay siege to Jerusalem and capture the city; wide-scale massacre of almost 40,000 Jews and Moslems; Crusaders declare Jerusalem capital of their Latin Kingdom
1187	Moslems recapture Jerusalem under Saladin, who encourages Jews and Eastern Christians to settle in Jerusalem and help him fight Latin Crusaders
1241	Saladin dies; heirs battle each other; Germany brokers deal to return all of Jerusalem except Temple Mount to Crusader control
1244	Crusaders expelled from Jerusalem by mercenaries hired by Egyptian Sultan
1291	Mamelukes rule from Cairo; Jerusalem becomes city of exile for dangerous criminals or disfavored government officials
1516	Ottoman empire succeeds Mameluke Empire
1517	Jerusalem in Turkish hands (for next 400 years)
1537–41	walls of Jerusalem rebuilt under Suleiman the Magnificent
1799	Napoleon moves against Ottoman Empire from Egyptian front; stopped before he reaches Jerusalem

1860	Mishkenot Sha'ananim, first Jewish neighborhood built outside Jerusalem walls

Zionism and the Modern State of Israel

1882–1903	*First Aliya,* large-scale immigration of Jews to Palestine begins as persecution in Russia and eastern Europe increases
1896	Theodor Herzl, founder of Zionism, publishes *The Jewish State* and argues for the creation of a Jewish state in Palestine
1897	First Zionist Congress convened in Switzerland; immigration to Palestine promoted
1904–14	*Second Aliya,* primarily from Russia and Poland
1916	Sykes-Picot Agreement signed by Britain, France and Russia carving up the former Ottoman empire, defeated in World War I; Britain gains control of Palestine; France gains control of what is now Lebanon and Syria
1917	Balfour Declaration endorses establishment of a "national home" for the Jews in Palestine; British capture Jerusalem; beginning of Mandatory rule
1919–23	*Third Aliya,* mainly from Russia
1920	*Haganah,* Jewish defense organization founded; Arabs riot against Jews in Jerusalem

1921	Haj Amin al-Husseini appointed grand mufti of Jerusalem
1922	Churchill White Paper establishes Transjordan east of river, taking 78% of land allocated for Mandate
1925	Vladimir Jabotinsky founds movement called Zionist Revisionism, forerunner of the Herut political party and the modern Likud Party
1929	Arab riots against Jews praying at Western Wall in Jerusalem
1924–32	*Fourth Aliya,* mainly from Poland
1933–39	*Fifth Aliya,* mainly from Germany
1936–39	Arab nationalist movements riot to stop Jewish homeland in Palestine; throw their support to Hitler in World War II
1939	British White Paper effectively overturns Balfour Declaration; halts Jewish immigration to Palestine, condemning millions of European Jews to Holocaust
1944–45	Jewish Brigade, part of British forces, fights alongside Allies
1946	Irgun bombs King David Hotel

1947	UN votes to partition Palestine; Arab states reject partition
1948	British Mandate ends May 14; Israel declared a state and recognized by US; May 15, five Arab states invade the new nation; Jordan lays siege to Jerusalem; Old City lost to Jordan, which annexes East Jerusalem
1948–52	large-scale immigration from European and Arab countries
1949	Armistice agreements signed with Egypt, Jordan, Syria and Lebanon; Israel becomes 59th member of United Nations
1951	King Abdullah of Jordan assassinated at Al-Aksa mosque in Jerusalem
1956	Sinai Campaign
1964	Palestine Liberation Organization (PLO) established in Cairo
1967	Six-Day War ends Jordanian occupation of East Jerusalem; Israel gains Sinai and Golan Heights
1969	Yasser Arafat, head of the *Fatah* guerrilla wing, gains control of the PLO
1970	PLO initiates civil war in Jordan; Hussein evicts Arafat and PLO

1973	Yom Kippur War, started by surprise attack of Egypt in the south and Syria in the north; Israel makes tremendous gains and Arabs ask for cease-fire after three weeks of fighting
1977	Anwar Sadat of Egypt visits Jerusalem; leads to peace treaty in 1979
1982	Israel invades Lebanon to stop PLO terrorist attacks launched from that country
1987	*Intifada,* the Palestinian uprising, begins
1988	PLO pressures Jordan's King Hussein into renouncing all claims to the West Bank; from Algiers, PLO declares establishment of Palestinian state with capital in Jerusalem; 43rd General Assembly of the United Nations meets in Geneva
1989	Mass immigration of Soviet Jews begins; almost 600,000 arrive in five-year period
1991	Iraqi Scud missiles hit Israel during Persian Gulf War; Middle East peace conference in Madrid
1992–93	secret negotiations with PLO in Oslo
1993	Declaration of Principles (Oslo I) signed at White House ceremony, transferring control of Jericho and Gaza to PLO control

1994	Peace treaty signed with Jordan
1995	Interim Agreement (Oslo II) signed with the PLO cedes Bethlehem, Hebron and over 450 villages to Palestinian control; Prime Minister Yitzhak Rabin assassinated; Shimon Peres succeeds Rabin
1996	Benjamin Netanyahu wins first national election for Prime Minister; final status talks begin that will decide the fate of Jerusalem

Mike Evans is widely recognized as one of America's leading experts on Israel and the Middle East. As a bold advocate for the rights of the Jewish people to the land of Israel, his voice has been heard worldwide, from the Forty-Third General Assembly of the United Nations in Geneva to the Middle East Peace Conference in Madrid. His personal friendship with key leaders in the Israeli government has opened doors to evangelical Christians. Mr. Evans has met on numerous occasions with the last five prime ministers of Israel and the last two mayors of Jerusalem.

An internationally known speaker, Mr. Evans has addressed millions of people across the globe. He has produced five television specials; authored eleven books, including the bestseller *The Return*; and written numerous articles on Israel and Bible prophecy.

Mike Evans's organization, Bridge of Love, has made a commitment to assist in emergency ambulance service for victims of terrorism; programs to help children with cancer and their families; a school for the handicapped; a clinic for the treatment of diabetes; improvements to the Via Dolorosa; equipment and activities for blind and visually impaired school children; medical alert devices for the elderly; special fund for the victims of terrorism; medical center for Arabs and Jews; and support and assistance to Russian immigrants.

For more information on these and other compassionate projects, or for a catalog of books and tapes by Mr. Evans, write to the address below. A complimentary copy of *Jerusalem Prophecy* newsletter is also available. This monthly publication will keep you informed on current events in Israel and the Middle East as well as Bible prophecy.

Bridge of Love
P.O. Box 612128
Dallas, Texas, 75261-2128